Treatment Resistance

Related Titles of Interest

Treatment Resistance

A Guide for Practitioners

Salvatore Cullari
Lebanon Valley College

Allyn and Bacon
Boston • London • Toronto • Sydney • Tokyo • Singapore

Library of Congress Cataloging-in-Publication Data

Cullari, Salvatore.
    Treatment resistance : a guide for practitioners / Salvatore
Cullari.
       p.   cm.
    Includes bibliographical references.
    ISBN 0-205-15572-3
    1. Impasse (Psychotherapy)   2. Therapeutic alliance.   I. Title.
    [DNLM: 1. Physician–Patient Relations.   2. Treatment Refusal—
psychology.   3. Psychotherapy—methods.   WM 62 C967t 1996]
    RC489.I45C85   1996
    616.89´14—dc20
    DNLM/DLC
    for Library of Congress   95-43196
                                                                   CIP

Printed in the United States of America

10   9   8   7   6   5   4   3   2   1   00   99   98   97   96

I would like to dedicate this book to my wife (Kathi), children (Dante and Catherine), and parents (Carmelo and Carmela).

Contents

Preface

Before I started to write this book, I thought I knew a lot about treatment resistance. After all, I have nearly twenty years' experience in the mental health field, and working with difficult clients has been a favorite challenge of mine for more than a decade. I must admit that this project was a real eye opener for me. In fact, I like to think of it as something akin to being lost in a haunted house. At times, I was faced with darkened rooms, trap doors, and dead-end hallways. In other instances, I was merely overwhelmed. It was, in retrospect, a very exciting experience.

Before you read major sections of this book, I want to tell you a few things that might better prepare you. You might think of this as something like a role induction. One way to use this book is to read only those chapters or sections that are relevant to you at a given time. In this way you will avoid being overwhelmed with information. I have provided hundreds of references for those of you who want to learn more about a particular topic. In addition, I have included several optional sections for you to read at your own discretion.

I have tried to incorporate material that is broadly research-based rather than simply relying on my own clinical experience. To balance the research material, I have presented my own thoughts and viewpoints. Often these are not empirically based, and you can accept or reject them as you wish. I have tried to use information that is relevant to those who practice psychotherapy, but at times I review some theoretically oriented topics. My ultimate goal in writing this book was to provide material that is both research-based and practical.

I offer literally hundreds of ideas and suggestions for decreasing the many forms of resistance you encounter in your practice. If only *one* of these ideas makes only *one* of your clients attend only *one* more session than he or she might have otherwise, you will recoup the cost of this book. I strongly believe that the material and the corresponding references will help you as you work with many of your clients. The most important reason for reading this book is that you will be able to help some clients you otherwise would not have been able to reach.

As you will discover, I believe that in some respects the term *resistance* is a misnomer and perhaps an outdated concept. It will soon be clear that I generally do not subscribe to the Freudian notion that all resistance is due to unconscious conflicts or to a compulsion to repeat. Admittedly, there may be some instances in which these factors play a role. I agree that resistance often involves a client's fear of or anxiety associated with change. Resistance may also stem from the effort or discomfort involved with undertaking new and perhaps ineffectual patterns of behavior. From my viewpoint, treatment resistance can be conceptualized as a broad category of complex interactive factors associated with the process of change. Sometimes resistance originates within the client. Treatment resistance, as described in this book, is not equivalent to the general term *client resistance*. For example, resistance may result from a therapist's influence or from factors related to our social environment or to our culture. In this case, I believe that as therapists we should be careful not to blame the victim or assume that we always know what is right for the individuals we treat.

This book covers a number of key topics related to resistance. Included are motivation (Chapter 2), treatment process and compliance (Chapter 3), self-disclosure (Chapter 4), client–therapist interactions (Chapters 5 and 6), severe or persistent psychological disorders (Chapter 7), and cultural influences (Chapter 8). Included in Chapter 8 are numerous recommendations for treating multicultural clients. This book also includes chapters on treatment resistance, premature treatment termination, and client deception (Appendixes A, B, and C). To further enhance the practical nature of this book, I have created brief helpful hints, called "Recommendations," that appear at the tops of certain pages. These little hints can be quick reminders for you to use in your daily practice.

Acknowledgments

I am indebted to a number of people who made this book possible. First, I want to thank the hundreds of clients I have worked with through the years for teaching me a great deal about human nature. I would like to thank Lynne Kellner (North Central Human Services, Gardner, Massachusetts, and Mt. Wachusett Community College), Gary F. Ganahl (private practice, Stone Mountain, Georgia), and Ted L. Orcutt (private practice, San Diego, California), who reviewed significant portions of the manuscript and provided many valuable comments and suggestions. In a similar manner, I owe a special debt to my friends and colleagues, Janet Kelley (private practice, Harrisburg, Pennsylvania), Richard Small (private practice, Reading, Pennsylvania), and Hank Weeks (Harrisburg State Hospital), for reviewing my first draft and providing numerous helpful suggestions. I appreciate the help of Juris Draguns (Penn State University), who provided an excellent review of Chapter 8 and offered much thoughtful advice. Fred Frese (Director of Psychology, Western Reserve Psychiatric Hospital, Hudson, Ohio) has been one of my inspirations for working with chronic mental patients, and his review of Chapter 7 provided me with a number of new insights.

I would like to thank John Synodinos (president) and William McGill (dean of the faculty) of Lebanon Valley College for allowing me to take a sabbatical leave in order to write this book and for their overall support.

I would especially like to thank my wife, Kathi, for her support and my children, Dante and Catie, for their patience and for allowing me to miss some of their baseball games.

I am very grateful to the staff of Allyn and Bacon, especially Mylan Jaixen and Susan Hutchinson, for their helpful suggestions and guidance in preparing this book.

Finally, I wish to extend a great deal of credit to the library staff of Lebanon Valley College, especially Donna Miller, whose help was instrumental in allowing me to write this book.

About the Author

Salvatore Cullari received his Ph.D. in psychology from Western Michigan University in 1981. He began his work in the mental health field in 1976. Since then he has worked with virtually all age groups and diagnostic disorders. He has over thirty publications on eating disorders, treatment of psychiatric disorders and mental retardation, community psychology, testing and assessment, psychopharmacology, and other areas. He has written book chapters on treating mental retardation and community psychology. He has directed the psychology departments in both mental retardation centers and psychiatric facilities. He has consulted with state departments of mental health, psychiatric facilities, nursing homes, community halfway houses, the Bureau of Disability Determination, Veterans Administration centers, and inpatient drug and alcohol centers. He has worked in private practice and has presented numerous workshops on treatment issues to various organizations.

A licensed psychologist since 1979, Dr. Cullari is a member of the American Psychological Association (divisions 25, 28, 29, and 42) and of the Association for Behavior Therapy and the Pennsylvania Psychological Association. He serves on the board of directors for the Institute for Psychotherapy.

Dr. Cullari is currently chairman of the psychology department of Lebanon Valley College, where he also teaches courses in clinical psychology. His current research interests include the treatment of schizophrenia and eating disorders, and the treatment of resistant clients.

Nasrudin stood up in the market-place and started to address the throng. "O people! Do you want knowledge without difficulty, truth without falsehood, attainment without effort, progress without sacrifice?"

Very soon a large crowd gathered, everyone shouting "Yes, yes!"

"Excellent!" said the Mulla. "I only wanted to know. You may rely upon me to tell you all about it if I ever discover any such thing."

From *The Pleasantries of the Incredible Mulla Nasrudin* by I. Shah. Copyright 1968 by Mulla Nasrudin Enterprises. London: Octagon Press.

1

Resistance

Overview

Regardless of whether we are dealing with a client's personality, attitudes, behavior, or other factors, the underlying theme of all psychotherapy is change. At the same time, proposing change, both inside and outside of the therapy room, almost inevitably leads to some resistance. The human tendency to challenge the influence of others is as old as our time on earth. In the case of Adam and Eve, I suppose the first to experience resistance was God.

There is no doubt about the importance of Freud's role to the understanding of resistance. Perhaps his most important contributions to this area are the identification of conflict as a key ingredient in resistance and the introduction of transference. Freud has influenced virtually every Western theorist on this topic, either by stimulating additional viewpoints consistent with his theory or by motivating individuals to find alternatives to his beliefs. Nevertheless, the psychoanalytic model of resistance based on Freud's writings appears to be deficient in three major ways. First, the basic tenets of psychoanalysis have never been empirically proved; Second, there is too much emphasis on intrapsychic factors. Third, the role of social factors outside of therapy in resistance have largely been downplayed or ignored. This book explores these issues and suggests an alternative model for dealing with resistance in psychotherapy.

Freud and the Concept of Resistance

Resistance, as it was originally conceived by Freud, assumes some type of intrapsychic opposing force to treatment. In a simplified view of this model, as pathogenic material begins to be exposed during therapy, the threatened ego unconsciously attempts to abort the process. In this case, resistance functions as the agent that prevents painful memories, feelings, or emotions from becoming conscious once they are repressed. According to Freud, both the repressed content and the repressing force are dynamically unconscious. The theory further suggests that, during therapy, the client will develop a regressive transference neurosis, which represents the core themes of his or her neurotic conflicts. Through the analysis and interpretation of this transference, including the resistance associated with its formation, the client's neurotic conflicts are made conscious and resolved.

Freud's view of resistance was based on a biological model and makes perfect sense if one accepts the notion of behavior and personality as being due primarily to instinctual forces and intrapsychic conflicts. Similarly, on the basis of the scientific premises of his time, Freud was simply making a causal attribution to try to explain the seemingly inconsistent resistive behavior of his patients. His ideas were consistent with the nineteenth-century mechanist movement, which had revolutionized the field of physiology during Freud's lifetime and which led to his principle of psychic determinism. Freud's emphasis on intrapsychic factors was part of his attempt to make psychotherapy as objective and scientific as possible. His beliefs were also consistent with his medical training, where the focus of treatment was on the individual and where the therapist functioned as a detached and impartial expert observer. For example, the nineteenth-century physician was taught that the most important aspect of treatment is what you do *to* your patients, rather than what to do with them. This autocratic approach is found in other psychoanalytic practices as well, including its interpretation of resistance.

Resistance as Ideology

Despite the wide acceptance of many of Freud's ideas, the basic theoretical assumptions of psychoanalysis, including its explanation of resistance, have never been empirically validated. In part, this results from the difficulty of operationally defining some of the major constructs of psychoanalysis. A related problem is the inability to make direct observations (for example, of repression or the unconscious). Another difficulty has been the willingness of many psychoanalytic researchers to accept much of Freud's writings at face value. Spence (1994) supports this viewpoint and suggests that the problem stems largely from the failure of psychoanalytic researchers to ask the "hard questions." For example, Spence states: "Believing that everything important is largely already known (and this position has a disturbingly medieval ring to it), authors present us with some new examples of the obvious" (p. 34). As a result, much of the psychoanalytic writings about topics such as resistance are based on dogma, subjective case studies, anecdotal information, or similarly unreliable methods. In this case, the preconceived notions of resistance become a self-validating and self-perpetuating system.

Along the same lines, the psychoanalytic model of resistance tends to ignore social influences that operate both within the client and between the client and the therapist. As a result, in many ways the traditional concept of resistance parallels the controversy of the notion of mental illness (e.g., Szasz, 1970). For example, in both instances a number of value judgments must be made. In the case of resistance, the therapist decides that some of the client's thoughts and behaviors are harmful or at least not useful. The client, however, may have a different viewpoint, and it is not clear whose opinion is correct. If psychotherapists were always absolutely sure of what exactly was wrong with their clients and how best to treat them, this concept of resistance would be more secure.

Even in this unlikely scenario, the role of values cannot be completely eliminated. Labeling a client resistive involves a comparison between the ideas or beliefs of the individual and those of the therapist. Thus, a therapist decides that a person would be better off by making changes in a particular direction. If the client does not agree with these proposed changes or is not cooperative, he or she may be labeled resistive.

However, none of this occurs in a vacuum. Typically, it is the therapist who makes an interpretation of resistance or perhaps even sets the resistance in motion. In other words, something that the therapist says or does brings about a reaction, which, depending on the context, may be labeled resistance. In this case, what we consider to be resistance may be a relative rather than an absolute explanation of behavior. Furthermore, it virtually always involves some type of interpersonal interaction and subjective judgment.

I once worked with a client who committed suicide. Afterwards, I constantly thought about what I could have done to have prevented her from taking her life. It seemed as if all my years of training and experience were overpowered by her determination. Yet, probably for my own sense of stability, I finally accepted the fact that there was nothing I could have done differently. From the moment I met her, she seemed set on a course toward self-destruction. From her point of view, she was not being resistive but, rather, doing what she thought was necessary. If our lives had never crossed, I assume she still would have killed herself, and the notion of resistance would have had no relevance.

My point is that resistance is an interactive process: It always involves at least two of something. In psychotherapy, this includes the client, the therapist, and the social systems of both of these persons. Perceiving a client to be resistive and assuming that the resistance is due primarily to isolated intrapsychic factors detracts us from understanding the clients' behavior and from exposing other contributions to the process, including our own role. For example, if we become angry or frustrated with a client who is being "resistive," these feelings will have an obvious impact on our thoughts, behaviors, and communications with the client. Thus, it becomes difficult to determine which person is being reactive.

Other writers have looked at these issues. For example, to help differentiate resistance due to intrapsychic factors from that due to the interactions of the client and therapist, some writers (e.g., Pipes & Davenport, 1990; Kris, 1990) have suggested the use of two terms. *Resistance* is the recommended term for the unconscious process that takes place within the client. *Reluctance,* on the other hand, should characterize the conscious ambivalence that results from the interactions between client and therapist. Although this sounds like a reasonable distinction, it is again based largely on the unsupported concept of a detached and isolated inner psychic world. Even Freud's early supporters, such as Otto Rank and Alfred Adler, seriously questioned this assumption. Otto Rank (Karpf, 1953) stressed the interdependence of the individual and the social system and argued that the two cannot be disassociated. "In effect, he replaces the Freudian antithetical view of libido striving and social restriction with a view of the dynamic interdependent relation of the individual and the social world" (Karpf, 1953; p. 60).

Atwood and Stolorow (1993) expand on this theme and discuss similar problems resulting from the introspective nature of psychoanalysis. Their theory of intersubjectivity is based on three principles that highlight some of the points made here. In their own words, "The first principle claims that human experience is always embedded in an irreducible engagement with others." "The second highlights the essential inseparability of the psychological investigator from the world of experience he investigates." "The third holds that every individual's personal reality is subjectively and historically shaped and that therefore no one's personal reality is inherently more true or valid than another's" (p. 189). Although the material in this book is not directly based on this theory, most of it is consistent with these three principles. In short, resistance appears to be a dynamic interactive social force rather than an isolated intrapsychic biological mechanism.

The Role of Cognitions

A recent line of investigation that is also relevant to the concept of resistance is associated with memory and cognitions. The growing body of evidence accumulating in this field appears to have implications not only for understanding resistance, but for psychotherapy as a whole. For example, despite extensive reviews of the literature, there seems to be little empirical evidence for the existence of repression (see Loftus & Ketcham, 1994). This is a complex topic that has been debated for many years, and I do not mean to trivialize it. Clearly, the research findings in this area vary depending on the definition of repression and the methods used to study it. For example, there seems to be a lot of clinical evidence in support of repression (see Erdelyi, 1985; Fox, 1995). However, a number of controlled studies done with subjects such as concentration camp survivors, children who have witnessed a parent's death, or subjects with similar traumatic experiences suggest that repression is a rare event. Rather than being repressed, memories of highly emotional or disturbing experiences are often vividly remembered, even when a conscious effort is made to forget them.

On the other hand, less salient memories may be biased by events occurring long after the episode. For example, one of the arguments in the current controversy over "false memory syndrome" is that a client's recollections may be influenced by postevent factors, such as what a person reads or even the suggestions of a therapist. A number of experimental studies investigating the accuracy of memory support this view. To illustrate, Loftus and Ketcham (1994) report that new and misleading postevent information can lead subjects to believe they witnessed events that did not really occur and that false memories can be implanted by trusted authority figures. Loftus summarizes her findings as follows: "My work has helped to create a new paradigm of memory, shifting our view from the video-recorder model . . . to a reconstructionist model in which memories are understood as creative blendings of fact and fiction" (1994, p. 5).

The investigations of cognitive scientists who study schemas also support the unreliability of memory. Briefly, *schemas* are cognitive frameworks that are used to process, store and retrieve information. They allow people to focus their attention on specific stimuli, fill in missing information, and behave in a schema-consistent manner. For example, transference may be viewed as a type of schema. Research studies in this area suggest that schematic-consistent information is recalled more accurately than other types. In addition, schemas can facilitate inaccurate memories, and some subjects "recall" schema-consistent information that was never presented (see Horowitz, 1991, for a review). Because schemas are learned and evolve through our contact with the environment, this again underscores the importance of social interactions on our thoughts, memory, and behavior.

This interconnectedness seems to be especially salient in the context of psychotherapy. Everything a client says is filtered through the therapist's already established cognitive schemata, and vice versa. Therapists largely attend to and remember material that is consistent with their own therapeutic paradigms and, either verbally or nonverbally, communicate these impressions to the client. Through this process, schema-consistent information is assimilated by both parties, and that which is inconsistent is often distorted or ignored. For example, in the case of interpretations, the therapists' own cognitive structures are used to make inferences about clients' verbalizations and behaviors.

The danger here is that the schemas of the therapist will become entwined with those of the clients. This can occur when clients' "missing" information is automatically filled in by the therapist. In this case, it is never really clear whose material is being evaluated. Another example occurs when clinicians cling to an initial diagnosis because their initial schema restricts their attention to harmonious information and away from incompatible evidence.

A third example of how schemas can influence psychotherapy relates to case study reports. Unless proper controls are used with this method (such as recording and analyzing treatment sessions), the material that the therapist remembers may be grossly distorted to agree with his or her own theoretical paradigm. Even with therapists who attempt to maintain a blank screen, the idea of a totally detached and objective model of psychotherapy seems to be more myth than reality.

Given the many factors cited here, the term *resistance,* implying primarily an intrapsychic opposing force in therapy, has probably outlived its usefulness. In this book, I propose a view of resistance that focuses on the interactions of the client, the therapist, and the culture at large. Given that psychotherapists are only human and treatment errors are unavoidable, clients are often resistive for justifiable reasons (Lazarus & Fay, 1982; Ellis, 1985). Harris and Watkins (1987) explain it this way: "Put simply, any counseling practice that is threatening, degrading, dehumanizing, demeaning, impolite, or generally annoying will elicit resistance. Antagonistic receptionists, excessive paperwork, and long waits for appointments are just a few examples that cause problems" (p. 23).

Considering all the useless and even dangerous types of medical and psychological treatments that have been used over the centuries and even recently (e.g., purging, leeching, bloodletting, ice packs, hydrotherapy, psychosurgery), it is no wonder that people are often hesitant to cooperate with professionals. As DiMatteo and DiNicola (1982) point out, "it is quite likely that before this century patients who ignored their physician's recommendations were much the better for it" (p. 3). Although most psychological techniques are currently not dangerous in the physical sense, often they are not necessarily useful either. We still have a long way to go in terms of fully understanding human behavior and developing universally effective treatment programs. In some cases, psychotherapeutic techniques may appear as illogical to our clients as prescientific treatment methods appear to modern practitioners. Along the same lines, some forms of resistance may be the client's way of striving for independence and, in those cases, should be encouraged rather than eliminated.

Because of the emphasis on individual change in contemporary psychotherapy, we often ignore the fact that the client is part of a larger social system that includes the family, peers, and the overall society. Resistance appears to be a complicated interactive psychosocial phenomenon and should be treated as such. I am not suggesting that resistance is never intrapsychic or even unconscious. It is important, however, for the therapist not to have any preconceived notions of the origins of resistance and to evaluate the source objectively.

Reducing Resistance in the Initial Session

To begin to demonstrate how this model can be used in psychotherapy, I would like to explore briefly how resistance can be reduced in the first session. This is important because, as Appendix B explains, up to one-half of all psychotherapy clients may drop out at this time.

Many clients come to the first therapy session in a state of uncertainty. Their typical coping strategies are no longer effective in dealing with some stressor. Often they will say that they do not know what to do next. Uncertainty often leads to fear, and I believe that much of the client's initial resistance stems from feelings of fear. That is why it is important for clients to be aware that this state of uncertainty may be a fundamental step toward change. In other words, the uncomfortable emotions that often accompany uncertainty are frequently the inspiration for self-examination and development. Uncertainty should be a sign to clients that at least some (but not all) of their old ways of doing things, whether conscious or unconscious, are no longer adequate. Thus, uncertainty serves as an opportunity to change and grow.

To a large extent, what a therapist does during the first session sets the tone for the subsequent treatment process and has a great deal of influence on outcome. This is especially true in light of the current popularity of brief forms of treatment. The model of resistance that is promoted in this book encourages a proactive rather than a reactive process. That is, we need to prevent resistance from occurring in the first place. Because of the initial state of uncertainly of new clients as described here, the therapist should address at least two issues in the beginning session. First, when one is facing an overwhelming stressor, which is common at this stage, it is easy to fall into the trap of blaming others or just doing nothing. This often has the effect of making the problem worse, and clients may get caught up in a negatively accelerating behavior trap. Thus, the first step is getting the client to reverse their direction and start engaging in positive adaptive behaviors. This process may be as simple as getting clients to view their problems in a different light as long as they realize they have taken their first step toward change.

Second, in most cases clients have tried to deal with their problem for some time without success. Thus, in many instances, simply going to psychotherapy is an indication that the client's level of self-efficacy is probably very low. As most of us have experienced, failure in one area tends to reduce our confidence in other areas as well, so it is crucial that clients' self-efficacy be addressed in this session. One way to do this is to focus on clients' positive coping strategies. I have never met a client who is a failure at everything, and most people do more things right than they do wrong. At times, clinicians have a tendency to focus too much on what clients are doing wrong and to ignore their positive resources. In this case, reviewing how clients are coping successfully with their other problems may not only increase their confidence but also suggest methods that may be used or modified to address their target issues. I will have more to say about both of these topics in subsequent chapters.

Outside-Therapy Influences

Because of the traditional focus on intrapsychic factors, some clinicians object to linking factors outside of therapy to resistance. I do not agree with such an approach. For example, what happens when the client is being cooperative but the funding source (HMO, workmen's compensation department, etc.) is not? Do these factors have an influence on resistance? I believe they do. Anyone who has dealt with HMOs knows that they often put restrictions on the type or length of treatment that can be offered. It is almost as if the therapist has to deal with two clients at the same time. At the most basic level, a restriction on the number of sessions that the client can be seen often precludes dealing with resistance in the traditional manner. There simply will be not be enough time, and thus new ways of dealing with resistance need to be developed. This is the object of this book.

Some clients really want to change, but overwhelming social forces prevent or reduce their ability to do so. A myopic view of resistance leads therapists to blame the client when the real factor lies outside their control. It is very important to consider the effects of the macro-environment on both the treatment process and the outcome. This potentially will allow clinicians to be more realistic and become more aware of their limitations within a given social context. For example, the resistance that African-American clients bring to therapy may be based on years of societal racism and economic deprivation. It may be unrealistic to expect a few hours of therapy to have a major impact on their attitudes, especially when we have little control over their living environment. Factors like these will be addressed throughout the book.

Summary: An Interrelational Approach

The traditional view of resistance tends to place most of the blame for treatment ineffectiveness on the client. Often, this is not warranted. My view assumes that psychotherapy is a dynamic interrelational process where both client and therapist influence each other. This book is largely about change, flexibility, and treatment effectiveness rather than simply resistance. This is an important point because without this in mind many of the topics covered in the following chapters may seem out of place. Change is seen as a continuous, multifaceted process. Resistance is viewed as being due primarily to conflicts arising from simultaneous attempts at self-preservation and self-transformation both within the client and between the client, the therapist, and society.

The interactive model I am presenting is not unique. Some of the ideas I will discuss in this book have been addressed by writers such as Langs, Kohut, Atwood and Stolorow, Kiesler, Strupp, Lazarus, and many others. However, my extensive review of the resistance literature suggests that many therapists still exclusively follow the traditional intrapsychic model. Second, I have not come across any works that deal extensively with resistance using an interpersonal and interactive approach, which is the basis for this book. Consistent with this model, Table 1-1 presents a number of behaviors that may be regarded as resistance and some possible reasons for each of them. Although some of these may be due to the characteristics of the client, many others may be a function of the therapist or social factors and the interactions among them.

In Table 1-1, I am merely trying to show that resistance may have a number of different origins. In this book, I am proposing a paradigm shift away from the traditional reductionist view of resistance in psychotherapy. Rather than assuming that we know why the client is being resistive, I am suggesting that we take an objective approach. As in our legal system, let us assume the client is innocent until proved guilty. Furthermore, resistance probably stems from a number of different factors, and it is important to consider all of these. The basic premises of this model are given in Table 1-2 and will be fully explored in the chapters that follow.

TABLE 1-1   Interactional Factors That May Lead to Resistance

Clients' "Resistive" Behaviors	Possible Causes
Seductiveness	Unconscious therapist cues
Missing therapy	Ineffective procedures
Avoidance	Poor treatment timing
Ambivalence	Inability to trust therapist
Blaming others	Societal racism
Coming late	Client–therapist mismatch
Anger/hostility	Treatment aversiveness
Uncooperativeness	Misdiagnosis
Silence	Negative expectations
Talking too much or too little	Lack of role induction
Intellectualization	Therapist's overuse of techniques
Boredom	Interpersonal skills of therapist
Nonadherence	Negative therapy experiences
Restlessness	Dissatisfaction with treatment
Defiance	Involuntary treatment
Manipulativeness	Inappropriate treatment procedures
Acting out	Inability to relate to therapist
Lack of effort	Clients' skill deficiencies
Defensiveness	Inability to form a relationship
Reluctance	Fear of failure
Passivity	Nondirective therapist approach

TABLE 1-2   Basic Premises of an Interrelational Approach to Resistance

1. Resistance is an interactive rather than a simple intrapsychic event. Rather than having one underlying cause, resistance is assumed to be the product of the mutual influence of a number of interrelated factors.

2. There is no such thing as an unmotivated client.

3. Many clients are perceived to be difficult because of the effect they have on the therapist.

4. All psychotherapy is at least partially coercive and aversive. In this case, resistance appears to be a natural consequence of the change process and of the therapist's attempt to influence an individual.

5. Resistance is often a form of communication between client and therapist.

Appendix A presents a history of the concept of treatment resistance. Although most of these theoretical orientations see resistance as a client-emanated problem, a number of important points are made. Anyone who is not already familiar with this topic should read this section now. Examining the various viewpoints presented by different theories will help reinforce some of the ideas that will be presented in this book.

2

Motivation and Change

Overview

Motivation and resistance are closely linked concepts. Freud's theory of resistance is largely based on the idea of unconscious motivation. At the same time, when clients do not change, we often blame it on a lack of motivation. If we can increase the client's motivational level, we are likely to encounter less resistance. Of course, how to do the latter is the ten million dollar question.

This chapter is based on several premises. The first is that all clients are motivated in some sense. Their motivation may be to engage in inappropriate behaviors or to remain the same or whatever, but it is not useful to say that clients are unmotivated.

The second premise is that motivation should be viewed neither as a stable personality trait nor as an isolated construct. For example, people who have drug and alcohol problems are often described as being difficult to treat because they lack motivation. But anyone who has worked with these clients knows that their motivation for certain behaviors is enormous. While addicted to drugs, they will do literally anything to get more drugs. Thus, when we talk about motivation, it always needs to be linked with some end-state or goal. Therapists have a tendency to conclude that people are not motivated when, in fact, the problem is that the goals of the client and our own goals are different. When clients do not do what we want them to do, we label them as unmotivated, resistive or in a state of denial. In fact, we may simply be going in different directions or perhaps may endorse different values.

Third, clients' levels of motivation tend to change very quickly and thus may be difficult to measure. Even within a very short time period

---

Recommendations: Motivation

1. Help clients make the decision to change by discussing the costs and benefits of changing versus staying the same.

Recommendations: Motivation

2. Deal with clients' sense of demoralization or hopelessness during the first few sessions of therapy.

(e.g., a few minutes), a person's motivation to engage in a certain behavior may change. For example, while watching television, you may feel like getting a can of soda and then may change your mind. This is probably why measures of client motivation have shown very poor predictive validity (Miller, 1985). We need to treat motivation as a dynamic rather than a stable characteristic; at best, it can be measured only as a state at a given point in time. This does not mean that motivation cannot be assessed, but it may need to be assessed frequently.

The motivational level that clients present in your session may not be the same as the one they have in the "real world." We have all worked with clients who seem highly motivated while they are with us but never seem to make any progress. In fact, most clients' motivation for change is likely to be at its highest level in the treatment session.

Fourth, people tend to have multiple goals, many of which may be inconsistent or incompatible with their other goals, or may be more and less important at any given point. This is probably why we sometimes label a person's behavior as erratic or inconsistent. If we knew or were able to see the person's motivational system as a whole, it would not appear that way.

The fifth premise of this chapter is that motivation, in the sense that I will describe it, is not based on homeostasis (e.g., a return to equilibrium; see Weiner, 1986; Mahoney, 1982) but, rather, on action or change. It is difficult if not impossible to isolate the concept of motivation from the change process itself.

Finally, a person's motivational level is affected by their biological make-up, social and physical environment, cognitions, the interactions of all of these, and possibly other unknown factors. This multiplicity of interacting factors makes the concept of motivation a very complex phenomenon. Figure 2-1 summarizes the major topics covered in this chapter.

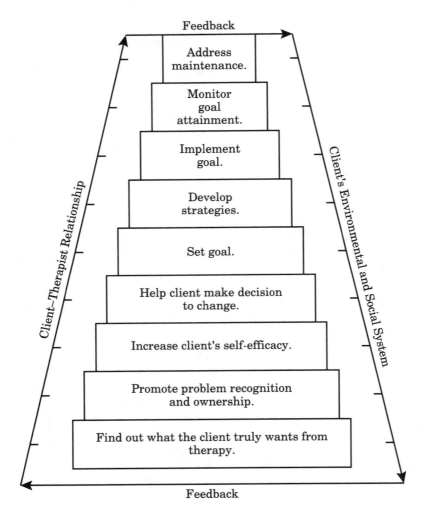

FIGURE 2-1   Steps to Increasing a Client's Motivation

Change

Most therapists would probably agree that motivation is a construct. A *construct* is an idea that is invented to help explain behavior. It does not exist in the physical sense. For this reason, constructs must be correlated with concrete or observable events and measured indirectly. The only way we "know" that motivation exists is when measures of motiva-

Recommendations: Motivation
3. Identify some of the reasons for previous treatment failures.

Recommendations: Motivation
4. Find out from clients what some of the factors and incentives are for maintaining their current behaviors so that these can be addressed.

tion (assuming these are valid) are correlated with some behavior or change in that person. Therefore, motivating a person can be construed as facilitating certain behaviors or behavior changes in that person. Virtually all types of psychotherapy aim, ultimately, to change clients' behavior, cognitions, and/or emotions. My own bias is that effective psychotherapy directly or indirectly modifies all three of these, but I will not address this issue in this book.

Humans can change through a number of different modes. The first is through maturation and aging. This includes both cognitive and physical changes that open up entirely new repertoires for individuals. For example, changes in gross and fine motor skills allow children to learn or engage in behaviors that were not previously possible. Moving from concrete to abstract thinking similarly opens up a vast area of potential capabilities. Maturation would also include some of the detrimental effects of aging, such as memory loss.

A second way we change is by learning something new or by forming new associations. This category includes classical and operant conditioning. It also includes forming new perceptions of the world; acquiring new facts, information, feedback, skills, attitudes, values, or insights; and achieving "transformations of personal meanings" (Mahoney, 1982). This category also incorporates combining already established or learned elements into novel or creative patterns. I will also include here forgetting or unlearning previous cognitions or behavior patterns, although the argument can be made that this is (or should be) a separate channel.

A third course for change is through environmental or social influences. Included here are effects of the physical environment, as well as the multitude of social influencers such as attraction, conformity, modeling, reciprocity, the various social power bases, and so on.

A fourth way that a person can change is through physical or biochemical transformation. This would include the effects of hormones, drugs, or other chemicals, and of bodily changes such as brain damage.

All of the various types of psychotherapies we use promote change through one or more of these channels. Typically, psychotherapy promotes change through the second and third factors described here, but all four of these channels are interrelated, and in some cases it is difficult to separate one from another totally. It appears that all human change sequences involve these processes.

Stages of Change

Prochaska and DiClemente (1984, 1986) have described a model of change based on studies with people both inside and outside of therapy (see also Miller, 1989; Miller & Rollnick, 1991; and Prochaska, DiClemente, & Norcross, 1992). They suggest that change occurs in repeating phases or cycles, which typically involve five stages.

The first level is called the *precontemplation* stage. Therapists usually do not see clients in this stage because the prospective clients have not yet determined that there is anything wrong with them that needs to be changed (although others often have). This stage assumes that there is a problem, but the person is not aware of it yet.

The second stage is called *contemplation*. Here, the person is aware that a problem exists but is ambivalent about whether to change it. Often people seek help at this stage but are not yet fully convinced that a change is needed. This is probably one reason that so many clients drop out of therapy after the first session (see Appendix A). In addition to contemplating whether they want to change or not and considering various types of changes, clients have a number of other decisions to make as well: Do they need to be in formal therapy in order to make these changes? Is this therapist the right one? We can also say that therapists are in a contemplation stage because they have to decide on a number of parallel matters, such as whether clients need to be in treatment or whether they are the appropriate persons to deal with clients' problems. Like all other stages of therapy, the contemplation stage involves an interactive process between client and therapist.

The third stage is called *determination* or *preparation*. Although some ambivalence may still be present, clients have decided (at least temporarily) that a change is necessary. The therapist's goal is to prevent clients from slipping back to the previous stage and to help them decide on the best approach to use in order to achieve the desired changes.

The fourth stage, *action,* is what we typically think of as treatment. In this phase, the therapist helps clients to take the necessary steps for change. It important to maintain clients' levels of motivation and to promote the idea that in the long run change offers more advantages or payoffs than remaining the same.

Recommendations: Motivation
5. Help clients take responsibility for their behavior and behavior change program.

Recommendations: Motivation
6. Allow clients to choose among various treatment goals and procedures. Be willing to negotiate any changes as needed even after goals have been set.

The fifth stage is called *maintenance*. The desired changes have occurred, but clients must be assisted in maintaining these changes and preventing relapse. Mental health professionals have a number of effective techniques for helping clients change their behaviors, but until recently maintenance was relatively ignored. It is usually much easier to produce changes than to maintain them. As many therapists have pointed out, the skills necessary for maintaining behavior changes may be different from those needed to produce the changes. Therefore, maintenance interventions should be specifically built into any treatment program.

Even if maintenance is addressed appropriately, some clients enter an additional stage, called *relapse*. In this phase, the task of the therapist, assuming that you still have contact with clients, is to prevent them from becoming stuck in relapse and to get them back into the change cycle again. However, it may not be necessary to start from the beginning.

As Prochaska and DiClemente (1986) point out, clients may begin or reinitiate therapy at various points in the five stages. An assessment of where individuals are in this cycle and what processes they are already using to change is crucial. For example, these authors maintain that the various stages of change require different interventions to help the client move from one level to another. They have developed the University of Rhode Island Change Assessment Scale (URICA) to assess clients' stages in the change process. If this instrument is not available, therapists should be able to do a less formal assessment. After evaluating at what stage clients enter therapy, appropriate interventions can be identified for them. The following section reviews the major tasks that the therapist needs to accomplish at each stage, based on this model.

Clients in the contemplation stage are most likely to be ambivalent and need stronger reasons for changing than for staying the same. Sometimes they may not really know what their problem is and may need some help in problem clarification. Reframing may also be useful. Very often they have tried to change in the past and were not successful. Reviewing these previous attempts may identify reasons that they were not successful. In addition, some clients need to be convinced that change is possible and that they have the ability to change. Moving too quickly in this stage however may lead to premature termination. Miller and Rollnick (1991, p. 115) describe various signs that may signal when clients are ready to move on. For example, clients may stop arguing or objecting, they may have more questions about how to change, or they may begin to talk about how their life will be after the change takes place. These actions may be taken as a signs that clients are ready to move on.

In the determination stage, clients need help in setting goals and selecting a plan of action. They also need to make a strong private and public commitment to change. In the action stage, therapists should help clients stay on course. Clients benefit from further evidence that they have made the right choice to change, and from feedback on their progress. It is especially helpful to encourage them to take credit for their improvement. They also need a lot of therapist support, so this is the stage when a strong client–therapist relationship is most useful.

In the maintenance stage, clients need to be aware of and use strategies to prevent relapse. Unfortunately, clients often are not in contact with their therapists during this stage, but every effort should be made to facilitate communication if and when the need arises. Even if treatment was successful, a post-treatment evaluation can be helpful in identifying the most and least useful aspects of the program, and what clients would have changed if they had to do the whole thing over again. Such information is useful not only for other clients but also for the same person in case of relapse. Prochaska and DiClemente (1984, 1986) and Miller and Rollnick (1991) provide more detailed explanations and case examples of this process.

Helping Clients Change

An important agent that promotes motivation to change is a difference between people's current functional or affective state and what they would like it to be. In a therapy setting, this is sometimes labeled self-dissatisfaction. Some studies show that a measure of *self-dissatisfaction* is predictive of efforts expended toward reducing this dissatisfaction (see Miller, 1985; Locke, Shaw, Saari, & Latham, 1981). The greater the dissatisfaction, the greater the effort the client will expend to achieve change. This state of self-dissatisfaction is probably similar to what some therapists call distress or demoralization (e.g., Frank, 1982) In Chapter 1, I described this as a state of uncertainty.

Recommendations: Motivation

7. Focus on goals that are meaningful to clients and those that the clients believe they can achieve.

Recommendations: Motivation

8. Promote the attitude that change is possible and that clients have the ability to change.

Many clients seek therapy not because of symptoms alone but as a result of a combination of symptoms and demoralization. The latter can be defined as a subjective feeling of incompetence. These feelings surface when clients cannot live up to their own expectations or the expectations of others, or when they have significant problems that they cannot solve. In this case, clients seek therapy only when other attempts to change have failed. In my experience, clients such as these come to therapy functionally immobilized. They simply do not know what to do next, and every potential move seems to have both positive and negative repercussions. In short, they find themselves in a classic approach–avoidance conflict. Such clients generally present themselves for therapy because of feelings of helplessness and hopelessness.

Given that many clients enter therapy feeling lost and confused, the following partially overlapping conditions must be established in order to help them change:

1. Clients must be aware of a problem or condition that needs attention and must make a decision to do something about it.
2. Clients must be ready to accept influence.
3. Clients must have sufficient motivation to engage in activities related to change.
4. Clients must have a goal.
5. Clients must be mentally and physically able to reach the goal.
6. Clients must be in an environment that allows movement toward the goal.

The absence of any of these conditions makes purposeful change much more difficult and is likely to produce resistance (see also Ford, 1992).

Problem Awareness and the Decision to Change

In terms of psychotherapy, in my opinion the most important stage in Prochaska and DiClemente's system and the one most relevant to the concept of motivation is that of contemplation. Clients are often at this stage when they decide to begin therapy and perhaps when they decide to drop out. The contemplation stage is likely to be the time when clients are most vulnerable to influence, and therapists should be prepared to take advantage of this. As stated before, this stage is often marked by ambivalence. Miller and Rollnick (1991) point out that therapists often react to this ambivalence negatively. That is, therapists respond as if its occurrence is unusual, a sign of resistance or a personality problem. However, we all tend to be ambivalent before we make a major change in our lives (e.g., looking for a new job, buying a house, getting married). Thus, ambivalence should be expected and even welcomed. If clients are not ambivalent, it may mean that awareness of some discrepancy, which is a crucial precursor to change, has not been reached. On the other hand, clients may have decided they do not want to change, or a lack of ambivalence may indicate that clients have already reached the determination stage, which would call for different procedures than those for contemplation. The latter is an example of why it is important to assess clients' stage of change on entering therapy.

The Decision-Making Process

At the contemplation stage, clients are often trying to make decisions about important aspects of their lives. It may be helpful to look at ways that people typically reach their decisions. A model of decision making that shares some similarities with Prochaska and DiClemente's theory of change was developed by Irving Janis and described in Janis and Mann (1977, pp. 171–200; see also the "help seeking" section in Appendix B). In studying people who have made difficult decisions and subsequently carried them out, the authors have identified five major stages that people are likely to experience:

1. *Appraising the challenge:* The key question relates to the potential risks involved if they do not change.
2. *Surveying alternatives:* In this stage, people seek advice from significant others and information from various sources related to alternatives they can pursue.
3. *Weighing alternatives:* In this step, people continue to seek out infor-

---

Recommendations: Motivation

9. Use the positive relationship with your clients to help ensure that they trust you and feel safe in therapy.

Recommendations: Motivation

10. Consider starting off with small requests for change (those that are very likely to be successful).

---

mation about the pros and cons of the remaining alternatives in order to select the best one.

4. *Deliberating about commitment:* This involves a tentative decision to make a change. Typically, people will first announce his decision to change to others from whom they expect to get positive feedback and will withhold the information from people they expect will disapprove of the plan. At this stage, having clients make a public commitment to change is often effective in getting them to stay on course.

5. *Adhering despite negative feedback:* Most people go through a relatively stress-free ("honeymoon") period right after they have made a decision to change, but this is often interrupted by negative feedback from the change process itself or from significant others. This is the time when some of the costs of change become evident or when the benefits do not arrive as soon as expected, so it tends to be a crucial stage in terms of follow-through.

Although the decision to change can derail at any one of these levels, the authors maintain that it is most likely to occur between stages 1 and 3. Because people are likely to get stuck here, these authors label this the "short-circuited decision loop" (Janis & Mann, 1977, p. 342). To help clients in this situation stay on track, the authors suggest that the following issues need to be reviewed accurately and thoroughly by the therapist:

- Do individuals truly believe the risks are serious if they do not change?
- Do they believe the risks are serious if they do change?
- What are the significant losses and gains for individuals if change occurs?
- What are the significant losses and gains for their significant others?
- How will they feel about themselves if they do or do not change?

- What types of social approval or disapproval can they expect if they do or do not change?

The answers to these questions may help a client make a commitment to change, or indicate that a change is not necessary, or show that a client is not yet ready to change. Clients who are caught in this loop have two options. The first is to accept that they have a significant problem that requires some intervention. The second is to minimize or deny that they have a problem or to use other defense mechanisms, such as rationalization, which are likely to maintain them in an ambivalent state. The job of the therapist, assuming the circumstances justify this, is to get clients to turn to the first option.

Accepting Influence

To get clients to a level where they are ready to accept influence from a therapist, a number of tasks need to be accomplished. One of the most important and complex tasks of a therapist is to determine accurately what clients want from therapy. It is difficult to give people directions unless we know where they want to go. And as Ford (1992) points out, this is often complicated because people may not know what they want or may be unable to communicate it. Some clients may not want to tell you. Some clients have multiple problems, and their goals may change during the course of therapy. However, we need to get some idea of clients' expectations because these may not be what we think they are, and our treatment approach needs to be consistent with them.

Second, with some clients, we may need to develop the perception that change is possible and that they have the ability to accomplish it. Whether you call this self-efficacy or remoralization, it is unlikely that we will be able to motivate clients without these types of beliefs.

Third, as I have already described, we need to review with clients the costs and benefits of making a change as well as the costs and benefits of remaining the same. As Miller and Rollnick (1991) suggest, it is important for the therapist to know what some of the incentives are for continuing a problem behavior from clients' point of view. This will better inform us about what we are up against in terms of trying to tip the momentum in favor of change, and will allow us to address these issues in the treatment program. For example, I once had a client who wanted to lose weight but at the same time was afraid of becoming more sexually attractive to her husband. Once this was out in the open, we were able to deal with her ambivalence.

It is also important for clients to get a sense of what is realistic and to

Recommendations: Motivation

11. If appropriate, have clients make a public commitment to change.

Recommendations: Motivation

12. Find out what clients have already done about their problem behaviors that has been successful and incorporate this in the treatment plan.

dispel any grandiose or unreachable goals. Doing this may increase the risk of clients dropping out of therapy if they decide that the costs of therapy outweigh the benefits or that the benefits of their behaviors outweigh the costs. In the long run, however, inappropriate goals tend to do more harm than good.

The next task that needs to be accomplished is that clients must take responsibility for the change process. Even in disorders that are due primarily to biological or organic factors, clients still have some control over their symptoms—for example, by following a treatment plan (taking medications, doing homework assignments), being aware of prodromal signs, seeking help at the first signs of a relapse, and so on.

At best we will be spending only one hour per week with our clients, so it is clear that the lion's share of the change process will fall on them. This is even more crucial in the maintenance stage. In this case, clients must know how to examine—and be willing to examine—their own thoughts, feelings, and behaviors, and must be able to recognize how these influence their condition. Through this recognition, clients will be better able to make appropriate choices in their behavior.

Clients also need to be convinced that ultimately they are the only ones who can accomplish change. Because psychotherapy's long association with the medical model, many clients assume the "sick" role while attending therapy. This tends to promote passivity, dependence, and a sense of vulnerability. Of course, this needs to be reversed. However, while clients must assume responsibility for changing their lives, at the same time the therapist must also be willing to surrender his or her control. For an excellent review of this possible power struggle in psychotherapy, see Goldberg (1986).

Finally, clients have to be able to trust the therapist and must believe that he or she has the ability and expertise to help them reach their goals. We can accomplish this last task by (1) using basic "Rogerian" techniques (accurate empathy, unconditional positive regard, etc.); (2) developing a positive relationship; (3) making the client feel safe; and

(4) using various social power bases (especially referent power), which I will describe in Chapter 4.

Depending on the characteristics of the client, the process described here might take some time. Often therapists feel pressured to make changes too quickly, when the client may not be ready for them. As I will describe in Chapter 4, it is often better to start off with small requests for change. This allows clients to experience success and increase their self-efficacy progressively as therapy unfolds. One potential problem with managed care systems is the inclination to treat all clients alike. Obviously, some clients may do very well with brief forms of treatment, but others will not. One of the important challenges therapists will face is assessing and matching clients with appropriate procedures (see Bennett, 1989). In some cases, the goal of therapy might be to teach clients how to change on their own or with the help of individuals in their social network. For others, it may be most appropriate for the client not to begin therapy at all at that point in time. Alternatively, some clients will require an extended period to make any significant improvements, and, as we will see later in this book, a small minority of clients may need therapy throughout their lives. I will return to the topic of treatment matching in a later chapter.

Motivation

Although a concept of motivation is central to the process of psychotherapy and the notion of resistance, an accepted definition of the term has been elusive. As Ford notes (1992, p. 9), "vagueness and ambiguity have characterized efforts to define and conceptualize motivation throughout the history of psychology." This problem is not due to a lack of effort. For example, Pinder (1984, p. 7) writes, "it is only a slight exaggeration to say that there have been almost as many definitions of motivation offered over the years as there have been thinkers who have considered the nature of human behavior." However, the end result of all this labor is aptly summarized by Mook (1987, p. xvii): "what is motivation, anyway? One can define it so broadly that it encompasses all of psychology, or so narrowly that it threatens to vanish entirely." Since most of you are probably not motivated enough to read a lengthy discourse on how the various definitions of motivation have evolved and changed through the last hundred years, I will not cover them in this section (those who are interested in a detailed background and history of this concept should see Weiner, 1992; Ford, 1992; Mook, 1987; or McClelland, 1987).

In their comprehensive review of motivation, Kleinginna and Kleinginna (1981) found 98 definitions for the term. A simple, though

Recommendations: Motivation
13. Give clients feedback on progress and change the procedures or goals as necessary.

Recommendations: Motivation
14. If clients are not progressing, try to determine the factors for this (lack of skills, social pressures, etc.).

not direct, summary of these explanations is that humans are either pushed, pulled, self-propelled or just coasting along. The common theme is *motion.* The root of the word *motivation* (and also *motor, moment,* and *emotion*) is the Latin *movere,* which means "to move." Attempting to go back to its roots, I am going to offer a simple definition of a *motive* as any variable that increases a person's probability of action (movement) or change. This would encompass cognitive, emotional, biochemical, social, and environmental factors.

Notice that this definition lacks directionality. The element that gives motivation its direction is the end-state or goal. A person's goal, however, can and often does vary within a given period of time, and goals can have more than one motivator. I favor the idea that most motivators can ultimately be linked to certain affective states or feelings. I will return to this idea and to the general topic of goals later on.

Another important variable of movement and change is the magnitude or intensity of the motivator. This can be viewed as the intrinsic value of the end-state and is measured in part by the energy or effort that is expended toward reaching the goal as well as the persistence of this effort. Rather than being a constant, the strength of a motivator most likely fluctuates over time and may need to be addressed and rekindled frequently in order to maintain performance. Strength of motivation may not be easy to assess. For example, it would not be appropriate to evaluate the intensity of motivation simply by looking at goal achievement or the amount of time it takes to reach a goal or even the amount of effort expended, because many factors other than the intensity of motivation affect these measures. For example, the tasks involved in reaching a goal vary in terms of difficulty. Obviously, difficult tasks will require more effort and persistence than easy ones, but task difficulty is not always correlated with the intensity of a motivator. The motivation to get intoxicated on drugs is very high for some individuals, yet the tasks involved in doing so may be minimal.

Assessing motivation is further complicated because a sequence of behavior may have more than one goal, and single goals are often steppingstones to other goals. A young woman, for example, may go to a certain college because her parents may want her to, because her boyfriend is going to that school, and also because she wants to become a lawyer someday.

In addition, persons often have multiple goals, and certain goals may conflict with each other. For example, I once worked with a Vietnam veteran with PTSD. His motivation for coming to therapy was to be able to cope better with his symptoms so he could go back to work. However, he was also applying for disability benefits in case the therapy "didn't work out." His inconsistent progress in therapy appeared to match whatever goal seemed (consciously or unconsciously) to be most important for him in any given time period. Similarly, a person's behavior may not always be consistent with his or her expressed motivation; (people often have hidden, ulterior, or unconscious motives). For example, I once worked with an interesting older woman who claimed to be depressed throughout the treatment process; but her real problem, as far as I could determine, was loneliness.

Finally, at times people withhold behaviors in order to reach certain goals (not speaking to someone or withholding information), which makes the connection between motivation and behavior even more difficult to assess. As with other psychological constructs, we have to depend on what people say and do in order to gauge the intensity of motivation, but because of its complexity and instability, this is a difficult task.

Affective End-States

Much, if not most, human behavior is motivated by our desire to experience certain feelings and sensations (sexual feelings, euphoria, happiness, pride, joy, etc.) and to avoid others (pain, fear, anxiety, etc.). In other words, the reason we like to watch a sunset or listen to music or like to be with certain people is that these activities make us feel a certain way. Many of our behaviors are geared to making such experiences possible, either in an immediate or a delayed fashion. Although a detailed description of this type of motivational system is beyond the scope of this chapter, Pervin (1983, 1991) has developed a theory that addresses the essential components of such an approach (see also Ford, 1992, for a similar process). Pervin's system is based on six principles, which are summarized as follows (1991, pp. 8–9):

1. Behavior is organized and directed toward certain end-points or goals.

Recommendations: Motivation
15. Address relapse and maintenance issues in the treatment program.

Recommendations: Motivation
16. Careful selection of goals should dramatically reduce the problem
of client motivation in treatment.

---

2. Goals include cognitive, affective and behavioral components, but the primary motivational force is affective. Goals may or may not be conscious.
3. Goals are organized in a highly fluid and dynamic hierarchical structure, where at any given point in time the dominance of any particular goal may change. Goals can be either consistent or in conflict with one another.
4. Goals may be activated by internal or external stimuli.
5. Sometimes a goal may be simply to engage in a particular behavior.
6. Some forms of psychopathology may be due to the absence of goals, goal conflicts, or an inability to reach desired goal states.

Although this model may not explain all behavior, it addresses many of the types of problems that we face in psychotherapy. Some people, for reasons we do not yet totally understand, become addicted to certain behaviors (eating, sex, drugs, gambling, etc.). According to the model given here, what they really become addicted to is the sensation that these behaviors produce. Unlike "normal" people, they cannot seem to get enough of that sensation, despite some potentially serious negative consequences. Thus, compulsive gamblers are not really motivated by the money they can win but, rather by the "rush" they feel when playing. According to Pervin, most addictive behaviors are maintained because of the powerful positive affect they produce, because goal substitutes are absent or too weak, and/or because various inhibitory responses that allow most people to control such urges and desires are ineffective (see Pervin, 1991, for a more detailed description).

Pervin (1983) suggests that affect directs movement on the basis of pleasure (approach), fear (withdraw) or anger (attack). Although the primary motivator is affect, the force that steers and maintains our behaviors is our thoughts. As we get feedback on our progress toward certain goals, we picture ourselves being successful, or imagine how it will feel to engage in an activity. Alternatively, we may decide that we will never be able to reach a goal or that the potential negative consequences are not worth the payoffs, and we may turn to something else. Cognitive aspects (including memory) help determine which goals are appropriate at any given time and determine the appropriate steps needed to reach the goal. Of course, behavior is also important because it is the enactment of our thoughts or plans.

Goals

A goal is a desired end-state toward which some effort or action is directed. In this case, we can differentiate goals from wishes or desires (see Ford, 1992, for a different viewpoint). In other words, wishes or desires do not become goals until some effort is expended toward reaching them. However, this effort need not be overt or behavioral and the goal may not necessarily be reached. Locke and Latham (1990, p. 320) summarize the roles that goals have in regulating human behavior. They state that goals: (1) direct attention and effort towards goal-related activities; (2) activate stored knowledge and skills that individuals have which are relevant to the goal; (3) prolong effort over time; (4) motivate individuals to develop appropriate task strategies for reaching goals; (5) serve as a benchmark for evaluating performance feedback; and (6) affect what and how information is processed in terms of retrieval, selection, and organization. Similarly, Srull and Wyer (1986) claim that "Goals often determine what we attend to, how we perceive objects and events, how we use reasoning processes to make inferences about causal connections, and how these events are organized and represented in memory" (pp. 541–542). They add that goals also influence our judgments and possibly trigger various affective reactions.

Goals can be separated into various broad categories. For example, Ford and Nichols (1991) make the distinction between intrinsic and extrinsic goals. An intrinsic or terminal goal is one where the consequence of goal achievement is valued for its own sake, as opposed to extrinsic or instrumental goals where attainment is valued because it leads to some other goal. These authors suggest that a given goal can be intrinsic, extrinsic, or both. In practice, however, it may be difficult to categorize goals accurately in this manner.

In a similar vein, Winell (1987) makes the distinction between outcome and process goals. Outcome goals have clear end-states, such as getting a degree or buying a car. Process goals, on the other hand, relate to things like being honest or always doing your best and, in a sense, are never actually achieved. Many of these goals are associated with our value systems.

Recommendations: Motivation

17. Make sure that the goals selected in therapy match clients' value systems and cultural backgrounds.

Recommendations: Motivation

18. Clients need to know how to examine their own thoughts, feelings, and behaviors, and some individuals may need training in this area.

The selection of goals in therapy has a major impact on outcome and therefore should be done carefully. If appropriate goals are chosen for therapy, we should not have to worry too much about motivating the client because motivation will come naturally from the goals themselves. Although the efficacy of goal setting in therapy is seriously reduced when the client lacks a strong interpersonal relationship with the therapist, selecting the right goals promotes a positive relationship.

As I have already suggested, when we speak of increasing a person's motivational level, we have to include some terminal goal. However, out of fear or the desire to maintain some secondary gain, at times a client's goal may be to avoid change. Although this process may not be conscious, such clients are not likely to make much progress in therapy. In this case, it is inaccurate to say that clients are not motivated. Their motivation may be very high, but, at least in the therapist's view it is not moving them in a direction that is beneficial for them. Kanfer and Schefft (1988) describe this as follows: "the clinician should consider not if a client is motivated but with what magnitude the client's behavior is directed towards what goal" (p. 164).

Similarly, a person's goals may conflict with one another. Consider a client who comes to therapy because he is a workaholic and his wife wants him to spend more time with her. His conflicting goals might include: to reduce the arguments he and his wife are having, to prevent his wife from leaving him, to make a lot of money and become president of his company. All of these taken together may lead to little or no progress in terms of changing his workaholic behaviors. However, the client's lack of improvement is due not to poor motivation but, rather, to inconsistent goals and motivators. In this case, the therapist's task is to clarify and select goals that will redirect the client's motivation and focus it toward agreed-on and internally consistent objectives for therapy.

Life Goals

It is useful to get an overview of our clients' predominant life goals before developing a treatment plan so that the plan can be consistent with the goals. Of course these are likely to be different for each person; some clients may not even be aware of what they are. To help us assess these possible motivators, we can use various tools such as the Ford and Nichols Taxonomy of Human Goals presented in Table 2-1. This assessment device presents a small number of general categories of goals that can be used to help identify integrative themes in clients' behavior patterns and to help us develop treatment strategies. It is interesting that most if not all of these 24 goals are related to experiencing some type of affective

TABLE 2.1   The Ford and Nichols Taxonomy of Human Goals

Desired Within-Person Consequences

Affective Goals

Entertainment: Experiencing excitement or heightened arousal; avoiding boredom or stressful inactivity.

Tranquility: Feeling relaxed and at ease; avoiding stressful overarousal.

Happiness: Experiencing feelings of joy, satisfaction, or well-being; avoiding feelings of emotional distress or dissatisfaction.

Bodily sensation: Experiencing pleasure related with physical sensations, physical movement, or bodily contact; avoiding unpleasant or uncomfortable bodily sensations.

Physical well-being: Feeling healthy, energetic, or physically robust; avoiding feelings of lethargy, weakness, or ill health.

Cognitive Goals

Exploration: Satisfying one's curiosity about personally meaningful events: avoiding a sense of being uninformed or not knowing what's going on.

Understanding: Gaining knowledge or making sense out of something; avoiding misconceptions, erroneous beliefs, or feelings of confusion.

Intellectual creativity: Engaging in activities involving original thinking or novel or interesting ideas; avoiding mindless or familiar ways of thinking.

Positive self-evaluations: Maintaining a sense of self-confidence, pride, or self-worth; avoiding feelings of failure, guilt or incompetence.

Subjective Organization Goals

Unity: Experiencing a profound or spiritual sense of connectedness, harmony, or oneness with people, nature, or a greater power; avoiding feelings of psychological disunity or disorganization.

Transcendence: Experiencing optimal or extraordinary states of functioning; avoiding feeling trapped within the boundaries of ordinary experience.

(Continued)

TABLE 2-1 *(Continued)*

Desired Person–Environment Consequences

Self-Assertive Social Relationship Goals

Individuality: Feeling unique, special, or different; avoiding similarity or conformity with others.

Self-determination: Experiencing a sense of freedom to act or make choices; avoiding the feeling of being pressured, constrained, or coerced.

Superiority: Comparing favorably to others in terms of winning, status, or success; avoiding unfavorable comparisons with others.

Resource acquisition: Obtaining approval, support, assistance, advice, or validation from others; avoiding social disapproval or rejection.

Integrative Social Relationship Goals

Belongingness: Building or maintaining attachments, friendships, intimacy, or a sense of community; avoiding feelings of social isolation.

Social responsibility: Keeping interpersonal commitments, meeting social role obligations, and conforming to social and moral rules; avoiding social transgressions and unethical or illegal conduct.

Equity: Promoting fairness, justice, reciprocity, or equality; avoiding unfair or unjust actions.

Resource provision: Giving approval, support, assistance, advice, or validation to others; avoiding selfish or uncaring behavior.

Task Goals

Mastery: Meeting a challenging standard of achievement or improvement; avoiding incompetence, mediocrity, or decrements in performance.

Task creativity: Engaging in activities involving artistic expression or creativity; avoiding tasks that do not provide opportunities for creative action.

Management: Maintaining order, organization, or productivity in daily life tasks; avoiding sloppiness, inefficiency, or disorganization.

Material gain: Increasing the amount of money or tangible goods one has. Avoiding the loss of money or material possessions.

Safety: Being unharmed, physically secure, and free from risk; avoiding threatening, depriving, or harmful circumstances.

Source: Martin E. Ford, *Motivating Humans: Goals, Emotions and Personal Agency Beliefs,* pp. 88–89, copyright © 1992 by Sage Publications. Reprinted by permission of Sage Publications, Inc.

state, which is consistent with the preceding premise. Ford and Nichols (1992) have developed the Assessment of Personal Goals questionnaire to measure the general strength of each of these 24 goals.

There are several other tools we can use to assess the global motivational system of our clients. One is the Rokeach Value Survey (Rokeach,

1973). With this measure, the person has to rank-order two lists of 18 values that serve as "guiding principles" in their lives.

Another approach is the life task assessment procedure described by Cantor and her associates (Cantor & Fleeson, 1991; Cantor & Kihlstrom, 1987). In this system, clients are asked to list and describe their major life tasks (e.g., making friends, getting tenure, getting into graduate school), and when, where, and how they go about reaching these goals.

A third useful idea is that of "possible selves" (Markus & Nurius, 1986) which links a person's self-concept and what he sees for himself in the future. Individuals' possible selves include what they would like to become, what they could become, and what they are afraid to become (Markus & Nurius, 1986). This approach seems especially relevant to the concept of motivation because clients' imagery of possible future selves allow them to organize and direct their behavior. A possible self becomes the person's mental map to reaching a goal. In some cases, however, the therapist may need to help clients develop some appropriate possible selves before starting a treatment plan.

Goal Orientation

The strategies described previously generally refer to the assessment of goal contents—the results or consequences one wants to achieve. Related to this are clients' goal orientations, or how they conceptualize their goals—in other words, an assessment of factors that influence how people set their goals. Ford (1992, pp. 112–114; see also Ford & Nichols, 1987) describes three general dimensions that people typically use in this regard:

1. *Approach–avoidance:* Here, goals are conceptualized in terms of wanting to achieve something positive (e.g., producing quality work) as opposed to avoiding negative consequences such as social disapproval. For example, a person may work extra hours in order to be more successful on the job or because everyone else does and the person doesn't want to appear different.
2. *Active-reactive:* This is related to whether goals are initiated by the person or imposed by external factors. Generally, people with a reactive tendency are not as committed or successful in reaching their goals as are those in the active group.
3. *Maintenance–growth:* Maintenance refers to goals that seek to maintain a certain stability or status quo, as opposed to growth, which seeks change and self-improvement.

Winell (1987) has suggested an orientation that combines these three into a coping versus thriving life-style. A coping orientation includes a reactive, avoidance, stability-maintaining approach, whereas a thriving organization involves an active, improvement, and positive-consequence intent. In a similar vein, Dweck and Leggett (1988) have come up with the concept of learning and performance goals. For learning goals, individuals attempt to increase their competence by understanding or learning something new. In performance goals, individuals are concerned with getting favorable judgments or avoiding negative judgments of their competence. The authors suggest that performance goals tend to lead to a helpless pattern, characterized by an avoidance of challenge and reduced performance when confronted with obstacles. On the other hand, learning goals lead to a "mastery-oriented pattern" whereby challenging tasks are sought out and performance does not suffer in the face of failure (Dweck & Leggett, 1988, p. 256).

Individuals who view ability as a relatively stable attribute are more likely to impose performance goals on themselves. Individuals who see ability as an acquirable entity are more likely to impose learning goals. Although most of the research done in this area deal with children in a school setting, the studies seem to have implications for psychotherapy as well. Obviously, in most cases we will want to promote a learning versus a performance style.

Individuals'goal orientations affect both the goals they choose and the behaviors related to reaching these goals. It is useful for the therapist to have an idea of what clients' goal orientation might be. A detailed description of the assessment of a individual's goal orientation can be obtained from the references given previously.

Goal Setting

Once we have an idea of the general categories of motivators that clients have and of their personal goal orientations, we can start to develop appropriate goals for their treatment. The following four suggestions can be used as guidelines (these are modified from the original presented by Ford, 1992, p. 116):

1. *Goal relevance:* Select goals that are meaningful or appropriate for this particular client in a particular case.
2. *Goal importance:* Select goals that are personally significant to the client.
3. *Goal attainability:* Select goals that clients believe they can achieve.

4. *Emotional salience:* Select goals for which the natural consequences of goal achievement are obvious or salient to clients.

In a similar manner, Kanfer and Schefft (1988, p. 135) suggest that: (1) the client's present situation be analyzed to determine what is discomforting or distressful; (2) the range of possible end-states that would reduce or eliminate the client's self-dissatisfaction be evaluated; and (3) the most appropriate methods and procedures to reach these end-states be used.

Other researchers suggest that goals should be specific rather than vague, demanding rather than easy, and accompanied by feedback (Locke, Shaw, Saari, & Latham, 1981; Miller, 1985). There has also been controversy over whether proximal or short-term goals are more effective than distal or long-term goals in maintaining performance (see Locke & Latham, 1990, for a review). In my view, distal goals are sufficient for most types of clients, and those persons who need proximal goals will develop their own. For example, de Shazer (1988) suggests that clients should describe what will be different in their lives once they reach their treatment goals. These end-states can then be used as a global measure of progress or goal completion. Further research is needed in this area to clarify the most effective approach.

We should also try to identify any goal(s) that clients may have that conflict with or are incompatible with the treatment objective. Conversely, we should identify (or help develop) other client goals that are consistent with this objective and, if possible, use procedures that might satisfy several goals at the same time. At the intrapersonal level, goals may conflict because of various factors:

1. *Limitations of time or other resources:* For example, people's work schedule may not allow them to carry out a plan or they may be unable to pay for additional psychotherapy sessions.
2. *Opportunity costs:* In a given situation, a person may prefer one activity over another. For example, going to therapy may interfere with working overtime.
3. *Conflicting intentions:* For example, a husband may want to save his marriage, but also to date other women.

At the interpersonal level, goals may conflict because they are incompatible with the goals of a significant other. For example, a female client may want to go to graduate school, but her husband wants to buy a new house. Similarly, a couple's individual goals may conflict because they do not have the time to complete both. Finally, achieving one's goals may result in significant changes in the life of a significant other. For example, a client may hate his job and want to change careers, but doing so would require his wife to go back to work. A detailed discussion of conflicting goals is given by Wilensky (1983).

Treatment goals must be consistent with what the person ultimately wants to accomplish. As Robertson (1988) points out, we should try to set goals that clients truly want as opposed to those we believe they should have or those that are set by others.

Some clients will have no goals, or will have unrealistic or unattainable goals or goals that are inconsistent with social norms (Kanfer & Schefft, 1988). With these challenging cases, we need to identify creative alternatives or use our persuasive abilities to the fullest.

Task Difficulty

Goals that are far beyond a client's ability level obviously will not be fruitful. Most studies suggest that performance levels off when task difficulty exceeds the ability of the person (Locke & Latham, 1990). Clients' ability levels may not be easy for the therapist to assess, especially early in treatment. Although clients may not be able to evaluate themselves accurately, in the end they are the best sources of information. Similarly, clients' perception of their abilities (self-efficacy) may be more important than their actual competence. As I mentioned earlier, some researchers suggest that demanding goals are often more appropriate than simple ones. Although this may be true in educational and industrial settings, it is not always the case in psychotherapy. Obviously, each client must be treated as an individual; but some simple rules are to use goals that clients believe are reachable and, if you have to err, do so on the less rather than more stringent side. The difficulty level of goals can always be increased as therapy progresses, but if you start off with ones that are too vigorous, the client may become demoralized or drop out. In Chapter 7, I will discuss the issue of goal setting with clients who have severe psychological disorders.

To summarize, it is important to note that there are a number of goal systems operating in therapy. One relates to the goals the client is striving to reach, such as reducing alcohol intake. A second includes the goals that the therapist has for the client—for example, coming to all the sessions, not dropping out, and so on. A third system includes the personal goals that the therapist has for him- or herself. These might include making a certain amount of money, increasing their practice or prestige, and so on. A fourth includes the goals of the client's family or significant others, which may be inconsistent with those above. The point here is that in designing the goals of therapy, the therapist should be aware of how other goal systems enhance or interfere with each other, and as much as possible an attempt should be made to establish consistency among the various components.

Treatment Strategy and Goal Implementation

After selecting the goal(s) to be worked on, the next step is to identify the cognitive and behavioral strategies needed to achieve it. The steps involved in goal setting and goal implementation are interdependent and need to complement each other. As Locke and Latham suggest, the perception of a task or goal should automatically bring up in the client a repertoire of cognitively stored potential plans or strategies (similar to schemas) based on previous experience. These would include what we typically call habits and skills that have been learned through modeling, formal instruction, reading, and so on. Some of these are simple and task-specific, such as buying a bottle of milk. Others are more general or complex and may require a number of subplans linked together. In addition, most individuals have a hierarchy of potential plans that can be used depending on the situation and the expected outcomes. Such stored plans improve people's efficiency in that they are relatively automatic and require little thinking.

In a related manner, most people develop general rules or heuristics—"honesty is the best policy," "Never trust a stranger," and so on. These types of mental templates guide behaviors in a wide number of areas, although not all of these are useful or appropriate. Often the task of the therapist is to get the client to stop using these old and ineffective behavior patterns. As much as possible, however, it is advantageous to use strategies that the client already has learned in order to reach treatment goals. For example, de Shazer (1988) suggests that by the time clients are in therapy, they have already attempted to solve their problems numerous times and probably have been somewhat successful. He recommends that therapists find out what is working, find out what has worked, find out what might work, and "prescribe the easiest" (p. 98). As I described in Chapter 1, it is often useful to find out what successful coping strategies the client uses with other problems and to use these if appropriate.

To summarize, this stage involves developing the treatment plan or method to reach the goal. If a client's current tactics are not perceived to be applicable or appropriate for the task or goal, combinations of other coping strategies that the client already uses or totally new approaches may need to be developed. To a large extent this is what therapists are paid to do. It is advantageous, however, for clients to make considerable contributions to this process or, if possible, to develop their own methods. This should improve not only compliance, but maintenance as well.

All this looks good on paper. The problem is making it work in the real world. That is why the treatment strategy should be flexible and the client should be given various options. If possible, variations of the treatment strategy should be developed based on potentially different situations. In everyday life, we all have a number of different ways of accomplishing a given task. Often the particular situation will determine which, if any, strategy we choose. If the strategy we prescribe is too rigid, it is not likely to be applicable to the complicated system in which we all live. As a simple illustration, I once worked with a client who was trying to quit smoking. The plan we developed was working fairly well, except that he was also an avid skier and had developed the habit of smoking a cigarette each time he went on the ski lift. Despite his efforts, he couldn't control his urge for a cigarette while on the lift. Thus, we simply excluded this particular situation from his smoking restrictions and left the rest of the plan intact. Not doing so would probably have scuttled the whole process.

Appraisal of the Plan

The assessment of the strategy is related to the next step of this model, which involves answering two questions:

1. Will the plan work?
2. Can the plan be implemented?

This process is also interrelated with the last two steps. Various factors are important here, including past success, time restraints, the client's ability level, and self-efficacy. The plan can break down either at the client's cognitive level or at a more concrete behavioral level. Again, client input is very important. The task of the therapist is to help develop not only a treatment plan that could work, but one that could with this particular client.

At this stage, at least three tasks must be accomplished:

1. Try to predict any stumbling blocks.
2. Encourage clients to anticipate cognitively possible positive and negative consequences of reaching the goal. For example, clients can be asked to try out the plan (or parts of it) mentally to envision how significant others will react and to forecast environmental responses.

This type of imagery may allow clients to experience the affect (either positive or negative) of reaching their goal.

3. Increase the client's self-efficacy.

Obviously, it will sometimes be necessary to return to the previous stages and make appropriate changes.

Part of this appraisal process involves evaluating the plan against the client's potential resources. Read and Miller (1989) have come up with a comprehensive list of resources that may be available to the client. Table 2-2 is based in part on their suggestions. Each of these possible resources should be evaluated as either a strength or a weakness in terms of facilitating or interfering with the treatment strategy.

TABLE 2-2 Potential Client Resources

I. *Personal Resources*

intelligence	capacity for self-monitoring
self-control	problem solving ability
imagery	memory
attention span	education
knowledge bases	special talents
health	energy level
sensory capacities	physical attractiveness
age	physical strength
social skills	social intelligence
expressive skills	ability to communicate
adaptation skills	determination
social status	spiritual resources
income	professional status
time	assertiveness
common sense	capacity for relationship
values	capacity for self-exploration
habits	personal beliefs or stereotypes
self-esteem	self-schemas, person schemas
mental health	

II. *Environmental Resources*

living environment	transportation
work environment	availability of other resources (library, recreational facilities, exercise facilities, vacation, etc.).

III. *Social Resources*

friends or social network	family or significant other
quality of relationships	support for change
emotional, physical, financial, or professional support	client's cultural background
social, norms, rules and roles	

It would be an understatement to say that environmental and social conditions are important variables that must be considered in designing a treatment program. The treatment strategy must be consistent with individuals' attributes, their interpersonal relationships, and their social environment and culture. The importance of an environment that allows changes to occur is comparable to that of client ability. However, Locke and Latham (1990) make an important point in regard to both of these variables. If the proper goals have been selected and if clients are sufficiently motivated and committed to change, they will often take steps to maximize their ability or find avenues to overcome environmental constraints. I will talk more about these issues in Chapters 4 and 8.

The next step is implementation of the plan. Feedback, of course, is an important and necessary component of goal achievement. Clients will get feedback from the therapist, from others in their environment, and from their own internal self-monitoring. Assuming that clients want to reach their goals, behaviors that are perceived (through feedback) to get them closer to their target should be naturally reinforcing and thus persist, whereas those that are not should decrease or disappear. Many factors will affect this. If the previous steps are done correctly, this stage should go smoothly. However, the therapist should be flexible enough to change either the goals or the plan when necessary. In some cases, the previous steps will need to be repeated. Many of the problems confronted at this stage relate to treatment adherence, which will be thoroughly covered in Chapter 4. A schematic representation of the steps outlined here is given in Figure 2-2.

A Physiological Model of Motivation

This section briefly describes another model of motivation that some readers may find interesting. Although it is related to the model just described, reading this section is optional.

The general model of motivation I presented appears to be consistent with some of the brain reward system studies currently being carried out (see Wise & Rompre, 1989, for a review). Although most of these involve animal research, they have implications for human behavior as well. Such studies show that animals such as rats will press a lever to obtain electrical stimulation to certain parts of the brain until they are literally exhausted or, sometimes, until they die. They will forego water, food, or sex partners and are willing to encounter high levels of shock in order to gain these effects. It appears that addictive drugs (cocaine, heroin, amphetamines, etc.) have the same effect as brain stimulation on these animals and that this reward mechanism involves the neurotransmitter

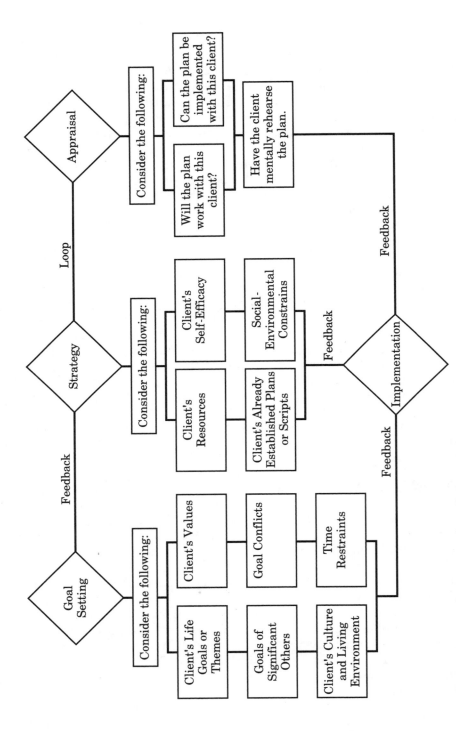

FIGURE 2-2 Goal Setting and Implementation

dopamine. Electrical stimulation, addictive drugs, and probably other reinforcers such as food, water, and sex appear to activate this reward system, which in turn produces two major effects in the animals. First, psychomotor activity increases; second, it intensifies the effects of subsequent "reinforcers." For example, rats will increase their rate of responding for electrical brain stimulation when injected with cocaine. This may help explain some of the binge behavior seen in drug and alcohol abuse and in other addictions. However, when these same animals are given drugs that block dopamine (such as neuroleptics), their rate of responding for brain stimulation decreases in a dose-related manner. That is, the higher the level of the neuroleptics, the lower the response rate; at very high doses, responding ceases altogether. It appears, then, that drugs that block dopamine reduce the motivating effects of various "reinforcers." Using older psychological terms, it is not the animal's drive that is reduced but, rather, the pull of the external stimuli.

Although the final implications of these studies for human behavior are not yet clear, they do raise several issues. First, the studies seem consistent with the premise that much of human behavior may be motivated by the intent to reach certain sensual or affective states. There is also evidence that this type of behavior involves a specific brain reward system at least partially associated with dopamine. Second, if the effect of drugs is similar in humans and in animals, the studies serve to highlight how powerful drugs are in motivating behaviors, making the lengths to which people will go to obtain them more understandable. Third, these studies may help explain why clients who have disorders such as schizophrenia (which is associated with dopamine) are so difficult to work with. For example, their apparent lack of motivation is probably due both to neuroleptics and to the effect the schizophrenic process itself has on the brain reward system. I hope that future studies in this area will help us better understand major psychiatric impairments such as schizophrenia, major depression, bipolar disorder, and motivation itself.

Summary

This chapter was based on five premises: (1) all clients are motivated in some sense; (2) motivation should not be viewed as a personality trait or isolated construct; (3) a person's motivational level may change quickly and thus may be difficult to assess; (4) people have multiple goals, many of which conflict with one another; and (5) motivation is based on action or change. To change, people must: (1) be aware of a problem; (2) be ready and able to accept influence; (3) have a goal or goals; (4) be motivated to move toward the goal; (5) be mentally and physically capable of reaching the goal; and (6) be in an environment that allows movement toward the goal.

Basic models of motivation, decision making, and stages of change were presented. A primary assumption of this chapter is that much of human behavior is motivated by a conscious or unconscious desire to reach certain affective end-states and to avoid others. Consistent with this view, a goal-based model of motivation was described.

The general stages of change described in this chapter include being aware of a problem or condition that needs to be modified; making the decision to change; selecting appropriate goals consistent with the desired changes; selecting procedures to reach these goals; implementing these procedures; getting feedback and modifying the goals and procedures as necessary; achieving these goals; and maintaining the change.

Recommended types of client assessment procedures include an assessment of the client's stage of the change process at the time of entering therapy and assessment of the client's life goals and goal orientation. Although many therapists tend to shy away from formal assessments, these may streamline treatment and make it more effective.

3

Self-Disclosure

Overview

Most practitioners would agree that the most important component of psychotherapy is the transfer of information from one person to another. Chelune (1979) points out that we constantly disclose information about ourselves. For example, our appearance indicates our sex, approximate age, weight, height, and possibly social status. Our body movements and posture also disclose various bits of information, such as moods or emotions. In therapy, however, one of the most important types of information conveyed is self-disclosure. Over the past twenty years, the number of books and articles written about self-disclosure has increased dramatically. Yet, as Archer (1987) maintains, to a large extent the field has remained isolated from the mainstream. Perhaps as a consequence, concrete research conclusions seem to be lacking, and no unified theory has yet been developed.

This chapter takes a broad look at self-disclosure. It is divided into three sections. The first is a literature review on the topic of self-disclosure. This may be useful for readers who are not familiar with this issue or with current developments in the field. The second section looks at the importance of self-disclosure for psychotherapy. Included in this segment is how therapists can help clients increase their disclosures, and a brief discussion of therapist disclosures. The third section explores the relationship between self-disclosure and resistance, and discusses how the two affect each other.

A Brief Literature Review of Self-Disclosure

Research on self-disclosure has been done by many different disciplines. Because psychotherapists may be unaware of some of the recent issues explored in this area, a brief literature review follows. Although this section is not always directly pertinent to psychotherapy or the topic of resistance, it does introduce some relevant issues

What Is Self-Disclosure?

A widely accepted definition of this term has not been established. Jourard, who pioneered the research on self-disclosure and was a major authority in this area, stated that "to disclose means to unveil, to make manifest, or to reveal" (1971, p. 19). Stricker (1990) defines self-disclosure "as a process by which the self is revealed" (p. 277). Chelune (1987) describes it as "the process of revealing personal information about oneself to another" (p. 9). In a similar vein, Derlega and Chaikin (1975) define it as "the process by which one person lets himself be known by another person" (p. 1). Derlega and Grzelak (1979) indicate that: "Self-disclosure includes any information exchange that refers to the self, including personal states, dispositions, events in the past, and plans for the future" (p. 152). After an extensive review of the literature on self-disclosure, Cozby (1973) operationally defines it as "any information about himself that Person A communicates verbally to Person B" (p. 73). A more restrictive definition is given by Worthy, Gary, and Kahn (1969): "when A knowingly communicates to B information about A which is not generally known and is not otherwise available to B" (p. 59). A similar one is given by Rosenfeld, Civikly, and Herron (1979): "Self-disclosure can be defined as a person's voluntary revelation of personal information that a receiver could not learn from any other source" (p. 80).

Although most of the published literature of self-disclosure involves verbal disclosures, some involves nonverbal behaviors (Kaplan, Firestone, Klein, & Sodikoff 1983), and some researchers restrict the term to disclosures that are intentional, are of a private nature, or occur within a relationship. For example, Allen (1974) describes self-disclosure as the "uncoerced exchanging of information in a positive relationship." Thus, self-disclosure may refer to verbal or nonverbal behavior, general or personal information, disclosures that are voluntary or coerced, information that is shallow or profound, information that is known or not generally known, and so on. These inconsistencies may arise from the fact that self-disclosure researchers come from many varied backgrounds and spe-

---

Recommendations: Self-Disclosure
1. Try to interpret the meaning of silence or low self-disclosure and deal with these issues during therapy sessions.

Recommendations: Self-Disclosure
2. Some clients may need training in how to disclose or how to put their feelings into words.

---

cialties—clinical, personality, counseling, or social psychology; communication theory; neuropsychology; and other fields (Berg & Derlega, 1987).

Chelune (1975) indicates that, at a minimum, self-disclosure includes five dimensions: (1) the amount or breadth of information disclosed, (2) the intimacy of the information revealed, (3) the rate of disclosure, (4) the affective manner of presentation (e.g., the consistency of affect with the material presented), and (5) self-disclosure flexibility, or the individual's ability to change disclosure levels based on the situation or partner. Since researchers typically study only one or two of these dimensions at a time, results may be inconsistent and ambiguous. As Chelune (1979) points out, the inconsistencies in the definitions of the term require different research methods and assessment techniques, and thus cross-study comparisons and outcome generalizations are difficult to formulate. Much of what Chelune said a number of years ago is still true today.

Self-Disclosure Measurement

Self-disclosure is not only hard to define but difficult to measure as well. Measurement has generally been done through three methods: (1) self-report inventories or self-ratings; (2) recipient ratings (e.g., a subject's reports of his or her partner's self-disclosures); and (3) objective measures. Each method produces somewhat different results (Chelune, 1979). For example, self-report methods may assess past disclosures, willingness to disclose, or disclosures to various targets and topic areas. There is also some question about the validity of self-reports (Cozby, 1973). Recipient measures may be biased by the target person's attitudes or perspective. Finally, objective methods may be influenced by the method used to collect data or by the way disclosure is defined. For example, using his rating scale, Jourard (1971) found some support for the positive relationship between self-disclosure and a "healthy" personality, but most behavioral measures of self-disclosure fail to replicate his finding. Even though much progress has been made in improving procedures to measure self-disclosure, it remains a difficult and elusive construct to quantify.

Self-Disclosure as a Personality Construct

A third factor that confounds the research findings in self-disclosure is that the term can refer to both a personality trait and a process. Self-disclosure as a personality trait has been researched extensively, but the results are, again, often inconsistent and contradictory. A possible reason is that many researchers ignore the effects of situational variables on disclosure, despite a number of published warnings against doing so (Hill & Stull, 1987).

A major question related to self-disclosure as a personality trait is the relationship between self-disclosure and gender. Jourard (1971) suggests that women are socialized in a feminine-expressive role, whereas men are brought up to be more secretive. He indicates that females are more open, self-disclosing, and empathic, whereas males are taught to be more concealing and unemotional. Jourard believes that this stereotyped male role can be "lethal" and that it results in higher rates of physical and mental disorders.

Overall about 75 percent of studies show that women disclose more than men do (e.g., Pederson & Breglio, 1968; Jourard, 1971; Chelune, 1977; Hendrick, 1981; Balswick 1988). In a recent study, Derlega, Metts, Pedronio, and Margulis (1993) speculate that gender differences may be related to the following factors:

1. Because of the effects of socialization, women enjoy intimate conversations and value self-disclosure more than men. For example, women are more likely to get together just to talk, whereas men usually get together to engage in some activity.
2. Males are more concerned about the negative consequences of self-disclosure. The traditional male role includes appearing self-confident and strong, and men learn to avoid disclosing any weaknesses or vulnerabilities.
3. Beliefs and stereotypes suggesting that women enjoy self-disclosing more than men do may influence how individuals behave toward members of each gender. This differential treatment may sway disclosure levels toward the expected direction.

Recommendations: Self-Disclosure

3. Use pretherapy interventions such as modeling, role induction, or instructional training.

Recommendations: Self-Disclosure

4. Consider the use of paradoxical techniques such as reframing or prescribing.

Some studies show no male–female differences in self-disclosure (e.g., Vondracek & Marshall, 1971; Feigenbaum, 1977; Shapiro & Swensen, 1977). Some actually show that, under certain circumstances, men will disclose more than women (e.g., Sermat & Smith, 1973; Derlega, Winstead, Wong, & Hunter, 1985). For example, men may disclose more than women in the initial stages of opposite-sex relationships (e.g., Davis, 1978). However, Hill and Stull (1987) suggest that in these situations women ask men a lot of questions as a way to get them to talk about themselves. After reviewing a number of studies, these authors conclude that women are generally more expressive than men but that various factors moderate the effects of gender on self-disclosure. These include the topic of disclosure, sex of target, relationship to target, sex-role attitudes, sex-role identity, sex-role norms, and measure of self-disclosure (see also Hendrick, 1987; Balswick, 1988; Shaffer, Pegalis, & Cornell, 1992).

In a further effort to resolve the research inconsistencies related to gender differences in self-disclosure, Dindia and Allen (1992) conducted a meta-analysis of the topic. They found that:

1. Gender differences do exist, but they are relatively small.
2. The target or partner moderates the effect of gender on disclosure in that female-to-female disclosures are greater than male-to-female or male-to-male disclosures. However, female-to-male disclosures are not greater than those of males to males.
3. Studies that use recipient (target) measures of self-disclosure show greater gender differences than self-report or observational measures and may be due to the effects of sexual stereotypes or expectations.
4. Despite recent changes in attitudes regarding gender roles in our society, no significant changes in gender-related self-disclosure levels were found over the last thirty years. These results were based on comparing studies done in the 1960s, 1970s and 1980s.

The authors also point out that individuals' goals or expectations may affect levels of disclosure and may partially explain previously found sex differences. In other words, men and women may set different goals in their interactions with others, and this in turn may lead to different disclosure levels. For example, the level of disclosure may fluctuate on the basis of whether a subject anticipates or desires future interaction with the target, whether the other person is perceived as a possible romantic partner, and so on. This appears to be a viable area for future research. In addition, because of the relatively small gender differences found, the authors question Jourard's (1971) assertion that men suffer more physical or psychological problems or that they are less likely to benefit from psychotherapy because of reduced levels of self-disclosure.

Other Factors Associated with Self-Disclosure

Similar research inconsistencies are seen in studies looking at the relationship between self-disclosure and various sociocultural or demographic variables. For example, a number of studies show that whites disclose more than do African Americans or Mexican Americans (Littlefield, 1974), but these differences may be due to social class influences rather than race (e.g., Cozby, 1973). Some studies (e.g., Diamond & Hellkamp, 1969) suggest that birth order may be important, with later-born disclosing more than first-born, but this finding is not always consistent. There is some evidence that disclosure increases with age and that extraverts are more likely to self-disclose than introverts (Archer, 1979). On the other hand, there is little relationship between self-disclosure and religion.

All things considered, Archer (1979) summarizes the search for variables associated with high-disclosing individuals as follows: "No categorical picture of the high discloser emerges from the personality research" (p. 37). Such findings have prompted some researchers to conclude that the use of a global construct of self-disclosure is not useful unless the "target" is also specified (Miller, Berg, & Archer, 1983). For example, Chelune (1979) maintains that the research surrounding self-disclosure parallels that of the state-versus-trait controversy, and suggests that complex behaviors such as self-disclosure must be viewed through the interaction of both person and situational variables. As an illustration, he describes the characteristic of self-disclosure flexibility: the ability of an individual to modify his or or her level of self-disclosure depending on the social context. This is similar to the process of self-monitoring. Chelune points out that factors such as alcohol consumption, sex, attractiveness and status of target, physical proximity, and other environmental factors have all been found to influence disclosure. He concludes that the factors

---

Recommendations: Self-Disclosure

5. With some clients, you may need to use nonverbal techniques such as drawings or checklists, or have them write down their responses.

Recommendations: Self-Disclosure

6. With some clients, you may have to slow down your pace until they are ready to self-disclose.

---

that influence self-disclosure include "When? To whom? On what topic? To what degree? Under what circumstances? And by whom?" (p. 16).

Self-Disclosure as a Process

Self-disclosure as a process has also been studied extensively. Jourard and many others have maintained that self-disclosure promotes disclosure in others. This process is generally known as self-disclosure reciprocity (Jourard, 1971; Jourard & Resnick, 1970; Ehrlich & Graeven, 1971). Berg (1987) suggests that reciprocity of disclosure is one of the most frequent and consistent research findings seen in the literature. Some possible reasons for this effect include modeling, showing that one likes the other person, and maintaining an "equitable social exchange" (Berg, 1987). For example, Balswick (1988) found that spouses exhibit the greatest levels of disclosure to each other and to same-sex friends. However, reciprocity does not appear to be a simple or automatic response. For example, in the initial stages of a friendship, the breadth of disclosure is high, but the depth or intimacy of disclosure is low. Derlega and Chaikin (1975) indicate that intimate disclosure reveals that the discloser trusts the listener, but at the same time he or she is making him- or herself vulnerable because the information may be used against the discloser. Thus, intimate disclosure is risky. The discloser "risks censure, ridicule, betrayal and worst of all, indifference from his confidant" (1975, p. 142). It appears, then, that reciprocity of intimate disclosure may be the crucial aspect of building a strong and trusting relationship. Altman (1973) indicates that the reciprocity for nonintimate information declines as a relationship develops, but reciprocity of intimate information shows a curvilinear effect, with maximum reciprocity occurring in the middle stages of the relationship. Thus, disclosure in the later stages of well-established relationships may be more flexible than reciprocal (Derlega, Wilson, & Chaikin, 1976; Hendrick, 1987; Berg, 1987). Derlega, Metts, Pedronio, and Margulis, (1993, pp. 34–35) summarize the main factors that appear to be important for reciprocity to occur:

1. The recipient must feel special.
2. The recipient must want to maintain or enhance the relationship.
3. The relationship must be in the appropriate interactional stage.

For example, as noted, reciprocity seems to be highest during the middle stages of a relationship.

Self-disclosure has also been linked to how much a person likes another (Halverson & Shore, 1969; Jourard, 1971). For example, receiving disclosing information may be a signal that one is liked by the discloser and may also increase attraction for that person (Berg, 1987; Worthy et al., 1969). Hendrick (1981) has also found a positive relationship between self-disclosure and marital satisfaction. Again, however, research suggests a number of qualifiers and inconsistencies between self-disclosing and liking. Although many studies show a positive relationship between self-disclosure and liking, this finding has not been consistent with males. Overall, there may be a curvilinear relationship between self-disclosure and liking (Cozby, 1973). Studies have found that high levels of self-disclosure may arouse anxiety and negative feelings in others, depending on the content of what is being disclosed. Jourard (1974) suggests that a major factor affecting self-disclosure is dependency. He maintains that people will not fully disclose to others on whom they are dependent because of a fear of losing their support: "any factor which promotes dependency and interferes with the attainment of independent security is a factor which interferes with full communication" (p. 224). Coates and Winston (1987), expanding on this, suggest that whereas too little disclosure may have negative consequences for our psychological (and possibly physical) health, too much "distress disclosure" may drive others away (p. 230).

Other studies suggest that the part of the conversation in which disclosure occurs is also important. For example, Archer and Burleson (1980) show that liking others increases when disclosure occurs later in the conversation because, when disclosure occurs early, the discloser may appear to be someone who shares intimate information with anyone. Chelune (1975) summarizes the functional qualities of self-disclosure as follows: It serves an expressive function to release pent up emotions; it increases personal clarification; it helps develop and maintain social relationships; and it controls outcomes in social relationships through impression management (p. 254).

> **Recommendations: Self-Disclosure**
> 7. Increase your own levels of self-disclosure to serve as a model.
>
> ---
>
> **Recommendations: Self-Disclosure**
> 8. Vary your expectations to match the type of client with whom you are working. Generally speaking, males, ethnic minorities, and children need more time for self-disclosure than other groups.

Models of Client Self-Disclosure and Their Relationship to Therapy

Doster and Nesbitt (1979) maintain that our knowledge base on self-disclosure has developed from four different models: (1) the fulfillment model, (2) the ambiguity-reduction model, (3) the interactional model, and (4) the social learning model. The fulfillment model is based primarily on humanistic psychology and views self-disclosure as both an interpersonal and intrapersonal process (Doster & Nesbitt, 1979), where clients learn to unrepress their "real" selves. The foundation of this model is that humans have a natural tendency to reach their full potential (self-actualization). However, the lack of an optimum environment during the developmental stage blocks this process and turns people's expressions primarily into a protective and defensive process. Self-disclosure is viewed as an essential process that allows individuals to experience self-awareness and thus to get back on track toward self-actualization. As such it is a crucial part of therapy. It not only allows the therapist to understand the client but also allows the client to understand more fully and accept him- or herself. Not surprisingly, this model emphasizes therapist self-disclosure more than any other model.

The ambiguity-reduction model is based on the notion that the reason clients do not open up to their therapists is that they are not fully aware of their role in therapy. As opposed to the passive or neutral tone that Freud suggested therapists take, this model promotes a proactive stance. For example, the use of pretherapy training, modeling, operant conditioning, role playing and other techniques that facilitate self-disclosure (Doster & Nesbitt, 1979). In this sense, this model shifts some of the responsibility for self-disclosure from the client to the therapist.

The interactionist model assumes that all human behavior is interactive and thus views self-disclosure as a dyadic process. Psychological symptoms are seen as being due to inadequate or inappropriate interpersonal relationships and pathological communication. For example, through improper communication, clients are able to control their relationships and advance those that are consistent with and reciprocal to their "sickness." As Doster and Nesbitt (1979) point out, "neurotic symptoms control relationships by defining how others are to become involved, whereas psychotic symptoms control relationships by preventing others from becoming involved" (p. 186). This model generally views therapy as the process of building a therapeutic relationship (Doster & Nesbitt, 1979; Sullivan, 1940), and self-disclosure as a process of metacommunication.

The social learning model sees self-disclosure as the product of the client's previous conditioning and learning history. Similar to the ambiguity reduction model, the social learning model assumes that self-disclosure is a skill that clients lack and therefore have to be taught. The techniques used for this include social skills and assertive training, modeling, cognitive therapy, and operant conditioning techniques.

Altman and Taylor (1973) offer a more objective and experimental approach to self-disclosure with their social penetration theory. "Social penetration refers to (1) overt interpersonal behaviors which take place in social interaction and (2) internal subjective processes which precede, accompany, and follow overt exchange" (Altman & Taylor, 1973, p. 5). Social penetration differs from self-disclosure in that it includes verbal and nonverbal communication, cognitive factors, and overt behaviors. The model involves a multilevel behavioral process of building a relationship in which self-disclosure is a part. The basic assumptions of this theory are, first, that interpersonal behavior is a gradual process in which information interchange progresses from superficial, biographical and nonintimate areas to "deeper layers of the selves" (p. 6), including emotions and attitudes; and, second, that people assess the rewards (positive aspects) and costs (time, effort, negative experiences) of these interactions, and the relationship progresses only when the balance is positive. The authors suggest that individuals predict implications of future interactions with deeper levels of exchange and then decide whether or not to move on. According to these authors, too much self-disclosure, especially early in a relationship, may actually hinder growth. They suggest that self-disclosure typically proceeds in an orderly fashion from nonintimate to intimate disclosures, and that it is but one of many processes that allow one person to be known by another. Thus, social penetration involves moving through the layers of each person's personality as the relationship proceeds. The authors suggest that the dissolution of a relationship also follows an orderly process that is the opposite of social penetration. That is, the movement is from more to less intimate disclosure, and from greater to lessor amounts of interaction.

> **Recommendations: Self-Disclosure**
> 9. In special cases, consider the use of silent sessions or conducting the session nonverbally.
>
> ---
>
> **Recommendations: Self-Disclosure**
> 10. Be careful not to elicit too much self-disclosure in the early stages of therapy, as this may have some negative impact with some clients.

Conclusion

The research findings described here have a number of implications for psychotherapy. These are briefly listed and will be further discussed.

1. Therapists should try to avoid forming expectations about client disclosures that are based on stereotypes. For example, women do not always self-disclose more than men.
2. Therapists should not expect high levels of client self-disclosure before an adequate relationship has been formed. In fact, promoting high levels of disclosure early in therapy may be detrimental to relationship building.
3. Research confirms that self-disclosure can be a useful therapeutic tool in therapy.
4. The reluctance of individuals to self-disclose to others can occur in any relationship and thus should not always be interpreted as a sign of resistance.
5. Self-disclosure can be used as an impression management tool by both the client and the therapist.
6. Rates of self-disclosure appear to be influenced by situational variables and by the characteristics of the listener.

Self-Disclosure and Psychotherapy

Self-disclosure in psychotherapy is important for a number of reasons. First, individuals' difficulties with self-disclosure may play an important role in the origination or maintenance of some of their emotional problems. For example, the inability to self-disclose has been linked to loneliness (Stokes, 1987), marital problems (Hendrick, 1981), and problems with the maintenance of social networks (Berg, 1987). In describing the relationship between self-disclosure and psychopathology, Carpenter (1987) makes a number of important points. First, by its very nature psychopathology disrupts normal functioning in a variety of ways. These include disruption of interpersonal behaviors and the motivation or ability to self-disclose. He gives as examples people who are paranoid, who view self-disclosure as very threatening, and schizophrenics, whose self-disclosures often include delusional and otherwise inappropriate material. Second, although there is no strong empirical support for a causal link between self-disclosure and psychopathology, poor self-disclosure may make pathology more persistent or more severe. As Carpenter states, "The act of requesting assistance for mental or behavior difficulties is itself a form of disclosure, and this likely prevents many persons from seeking therapy" (1987, p. 209). He adds that poor disclosure skills may prevent these individuals from utilizing supportive sources or using disclosure as a technique for dealing with emotional problems. Third, he maintains that the differences in self-disclosure between normal and abnormal groups is most likely in type rather than in quantity of self-disclosure.

A second reason that self-disclosure is important for psychotherapy involves two related assumptions: (1) People tend to disclose more when they are distressed, and (2) they obtain some benefit when they do so. Stiles (1987) has developed what he calls a "fever model" to explain this process. He uses fever as an analogy for disclosure because both tend to be a sign of disturbance and a part of the restorative process (p. 257). Stiles suggests that people in distress disclose more because they become almost totally preoccupied with themselves and their problems. He says, "upsetting or stressful events generate a subjective sense of pressure, of something being bottled up. Often the pressure incorporates emotion— usually anger, despair, fear, remorse, or some other negative feeling, though great joy and happiness can also impel people to disclose" (Stiles, 1987, p. 261). Stiles points out that clients come to therapy precisely because they are distressed and because therapy allows clients to disclose in a safe environment and without the risk of damaging social relationships. He has recently extended his research finding to a nontreatment (e.g., university student) population (Stiles, Shuster, & Harrigan, 1992).

Stiles also uses his fever model to resolve what he calls three paradoxes in psychotherapy research. The first, which is the association of disclosure with both "sickness and restoration," has already been described above. The second is the absence of a clear-cut positive relationship between levels of disclosure and therapy outcome. Stiles says that this occurs because clients who are very distressed disclose more, but because they are more dysfunctional, they are also likely to have poorer outcomes. The third paradox deals with the lack of differential effective-

---

Recommendations: Self-Disclosure

11. Some clients will not self-disclose when they are dissatisfied with treatment, so this factor should be considered.

Recommendations: Self-Disclosure

12. As much as possible, therapists should match their level of self-disclosure to the clients' expectations or preferences.

---

ness of various types of psychotherapy (e.g., Luborsky, Singer, & Luborsky, 1975). The solution here (though somewhat simplistic), is that the restorative powers of disclosure represent the common ingredient across all types of verbal therapies. Stiles warns, however, that more disclosure is not necessarily better and that not everyone benefits from high levels of disclosure. Janis (1983) makes a similar point about inducing high levels of disclosure in the initial stages of therapy, where it may actually increase the client's level of demoralization by revealing weaknesses and dissatisfactions. He suggests that high levels of self-disclosers may actually result in less treatment adherence or in dropping out, and suggests that moderate amounts are more appropriate.

Although the perceived importance of self-disclosure varies greatly among different treatment orientations, most therapists would argue that it does contribute significantly to the treatment process. At the very least, it helps the therapist understand the clients' problems more fully and, at the other extreme, is a major psychotherapeutic process. However, the relationship between self-disclosure and treatment outcome is murky at best. Doster and Nesbitt (1979) report that the greatest support for the contribution of self-disclosure to treatment outcome occurs with client-centered therapy, and less with psychoanalysis and behavior therapy. Likewise, these authors suggest that the general evidence supporting the contribution of self-disclosure to outcome is much greater for individual therapy than for group therapy approaches.

The intended purpose of self-disclosure also varies widely depending on treatment orientation. For example, one of the original uses of self-disclosure was to help promote *catharsis* (Freud & Breuer, 1895/1955). However, Freud later questioned both the effectiveness and the duration of this process, and suggested that the most important role of self-disclosure was to lead to self-understanding, which he believed was an absolute prerequisite for treatment progress (Strean, 1990). Currently, the use of self-disclosure to promote self-understanding is a core concept in various types of psychotherapy, and especially with the client-centered approach. In fact, a number of studies have found that the majority of client verbalizations in therapy sessions, regardless of therapeutic style, are of a self-disclosure nature (Stiles, 1987).

Increasing Self-Disclosure in Psychotherapy

Most therapists would agree that self-disclosure is a necessary part of therapy. Psychotherapy itself is often described as the "talking cure" (so named by Breuer's famous patient, Anna O). However, pertinent self-disclosure is not always easy for clients, who are often ashamed of their thoughts or behaviors or may not even know what to talk about. The first step in helping clients open up in therapy is to try to find out the reasons for their reluctance. For example, Harris and Watkins (1987, p. 37) suggest that clients may be silent for many reasons, including anger, shyness, anxiety, fear of hospitalization, a desire not to disappoint the therapist, involuntary presence in therapy, lack of understanding of the therapy process, unwillingness to take responsibility for their problems, fear that the therapist will reveal their disclosures to others, and an attempt to use silence to control the therapeutic process. Finding the cause of clients' reluctance to speak up will help determine the best way to handle the problem. Harris and Watkins suggest that it is often helpful to deal with the issues that induce clients to be silent rather than to confront the silence itself—for example, working with clients' resentment over being in therapy or their pessimism over being able to improve or change. In addition, some clients may not know what is expected from them in therapy. Explaining the therapeutic process or modeling may help. Role induction training or the use of pretherapy interventions may also be useful.

Manthei and Matthews (1982) offer a number of other suggestions for working with "silent" clients:

1. Interpret the silence. Clients may be silent to express various feelings, including fear, anger, boredom, embarrassment, sadness, and hostility. Because these distinct meanings of silence may need to be treated differently, they should first be analyzed and identified. Techniques that can be used for this purpose include direct questioning, nonverbal techniques (such as the use of drawings or pictures for extremely withdrawn or silent clients), and interpretation of body language.

Recommendations: Self-Disclosure

13. Clients who consistently answer, "I don't know," can be asked to make up invented answers. Many times the responses are consistent with the way the client truly feels.

---

2. Offer nonverbal words of responding. For example, clients can be encouraged to write down or draw representations of their thoughts or feelings rather than verbalize them. These can include the use of various checklists (problems, attitudes, etc.) or sentence completion instruments. Clients can also be asked to act out their feelings or to express themselves physically (using postures, mime, or role playing).

3. Work at the client's own pace. Some clients simply require more time in order to be able to trust the therapist and increase their self-disclosures. Not focusing in on the target problem immediately or delaying subsequent treatment sessions may be useful in some cases. Along the same lines, clients who come from different cultures may have unique problems with self-disclosure, which I will cover in Chapter 8.

Polansky (1965) developed the term "verbal accessibility" as a way to describe a person's readiness to self-disclose. He describes four personal characteristics that may prevent self-disclosure: (1) a chronically low need to self-disclose, (2) strong needs or desires to withhold disclosure, (3) fear of disclosure, and (4) deficiency in the ability to disclose. Polansky suggests that many clients are noncommunicative because they want to protect their self-esteem (this is similar to Rogers's theoretical orientation). He states: "They fear that should they expose their attitudes, they may not sound so 'nice,' or so perfect, as they like to think they are" (p. 35). In a sense, clients remain silent so that they themselves can avoid the awareness of any problems they may have. Other clients cannot tolerate closeness or allow themselves to trust anyone. These clients, who tend to be very lonely or to lack interpersonal relationships outside of therapy, use silence as a way of avoiding interpersonal involvement.

In working with clients with low verbal accessibility, Polansky suggests that talking itself be made a focus in therapy. In other words, the therapist should try to figure out the reasons for the lack of disclosures and then work on decreasing these blocks to communication. In some cases, clients may need to be taught how to communicate effectively or how to put their feelings or attitudes into words. Relationship-building techniques are also important in this effort.

Doster and Nesbitt (1979) suggest that individual characteristics result in different levels of self-disclosure. They describe three broad types of clients. Clients of the first type is generally well adjusted and attend therapy to obtain greater self-understanding or for similar reasons. These clients tend to be less anxious than others; they assume more responsibility for their own improvement and tend to be high self-disclosers. They are more likely to prefer expressive therapists and client-centered therapy. They are also more likely to continue and benefit from therapy. Clients of the second type tend to be less well adjusted and have more problems when beginning therapy, but they are not psychotic. Their disclosure levels tend to be low to moderate. They often prefer behavioral therapy to other techniques because they seek symptom reduction rather than self-understanding. These clients often require role induction training in order to elicit self-disclosure, and they are less likely to remain in therapy or to benefit from it than those in the first group. The third group includes clients who are low self-disclosers and who have serious mental health problems. They tend to respond poorly to role induction training, and they do best when high levels of disclosure are not requested. These clients generally do not respond as well to therapy as those in the previous two groups.

McHolland (1985) suggests a number of procedures for dealing with silence in adolescents. For example, when clients tells you they will not talk, paradoxical procedures such as prescribing and reframing, or scheduling a silent session, may help break the impasse. You can also tell clients that you will let others talk for them (e.g., the parents), which usually prompts these individuals to talk for themselves. Another technique is to carry out a nonverbal interview, wherein clients respond nonverbally through body language. McHolland also suggests that some shy adolescents need more time to open up so that the silence can simply be accepted during the first few sessions. Some of the nonverbal techniques described above by Manthei and Matthews (1982) can also be used.

Other approaches for increasing self-disclosure include assertiveness and social skill training programs. Some studies suggest that group therapy results in more disclosures than individual treatment, but this appears to depend on the makeup of the group and on the skill level of the group leader. On the other hand, as most of us would predict, research shows that audio- or videotaping tends to reduce self-disclosures.

The personality and behaviors of the therapist are also important in increasing self-disclosure. For example, Miller, Berg, and Archer (1983) found that some individuals seem to elicit more disclosures than others. Factors that appear to be important here are perceived trustfulness, level of attentiveness and eye contact, as well as ingredients that are often considered traditional therapist characteristics, such being warm, being responsive, and having good listening skills. Assuring the client of confidentiality seems to be important as well.

Sack (1988) describes various ways to deal with clients who routinely respond, "I don't know." He starts by suggesting that this type of resistance is often due to clients' unperceptiveness or defensiveness. In other words, clients may have little insight into the causes of their problems or may wish to protect their egos through the use of defense mechanisms such as denial and repression. One way a therapist can react to this is through silence. This gives clients a chance to think more about the question and to decide whether they want to risk a response at that particular time. Related to this, the therapist may ask if clients want to know. This helps to clarify clients' readiness to proceed with the topic or to determine whether there is a need to refocus the session toward the client's fears or ambivalence. Another suggestion Sack makes is to have clients pretend they know the answer or to make one up. This allows clients some flexibility in their response so that they do not have to worry about being totally honest (although their responses are likely to be relevant). Second, it allows clients to get in touch with aspects of themselves that they previously denied or distorted.

At times, the therapist may offer to answer the question for the client. This is a type of paradoxical technique designed to make clients aware that the real answers and real solutions to their problems lie within themselves. Like other paradoxical procedures, however, it needs to be used with caution.

Another technique that may be used if an adequate relationship has been established with clients is to challenge or confront their reluctance to respond. This might jolt some clients into facing real issues and also reveals that the therapist is aware of their resistance. Again, this technique needs to be used carefully, as it can result in greater withdrawal or resistance on the part of the client.

Often, therapist self-disclosure may be useful in terms of modeling openness and risk taking to the client, and to increase interpersonal trust. Also, as with the lack of self-disclosure in general, a therapist needs to explore possible reasons for clients' reluctance to respond. For example, female clients may not want to share certain personal or sexual information with a male therapist, or perhaps clients simply do not feel comfortable with the therapist. All of these techniques may help resolve the temporary impasse that often occurs when clients respond, "I don't know."

Therapist Self-Disclosure

Almost every practicing therapist would probably agree that psychotherapy is a complicated art form and will remain so for the foreseeable future. Answers to questions such as how honest we should be with our clients, how friendly, or how spontaneous remain largely unanswered. The same is true for therapist self-disclosure. As with other aspects of psychotherapy, different orientations offer various guidelines for practice. Classical psychoanalysts reveal very little, whereas Rogerians tend to be much more open. Therapist self-disclosure also varies as a function of the problem being treated. For example, it tends to be used more with substance abuse or in some cases of PTSD, where the sharing of similar backgrounds and information is thought to be necessary in order to achieve treatment goals. But comprehensive, hard and fast rules for therapist disclosures are lacking.

Research findings in this area have been inconsistent. As a rule, it appears that moderate amounts of therapist self-disclosure are more appropriate than extremes at either end. For example, some level of disclosure seems to be necessary to develop and maintain an effective relationship. Similarly, almost all clients want to know a little about the therapist's background, orientation, experience and values. In a study conducted to evaluate what clients want to know most about psychotherapy, Braaten, Otto, and Handelsman (1988) found that individuals prefer information about the type of intervention that will be used and some facts about the personal characteristics of the therapist.

On the other hand, I have frequently heard from clients that their previous therapist preferred to talk about him- or herself rather than to listen. Thus, the important question becomes what, when, and how much therapists should disclose to their clients. There is no simple answer, because self-disclosure results in some of the same vulnerabilities to the therapist as it does to the client. Thus, at a minimum, the client–therapist relationship must first be secure. Second, the therapist must be able to trust clients enough so that they do not misuse or take advantage of significant revelations either inside or outside of therapy. Timing is crucial. As in any type of relationship, self-disclosure has the potential to diminish a person's status and social power. Thus, therapist self-disclosures should be strategic in nature (i.e., having some type of planned outcome). In this case, therapists' self-disclosures will generally be of a different type and less extensive than those of clients. For example, therapists should emphasize their own competencies and focus less attention on their weaknesses, but there may be times when it is appropriate to admit to personal flaws that promote the idea that client and therapist are more alike than different.

An important related consideration involves the individual characteristics of the therapist. Some therapists find it very easy to self-disclose to their clients; others do so very reluctantly. In supervising therapist trainees, I have found that most clients can easily pick up these differences and that "forced disclosures" by therapists actually cause more harm than good. In cases where high levels of therapist self-disclosures are necessary for positive therapeutic outcomes and a mismatch between client and therapist exists, appropriate referrals may be the best solution.

Hendrick (1988) suggests that clients are the best source in terms of how much self-disclosure they want or expect from the therapist. She offers two ways of gaining this information—first, through direct questioning of the client and, second, through a disclosure rating scale that she has developed. Her research findings are consistent with the Braaten et al. study in that most clients want, at the very least, some personal information about the therapist and probable treatment procedures. As Hendrick points out, supplying this type of information in and of itself does not solve the problem of how much to disclose in therapy. As with other aspects of psychotherapy, therapist self-disclosure needs to be tailored to fit the needs and expectations of each individual client and to match the type of problem, length of intervention, and strength of the therapeutic relationship.

Strategic versus Spontaneous Disclosures

Palombo (1987) makes a number of important points about the disclosures of psychotherapists. First, he distinguishes between therapist disclosures that are made spontaneously during the course of therapy and those that are planned and delivered intentionally as part of the treatment strategy. Most of the controversy centers on the first type, but this differentiation is seldom made in research reports. This makes conclusions difficult to formulate. Palombo suggests that researchers should consider this issue in both the research design and published reports.

Palombo also suggests that spontaneous disclosures might constitute an attempt by the therapist to self-heal. In other words, he proposes that therapy with some clients develops into a completely interactive process in which both individuals are free to self-disclose spontaneously and each obtains therapeutic benefits. It is almost as if the client and therapist change roles at these times. This sets up a Pandora's box of psychotherapy issues, which may never be fully resolved. These include the questions of how close or intimate therapists should become with their clients and whether psychotherapy is (or ought to be) a healing process for both client and therapist. Obviously, there are no simple answers for these questions. Furthermore, concerns such as potential client victimization make them even more complicated. To some extent, however, I think they hold the key to better understanding what makes psychotherapy effective with some clients and not others.

Although I have no definitive answers, I do believe that psychotherapy always holds the potential to evolve into a close relationship between client and therapist. At the same time, I believe that at least some (if not many) therapists have problems with intimacy. Perhaps some therapists were attracted to this field as a possible means of overcoming their perceived deficiencies in this area. However, those who are not successful may place their clients in a classic double-bind situation: Their overt messages may be inconsistent with their unspoken hesitancy or uneasiness in forming a relationship. Possible client responses to this may be confusion, anger, or an inability to move on. Although I have not seen this topic investigated formally, I believe from anecdotal information that the problem exists and that some forms of client resistance result from it. In short, successful psychotherapy usually results when therapists are able to develop a special connection between themselves and clients. Therapist self-disclosure appears to be an integral aspect of this process and a necessary condition for effective psychotherapy. However, a number of questions raised here need further investigation. Table 3-1 summarizes some general approaches for therapist disclosure.

Self-Disclosure and Resistance

Self-disclosure is linked to resistance in a number of ways. First, therapists often interpret a lack of self-disclosure as a sign of resistance. This interpretation may or may not be accurate. Despite our society's relatively high level of sophistication, some clients simply may not know how much to talk or what to talk about in a therapy session. This may be especially true members of various ethnic groups in which psychotherapy is an unfamiliar concept or in individuals who have not been properly prepared for therapy. Thus, as mentioned earlier, the reasons for a lack of self-disclosure should always be explored.

At the same time, psychotherapy to some extent requires clients to relinquish control of some aspect of themselves to the therapist. One domain of therapy over which clients retain full control is the amount of information they are willing to share with the therapist. In this sense, self-disclosure is a neutralizing force between client and therapist, and can be used by the former to manipulate the process. For example, if a therapist wants to work on an area that is particularly sensitive for a client, the client can simply refuse to discuss it or can answer questions with "I don't know." In this way, clients are able to influence the process.

Along the same lines, the disclosures clients make in the early part of treatment can determine the focus of therapy, including its goals and procedures. Consequently, to a large extent clients can attempt to con-

TABLE 3-1 General Approaches to Therapist Self-Disclosure

1. Moderate amounts of self-disclosure appear to be more useful than either too little or too much.
2. Disclosures should generally reinforce or support clients' positions as opposed to challenging clients' perspectives.
3. Self-disclosures should produce some benefit in clients as opposed to serving the therapist's own needs.
4. In general, distressing facts or therapist weaknesses should be avoided unless there is a specific goal for these disclosures.
5. Therapists must disclose information that may have serious effects on clients or treatment (e.g., illness, extended leaves, etc.).
6. Therapists should not use disclosure when they feel emotionally vulnerable.
7. Disclosure rates need to be matched with clients' presenting problems, age, gender, expectations, ethnic group, and stage of relationship.
8. Disclosures should be used with caution when the therapist has strong positive or negative feelings about the client.
9. The therapist should be aware of clients' attempts to manipulate the therapy process by requesting disclosures.
10. As much as possible, disclosures should be natural rather than forced.

trol the path therapy takes. Thus, clients have a very strong arsenal on their side to counterbalance the power of the therapist to influence them.

A second way self-disclosure is linked with resistance is that withholding certain types of information allows clients to be resistive in ways that are not always obvious. For example, if a client does not admit to drinking excessive alcohol, it may be difficult to learn about this otherwise. In my experience, some clients like to play something analogous to the old television show *I've Got a Secret*. I imagine that the thoughts of some clients work something like this: *If the therapist is at all competent, he will know what my problem is without me having to tell him.* Or, *If the therapist cannot determine the general contents of my secret, the problem must not be so severe after all.* I am sure there are other themes as well, but these clients are not likely to reveal much relevant information, at least early in the treatment process.

Helping clients give up their secrets offers a number of advantages for the therapist. First, it is major step toward change. As I mentioned in the last chapter, clients often come to therapy in a demoralized state, not knowing what to do next. The process of self-disclosure helps to remove them from this demobilized position. As Shlien (1984) points out, the act of revelation is even more important than its contents in terms of the initiation of change. It often serves as the catalyst to move forward.

Second, clients' revelations allow painful or avoided topics to be brought to the forefront where they can fully explored. Hanna and Puhakka (1991) call the latter "resolute perception" and suggest that it is the common denominator of effective psychotherapy. For example, they point out that simply talking about a topic requires a client to attend to it so it can be fully discussed. This in turn helps them acknowledge a problem and help discover ways to overcome it. Whether this is called "working through," "dealing with," or confrontation, it appears to be a necessary component of psychotherapy. On the other hand, avoiding important personal issues may functionally paralyze a client because unresolved dilemmas make it difficult to move forward.

Helping clients reveal their secrets is important for a third reason: It helps to cement the relationship between the client and the therapist. A number of studies indicate that clients form a more positive attitude about their therapist after they have confided in him or her. Having once revealed important information, they are likely to do so again. In short, the process of client self-disclosure appears to increase the trustworthiness of the therapist and to improve the client–therapist relationship.

The factors discussed here highlight an important aspect of self-disclosure: When used appropriately, it appears to be the first step toward reversing the process of resistance. In other words, self-disclosure helps clients acknowledge their problems, bring them into focus, and initiate a change process. All of these actions appear to be the opposite of resistive or defensive reactions such as denial, avoidance, and stagnation. I am not suggesting that self-disclosure is the only ingredient necessary for decreasing resistance, but it does appear to be a prerequisite for it. At the same time, the behavior of the therapist greatly influences the amount and type of disclosures made by clients. Thus, self-disclosure in terms of both the client and the therapist appears to be an integral component of reducing resistance and achieving successful therapy.

Some therapists are, at times, overly zealous in their efforts to get clients to report "secrets" that do not really exist. Unfortunately, this may be just as damaging as clients retaining their real secrets. Some of the controversy surrounding the so-called false memory syndrome (see Chapter 1) is related to the bias that therapists can introduce into their clients' belief systems.

Sometimes this can occur very subtly. Consider the case of a therapist who starts to listen very keenly and take very careful notes any time a female client reports something evenly remotely related to sexual abuse. I do not think it is uncommon for clients to begin to talk more about these topics (either consciously or unconsciously) just to please the therapist. Soon the stories may be embellished somewhat, and before long it may be difficult for these clients to differentiate fact from fiction. It is not clear from the literature how extensive this problem is, but my experience and that of my colleagues suggest that it does occur. Therefore, it is equally important for the therapist not to look for secrets that really do not exist.

Summary

This chapter has reviewed the topic of self-disclosure and its implications for psychotherapy. Self-disclosure is important for psychotherapy because it allows the therapist to more fully understand clients and their problems, and is crucial for developing target goals and treatment plans. In addition, disclosure seems to reduce distress. Disclosure is also important in the development and maintenance of a therapeutic alliance, which can also have a positive impact on treatment.

Four general models of self-disclosure were presented, including (1) the fulfillment model, (2) the ambiguity-reduction model, (3) the interactional model, and (4) the social learning model. Some of the unresolved issues surrounding self-disclosure are that (1) a generally accepted definition is lacking; (2) there are a number of methodological issues associated with measuring this construct; and (3) it is not clear whether self-disclosure should be treated as a personality construct, a psychological process, or both.

Previous research indicates that women generally disclose more than men. However, factors such as the sex of the target, the topic of disclosure, the stage of the interpersonal relationship, circumstances of the situation, and how self-disclosure is measured all influence research findings. Thus, in some situations men disclose more than women.

A relatively consistent research finding is the reciprocity of disclosure. Again, however, a number of variables, such as the stage of the relationship, type of disclosure, and target, are important. In short, self-disclosure seems to be due to the interaction of individual characteristics, the situation, and the topic.

The relationship between self-disclosure and resistance was discussed. It appears that client self-disclosure can help reverse the process of resistance and make it more likely that clients will attend to and attempt to change problem behaviors. The role of therapist disclosures was also reviewed. A moderate amount of therapist self-disclosure appears to be most useful, but a number of treatment variables need to be considered.

4

Treatment Adherence

Overview

One of the most common outcomes associated with treatment resistance is noncompliance with treatment recommendations. This factor is often blamed for lack of progress in psychotherapy and for relapse. The problem is so widespread that hundreds of articles have been written about it. Although not completely overlapping, nonadherence and resistance share many similarities. This chapter touches on a number of topics that are more fully explored elsewhere in this book.

Treatment adherence covers a broad number of behaviors including cooperating with the therapy process, taking prescribed medications, completing "homework" assignments, not engaging in self-destructive behaviors, and following general treatment recommendations. Cummings, Becker, and Maile (1980) suggest that clients' health care behavior can be explained by looking at six categories of variables: (1) accessibility of services, including the client's awareness of services and ability to pay for them; (2) clients' attitudes toward health care, including belief in the benefits of treatment and perceptions of the quality of services offered; (3) threat of illness, including the perception of the consequences of clients' symptoms; (4) knowledge of their disorder; (5) clients' social system and social interactions; and (6) demographic characteristics. Because these factors appear to be relevant to psychotherapy as well as to general health care, this chapter reviews these areas and other factors associated with compliance and noncompliance. Many of the topics discussed next are interrelated and thus share some similarities. Figure 4-1 gives a general overview of the material covered in this chapter.

Recommendations: Adherence
1. Conduct a compliance history; find out what methods clients have tried in the past; which procedures were and were not successful; what obstacles prevented clients from carrying out previous treatment plans.

Recommendations: Adherence
2. Identify and reinforce clients' original reasons for seeking therapy in order to maintain their motivation and discuss the hazards of noncompliance.

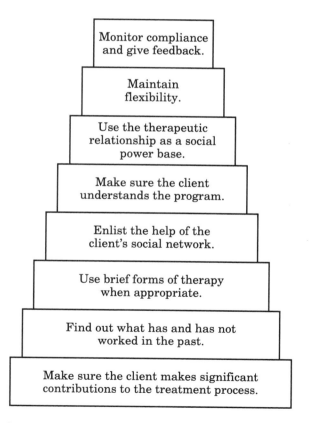

FIGURE 4-1   **Steps to Increasing Adherence to Treatment Programs**

In their comprehensive handbook on this topic, Meichenbaum and Turk (1987) begin by explaining the difference between the terms *adherence* and *compliance*. Briefly, some researchers maintain that *compliance* indicates a passive role on the part of the client and prefer the use of *adherence,* which suggests a more active cooperation between client and therapist. Although I agree with this distinction, the two terms have been used interchangeably in many previous studies, so I will do the same in this review. For the most part, the following discussion does not address attending therapy or dropping out of treatment, which will be discussed in a separate chapter.

Treatment adherence can fall along a broad continuum, from complete lack of cooperation to nearly full cooperation, and can fluctuate widely during the course of therapy. It is useful to view adherence as an active, ongoing process rather than a static one. Similarly, noncompliance is a complex phenomenon involving a number of interrelated variables, which often change over time, and this makes it difficult to pinpoint the cause. Note that compliance and noncompliance are not polar opposites: The absence of factors that lead to noncompliance will not necessarily ensure that compliance will occur. For example, not knowing how to carry out the treatment program usually leads to noncompliance, but complete understanding of the program does not necessarily lead to completing it. As much as possible, I will try to address both sides of this issue.

Like resistance, noncompliance should not be viewed simply as an intrapsychic process, and it should not always be viewed as negative. If clients are uncooperative, there usually is some reason for it. Clients are sometimes noncompliant to protect their self-esteem, to save their marriages or because of societal pressures. At other times these behaviors are due to characteristics of the therapist or treatment techniques.

Ultimately, the reason we want clients to be compliant in order to improve their condition. But this assumes that the treatment we propose will be effective and that we know what is best for the client— assumptions that are not always true. As Achterberg-Lawlis (1982) suggests, perhaps we are putting the cart before the horse by developing compliance technologies before perfecting treatment regimes. Similarly, Davidson (1982) points out that, "we have a much greater (and prior) ethical requirement to assure the efficacy of a treatment than to ensuring compliance" (p. 419).

Although I present a number of generalizations in the sections that follow, each case, as well as each client–therapist relationship, is unique. Therefore, noncompliance is best understood by using the idiographic approach and by evaluating the interactions between each client and yourself. One of the problems I found in reviewing the literature on com-

---

Recommendations: Adherence
3. Make sure you set realistic goals. Check with clients if you have any doubts, and negotiate the plan as necessary.

Recommendations: Adherence
4. Try to make the treatment plan as simple as possible (without compromising efficacy).

---

pliance is that much of it relates to physical disorders or health psychology in general. Therefore, caution must be used in generalizing from these types of studies to the treatment of psychological disorders. As much as possible, I have used studies that deal directly with mental disorders or research in which the results are relevant to psychotherapy.

General Findings

Overall, the incidence of nonadherence tends to increase as therapy progresses. However, this result varies depending on factors such as the characteristics of the client or disorder and the type of compliance. A general rule of thumb is to expect between one-third to one-half of clients to be noncompliant with significant aspects of your treatment recommendations, and up to three-quarters of clients with persistent or severe psychological disorders. Generally, it appears that clients are more likely to comply when they are required to learn new behaviors (e.g., an exercise program) as opposed to changing old behaviors (reducing fat in their diet). Similarly, they are least likely to comply with eliminating established behavior patterns or habits (smoking, overeating, substance abuse, etc.; Haynes, 1976). Stone (1979) suggests that acute or serious disorders with distressful symptoms elicit the highest levels of compliance, but this is probably more true of physical than of mental disorders. Clients are less likely to adhere when they have a chronic but non-life-threatening condition, or when the benefits of therapy are not immediately obvious (e.g., prevention programs). It is also important to remember that compliance behaviors are multidimensional (Davidson, 1982; Turk, Salovey, & Litt, 1986). In other words, clients may be compliant with one aspect of treatment but not with another.

DiMatteo and DiNicola (1982) maintain that cutting across the various factors that decrease compliance are two common elements, which they label the *process* and the *content* of influence. These are expressed by clients either resisting the influencer (process) or the influencer's advice (content). The client may resist the influencer because of various personal characteristics of the provider, a poor client–therapist relationship, or similar factors. This often results in no-shows, dropping out, or looking for another therapist. In the second type of resistance, clients accept the therapist, but not the advice. In this case, clients typically remain in therapy but tend not to comply with recommendations. The authors maintain that, in the second case, many clients are motivated to change but cannot do so because they lack the necessary skills or ability. These two conditions are similar to Ley's (1979) distinction between voluntary and involuntary noncompliance. Involuntary noncompliance occurs when clients agree to follow a treatment program but cannot do so for various reasons such as cost, time restraints, poor memory, or incorrect information. In this case, the treatment package should be modified to fit more closely the client's life-style, economic circumstances or personal characteristics. For some clients, additional training will also improve compliance. Clients who do not comply because they do not understand various aspects of the treatment regimen fit in this category as well.

In the case of voluntary noncompliance, the client understands the treatment plan but either disagrees with it, does not want to follow it, or does not want to change. Ley suggests that these clients require the use of more persuasive techniques to encourage compliance. In addition, clients should be allowed to participate in planning the treatment regimen and should approve it before it is formalized. As these studies suggest, it is important to identify the origins of noncompliance before attempting to modify it. Aside from the factors just described, other potential sources are reviewed next.

The problem with treatment adherence is obviously not limited to psychotherapy patients. For example, some of us with high cholesterol levels have problems giving up French fries. Research shows that about one-half of parents do not properly follow behavior modification techniques for their children, and many parents do not give their children medications for hyperactivity as directed (Firestone, 1982; Parrish, 1986; Pelham & Murphy, 1986). It is estimated that one-third to one-half of patients with high blood pressure, seizures, or diabetes do not regularly take their medications, and, across the board, about 60 percent of Americans do not take medications as prescribed (Sackett & Snow, 1979; Leventhal, Diefenback, & Leventhal, 1992). For example, many of us will stop taking an antibiotic as soon as we feel better instead of continuing for the prescribed number of days. In this case, the disorder may not be completely treated. Podell and Gary (1976) conclude that about one-third of all patients take their medications as directed, one-third take

---

Recommendations: Adherence

5. If possible, start off the first session with a simple assignment that you know clients will be able to do. Build up adherence requirements by starting off with small requests and increasing demands slowly as progress is made.

Recommendations: Adherence

6. Try initially to avoid procedures that are intrinsically aversive (for example, requesting an extremely shy person to ask someone out for a date). Phase these in slowly.

---

them sometimes, and one-third do not take them at all. On the other hand, patients facing a possible terminal disease such as cancer tend to comply with medication usage fairly well (Rodin & Salovey, 1989).

Measuring Compliance

There are a number of ways to measure treatment adherence (Gordis, 1979; Dunbar, 1979; DiMatteo & DiNicola, 1982; Masek, 1982; Meichenbaum & Turk, 1987). The most common are self-reports and self-monitoring; pill counts; therapist or clinical ratings; biochemical indicators (such as blood tests for lithium or antiseizure medications); records of broken appointments; direct observation and clinical outcome. Each of these methods has problems associated with it. For example, self-report or self-monitoring methods can be inaccurate and unreliable because clients are not telling the truth, because of poor memory, or as a result of imprecise measurement.

There is some evidence that the therapist might be able to increase the accuracy of self-reports by informing clients that he or she will be doing some type of reliability check—for example, using other family members to record behaviors or conducting covert observations of the patient in the natural environment. However, these procedures tend to be costly or difficult to carry out and may strain the client–therapist relationship. In general, while reliability checks may be useful for research, they do not seem to be widely used in general clinical practice.

Dunbar (1979) points out that clients tend to underreport poor compliance and overreport good compliance. She suggests that clients should be reinforced for both accuracy of reporting and compliance. Similarly, the therapist should create an accepting and nonthreatening atmosphere for reporting noncompliance. She emphasizes that it is important to tell clients what behaviors should be monitored and to provide training in how and when the behaviors should be measured. In addition, recording materials should be easy to use. This is not news for most of us, but I believe we often neglect this aspect of therapy.

The use of clinical outcome measures to assess adherence appears logical, but this assumes that there is a direct relationship between treatment adherence and desired results (Gordis, 1979; Masek, 1982). However, many factors unrelated to compliance can affect outcome. We all have worked with clients who improved even if they only minimally followed treatment recommendations, and with clients who regressed even though they followed our recommendations faithfully. Outcome measures also assume that the treatment we select will be effective with the particular client, which of course is not always the case (Eraker, Kirscht, & Becker, 1984). Therapeutic outcome tends to be an unspoken standard assessment of compliance, but the indirect relationship of treatment outcome to compliance makes its usefulness extremely limited (Masek, 1982).

Other methods of measuring compliance also have some drawbacks. Subjective ratings of clients' compliance behaviors by therapists have not been found to be very reliable (Dunbar, 1979; DiMatteo, & DiNicola, 1982). Overall, most studies indicate that therapists tend to overestimate the amount of compliance by clients and cannot accurately predict which clients are compliant or when (Kasl, 1975). Biological measures of compliance (blood tests for medication use, maintainenance of a certain diet, etc.) can be very useful, but they can also be expensive or intrusive, and the results may be difficult to interpret. Direct observation can be time-consuming and, depending on the observer's training or expertise, may be unreliable. Also, the act of observing people may affect their behavior and possibly invalidate the results. Some researchers have suggested that the use of unobtrusive measures (Webb, Campbell, Schwartz, & Sechrest, 1966) may be useful in measuring certain types of compliance, but most therapists have not utilized this approach. Finally, compliance levels may change over time, so frequent monitoring is necessary.

In general, attempting to measure treatment adherence can be difficult, but it is not impossible. Overall, it is important for the therapist to monitor adherence, to do so frequently, and to provide a nonthreatening environment for reporting nonadherence. It is also vital that the assessment procedure be relatively simple and the client know exactly what is being measured and how to measure it. Despite the problems outlined here, self-report methods or direct questioning by the therapist seem to be the most cost-effective and appropriate ways to gauge adherence. Once a satisfactory client–therapist relationship is formed, the feedback ob-

---

Recommendations: Adherence

7. Ask clients what they think about the treatment plan. Do they think it will work? If not, ask what modifications they would suggest.

Recommendations: Adherence

8. Try to reduce the overall number of treatment sessions if possible.

---

tained from clients should be sufficient. If not, a combination of the methods described here can be used, or creative alternatives may need to be developed (an interesting example is provided by Epstein & Masek, 1978).

Medication Compliance

As most of us have experienced, one of the biggest problems with clients with chronic or severe mental disorders is medication nonadherence. For example, between 25 and 50 percent of psychiatric outpatients do not take their medications correctly (Blackwell, 1976; Ley, 1979) and more than half of clients with schizophrenic or bipolar disorders stop taking their medications within the first year of treatment (Blackwell, 1982; Cochran, 1984; Pool & Elder, 1986; Corrigan, Liberman, & Engel, 1990). After a comprehensive review of several hundred articles, Sackett and Haynes (1976) found only a few variables that were related to medication noncompliance. These included complexity of medical procedures (e.g., more than one medication or multiple doses), duration of treatment, and clinic waiting time. They also found that factors such as family stability, compliance with other aspects of treatment, client satisfaction, close supervision, and belief in the efficacy of treatment increase compliance with medications. However, one of the problems with research investigating medication compliance is that objective measures are seldom used (Masek, 1982), and results therefore may not be reliable. Like compliance in general, medication adherence seems to be a complicated process involving a number of interacting factors, which makes prediction and control very difficult. However, many of the factors that increase or decrease medication compliance are similar to compliance in general, which is discussed next.

Factors Affecting Compliance

Past studies have identified hundreds of variables that can affect adherence, but they generally fall within these six major categories: client characteristics, treatment procedures, factors related to the disorder, client–therapist relationships, communication problems, and social-environmental factors. The importance of these varies depending on the type of compliance being studied. It is also important to note that compliance or noncompliance often results from a complex interaction of these factors. Table 4-1 presents a summary and examples of these variables with expanded descriptions in the accompanying text.

TABLE 4-1   Factors Related to Treatment Nonadherence

Client variables:
Characteristics of individuals
Sensory disabilities
Forgetfulness
Inappropriate or conflicting health benefits
Competing sociocultural and ethnic folk concepts of disease and treatment
Implicit model of illness
Apathy and pessimism
Failure to recognize that one is ill or in need of medication
Previous or present history of nonadherence with other regimens
Health beliefs (misconceptions about disorder; belief that medicine is necessary only in acute illness)
Dissatisfaction with practitioner or treatment
Resources
Expectations

Disorder variables:
Type and severity of psychiatric diagnosis
Stability of symptoms
Disorder-related characteristics (e.g., confusion, psychosis, cognitive distortions)

Treatment variables:
Characteristics of treatment setting
Absence of continuity of care
Long elapsed time between referral and actual appointment (more than eight days)
Timing of referral
Lack of cohesiveness of treatment delivery system
Inconvenience associated with treatment (inefficiency, unfriendly personnel)
Poor reputation of treatment facility
Inadequate supervision by professionals
Characteristics of treatment recommendations
Complexity of treatment regimen

(Continued)

> **Recommendations: Adherence**
> 9. Attempt to gain symptom relief as soon as feasible.
> _____
> **Recommendations: Adherence**
> 10. Work with only one major behavior change at a time.

TABLE 4-1 *(Continued)*

Treatment variables: (Cont.)
Degree of behavioral change (interferes with personal behavior and depends
  on alteration of one's life-style)
Inconvenience (e.g., location of treatment setting, lack of transportation)
Expense
Characteristics of medication (side effects, type of administration, inadequate
  labels)

Client–therapist relationship variables:
Client–therapist alliance
Client–therapist mismatch
Attitudinal or behavioral faults in either client or therapist
Inadequate supervision

Social / environmental factors:
Lack of social supports
Family instability or disharmony
Family expectations and attitudes toward treatment
Failure of family to supervise drug administration
Residential instability
Environment that supports nonadherent behaviors
Competing or conflicting demands (poverty, unemployment)
Lack of resources (transportation, time, money)

Communication variables:
Inadequate communication
Client forgets treatment instructions
Inadequate feedback from therapist or failure of therapist to elicit treatment
  feedback from client
Client anxiety that interferes with understanding treatment procedures

Source: Adapted and revised from *Facilitating Treatment Adherence: A Practitioner's Guidebook* by D. Meichenbaum & D. C. Turk, 1987, pp. 43–44, Table 4. Copyright 1987 by Plenum
Press. Reprinted by permission.

Client Variables

Thus far, strong and reliable predictors of compliance have not been identified, and therefore it is difficult if not impossible to predict precisely
which of your clients will or will not comply with treatment. A young,
highly educated self-referred patient may be just as difficult a problem
as a client with chronic schizophrenia. In general, nonadherence should
be considered a potential problem for all of your clients, but certain characteristics should be considered a warning sign. These include persons
who do not regard their problems as serious and clients who tend to be
hostile, demanding, aggressive, and overly self-sufficient. Other factors
are persons with a poor social support system, those who come from a
low socioeconomic environment, and those who require complex changes
in their life-styles (Gillum & Barsky, 1974). Age and sex do not seem to
be strongly correlated with compliance, although there is some evidence
that males may be more noncompliant than females. Interestingly,
Davidson (1982) reports that married women are more noncompliant than
single women and single men are more noncompliant than married men,
but the reasons for this are not well understood.

Some studies have found race and education to correlate positively
with compliance, but these results have not been consistent. Looking at
clients' past history of compliance seems to be a good indicator of future
behavior. Another is whether clients believe they can carry out the treatment procedure (e.g., self-efficacy; see Bandura, 1977). Clients who lack
insight or use denial are less likely to comply. In addition, some clients
believe that adherence will interfere with their self-concept, future goals,
or interpersonal relationships. For example, clients may fear becoming
too dependent on the treatment or the therapist, or may fear that getting
better will interfere with some aspect of their life.

Generally speaking, clients are more likely to comply if they believe
the disorder can be controlled by their own efforts or behaviors, as opposed to conditions that are perceived to be due to genetic, biochemical,
or external factors. Adherence is also influenced by clients' subjective
perception of the connection between their behavior and its outcome.
For example, an alcoholic who is near death may not stop drinking if he
sees no likelihood of improving his health by abstinence. Similarly, some
studies have looked at the relationship between clients' health locus of
control and compliance, but results have been mixed (Marston, 1977;
Haynes, Taylor, & Sacket, 1979; Wallston & Wallston; 1984; Marshall,
1991). It does appear that clients are more likely to comply with procedures with which they have had some success in the past. This seems to
effect both locus of control and self-efficacy. Also, there are clients whose
locus of control is so external that they place the entire outcome of their

---

Recommendations: Adherence

11. Adjust the treatment plan to fit clients' life-styles.

Recommendations: Adherence

12. Try to make the treatment plan the least intrusive possible.

---

disorder in the hands of fate or a higher power, which obviously will interfere with compliance. Intuitively, clients with an internal locus of control should be more compliant with treatment, and some studies have found this to be true. However, this general line of research has not yet produced many helpful interventions.

Self-Defeating Behaviors

Although it has not yet received much attention in the compliance literature, the broad area of self-defeating behaviors appears to influence nonadherence. Baumeister and Scher (1988) describe three models of self-destructiveness. The first is called primary or deliberate self-destruction. In this case, the person desires to harm him- or herself and engages in behaviors that will likely lead to that outcome. After a review of the literature, the authors conclude that there is little or no evidence to support the idea that *normal* individuals engage in this deliberate type of self-destruction. Although many of us can think of some obvious self-destructive behaviors in some of our clients, I believe that most instances of noncompliance are not motivated by a conscious desire to self-destruct. However, the psychoanalytic idea of resisting therapy because of an unconscious need to punish oneself may be an example of this.

Baumeister and Scher (1988) call the second model of self-destructiveness "trade-offs." Here the person chooses a response style that has certain benefits, but also some harmful costs, which are foreseeable but undesirable. This model assumes a situation in which the person has two conflicting and incompatible goals. The "reversing consequence gradient" (Mahoney, 1991) is an example of this. Here, the person gives in to the immediate gratification of behaviors such as smoking or drug use despite their potentially serious but delayed consequences. Compliance with treatment also seems to follow a reversing consequence gradient. For example, when costs of treatment are low and benefits are high (e.g., symptom relief), clients are more likely to follow treatment. However, when costs of treatment are high and benefits are low or slow in coming, clients are less likely to follow treatment even if the long-term (but delayed) effects of noncompliance are aversive. Examples of potential treatment costs are financial expenses, time, duration of treatment, embarrassment, or disruption of daily routines. According to this model, compliance behaviors can be increased by minimizing costs and maximizing benefits, and by using programs that favor short-term as opposed to long-term goals.

Another example of the trade-off model is self-handicapping behavior. There are two general types of self-handicapping. The first involves engaging in behaviors or creating barriers that interfere with performance or reduce the likelihood of success, but at the same time decrease personal responsibility for mediocrity or failure. This type of self-handicapping typically occurs when the outcome of one's behavior is important but uncertain. For example, a client can put little effort into a treatment program. The trade-off is that the person sacrifices his or her chance for successful treatment in exchange for an excuse for failure. This pay-off occurs if failure ensues and the person can blame it on the low effort rather than on ability. In addition, clients can then use their symptoms as further excuses for failure in life. Long ago, Adler spoke of client resistance in a manner that sounds very much like self-handicapping: He stated, "The so-called *resistance* is only a lack of courage to return to the useful side of life . . . for fear that his relation with the psychologist should force him into some useful activity in which he will be defeated" (Adler, 1929; p. 338; emphasis in the original).

In a related manner, people can use self-handicapping behaviors to increase their self-esteem. For example, if clients are successful despite all the obstacles against them, they may see themselves as having exceptional ability. Tice (1991) suggests that self-handicapping behaviors are always related to self-esteem. In her research, she found that persons with high self-esteem will typically engage in handicapping behaviors to enhance credit for success, whereas those with low self-esteem will do so to avoid the threat of blaming themselves for failure.

The second type of self-handicapping behavior occurs when individuals are confronted with failure or an inability to make a desired impression on others or perhaps on themselves. In this case, they may place the blame on external causes such as their psychological disorder. For example, clients may attribute their noncompliance to symptoms or personality traits (e.g., depression or a lack of will power) rather than to a lack of ability. Baumgardner (1991) found that depressive individuals may exaggerate their symptoms as a self-handicapping maneuver. Similar results have been found for test or social anxiety, shyness, and hypochondriacal symptoms (Arkin & Baumgardner, 1985). The question is

---

Recommendations: Adherence

13. Try to integrate the treatment plan into clients' daily routines so it is easier to carry it out.

Recommendations: Adherence

14. Encourage discussion of the costs and benefits of following the treatment plan. For example, how will clients' lives end up if they do or do not change? What costs are involved? Do clients trust the therapist enough to accept help?

---

whether this actually leads to more severe symptoms. Do clients start to believe their own self-presentations? This question has not yet been adequately answered (Baumgardner, 1991).

Another self-handicapping process involving external factors is choosing a goal that is difficult or nearly impossible to reach. For example, clients may present difficult problems to work on in therapy, as opposed to problems that are more amenable to treatment. Finally, some people seem to develop a self-handicapping life-style—for example, those who abuse drugs or alcohol (Higgins & Harris, 1988; Baumeister & Scher, 1988) or people who are chronic low achievers despite their high potential for success.

The third type of self-destructive behavior pattern is called a counterproductive strategy. In this case, the person neither desires nor anticipates aversive consequences but continues to engage in behaviors that produce negative payoffs. Perseveration would be included under this model (Baumeister & Scher, 1988), as would Freud's "compulsion to repeat." For example, some people continue to make the same mistakes over and over again or remain in a relationship despite abuse or other negative consequences. Factors that contribute to perseverative behaviors include underestimating or overestimating one's abilities, the amount of time and energy one has already put into an endeavor (and hence one's reluctant to let go), and the belief that things will work out eventually, as in an abusive relationship. There are numerous personal examples of such traps (e.g., pouring additional money into a business heading for bankruptcy), as well as national examples (the Vietnam War, Somalia). Some chronic psychological disorders may, in fact, result from or turn into these types of behavior patterns. For example, after putting a great deal of time and effort into trying to overcome a psychological problem, a person may (paradoxically) be unwilling to let go of it. It's as if getting better means that all the previous years of struggling were wasted. Strategies to reduce these types of behaviors in individuals include modeling and various cognitive therapy procedures, such as reducing the perception of personal responsibility for negative consequences (see Baumeister & Scher, 1988).

In conclusion, self-destructive behaviors may be the cause of at least some cases of noncompliance, but further research needs to be done to evaluate this and to identify procedures that can be used to alleviate this problem.

Clients' Belief Systems

A great deal has been written about the health belief model of adherence (see Rosenstock, 1974, for a history of this model; Becker, 1976; Kirscht & Rosenstock, 1979; Becker & Maiman, 1980). Becker and Maiman (1980) suggest that whether individuals follow professional advice depends on four factors: (1) health motivation or the person's interest in his or her health in general; (2) susceptibility, including perceptions of vulnerability to the disorder and acceptance of the diagnosis; (3) severity, including perceptions of the seriousness of consequences of the disorder if left untreated (e.g., it is more difficult to get clients to engage in behaviors that will prevent future problems, such as wearing seatbelts, losing weight, quitting smoking, as opposed to treating established symptoms); (4) benefits and costs, which is an evaluation of how effective the treatment behavior will be as compared to the barriers to treatment such as expense, discomfort, side effects, and so on. More recently, several other factors have been added to this model, including a client–therapist relationship, and a person's self-efficacy (Meichenbaum & Turk, 1987). Some of the recommendations made at the end of this chapter are based on this general area of research.

In a related manner, Foulks, Persons, and Merkel (1986) found that clients who perceive their problems in ways that are similar to or consistent with their therapists' perceptions are more likely to comply with treatment than are individuals who believe their symptoms are due to fate, "God's will," punishment for past sins, environmental toxins (pollution, food coloring, additives) or similar causes. In this study, the authors found that almost 27 percent of the subjects had some nonscientific beliefs about the cause of their symptoms. The authors suggest that it is important for therapists to be aware of their clients' beliefs about causation and to negotiate and amend treatment procedures (as much as possible) to make them more consistent with clients' belief system.

Recommendations: Adherence

15. Make sure that clients have the prerequisite skills needed to follow the treatment program.

Recommendations: Adherence

16. Monitor progress and give clients appropriate feedback and reinforcement.

More recently, Conoley, Padula, Payton, and Daniels (1994) found that three variables were related to whether a client would follow the psychotherapist's treatment recommendations. They were (1) making use of clients' strengths in the recommendations, (2) matching recommendations to clients' statement of the problem, and (3) designing recommendations with a perceived low difficulty level. The last two are obviously associated with the client's belief system; in addition to these, this study found several other variables related to client perceptions that seem to increase compliance.

The studies cited in this section underscore the importance of clients' belief systems for fostering adherence to treatment recommendations. Other related models are reviewed by Reimers, Wacker, and Koeppl (1987).

Client Satisfaction

Clients' satisfaction with treatment and with their therapist has consistently been found to be associated with compliance (Haynes, 1976; DiMatteo, 1979; DiMatteo & DiNicola, 1982; Corrigan, Liberman, & Engel, 1990), and treatment outcome (Kalman, 1983). Clients who are satisfied with their treatment experiences and feel that their expectations have been met are more likely to comply with treatment recommendations (Stone, 1979). Studies also report that mothers are more likely to comply with treatment for their children if they are satisfied with the practitioner (Becker, 1976). On the other hand, clients who are dissatisfied are more likely to drop out of treatment or change therapists, less likely to adhere to treatment recommendations, more likely to skip appointments, more likely to turn to nonprofessional "healers," and more likely to sue their therapist (Whitcher-Alagna, 1983).

Some factors identified as being related to client satisfaction are the physical characteristics of the setting, qualities of the therapist (returning phone calls, showing interest, cultivating client autonomy), qualities of treatment procedures, symptom relief, and progressing into normal functioning (Corrigan, 1990; Ankuta & Abeles, 1993; Corrigan & Jakus, 1993). Interestingly, most studies show only a moderate correlation between client satisfaction and outcome (Whitcher-Alagna, 1983). A possible reason is that client satisfaction may be due to subjective judgments that are unrelated to objective treatment outcomes. For example, in some cases clients may be satisfied with treatment even though they are not making any improvement. The suggestion that treatment satisfaction and outcome may be independent from each other at times has been shown in several studies (see Pekarik, 1992). Overall, however, it appears that client satisfaction facilitates progress.

Some clinicians shy away from assessing client satisfaction, but it appears to be an efficient way to enhance both adherence and treatment effectiveness. Assessing satisfaction can be done either formally or informally by the clinician or by someone other than the treating person. The latter method tends to reduce socially desirable responses or reactivity. Similarly, in some cases, it may be feasible for independent agencies to conduct these assessments in order to reduce response bias.

Methods of assessing client satisfaction include surveys, letters from clients, self-report measures, telephone interviews, follow-ups on complaints or positive statements, unobtrusive measures (dropout rates, missed sessions, promptness, etc.) or direct face-to-face inquiry (Corrigan, 1990; Lebow, 1982). Most therapists develop their own methods or questionnaires to assess satisfaction. Studies have shown that it is more effective to ask very specific questions concerning treatment rather than general, nondescript ones—for example, questions focusing on specific treatment procedures, communication problems, or personality compatibility. In addition, open-ended questions tend to bring out real client dissatisfaction more than rating scales.

A number of instruments have been developed to assess client satisfaction (Larsen, Attkisson, Hargreaves, & Nguyen, 1979; Essex, Fox, & Groom, 1981; Tanner, 1982; Kalman, 1983; Corrigan & Jakus, 1993; see also Meichenbaum & Turk, 1987). To have an effect on compliance, the assessment of satisfaction needs to be done while clients are still in therapy and while treatment changes can still be made, rather than after clients leave therapy. I recommend initially assessing client satisfaction after the first treatment session because this is when many clients drop out of therapy (see Appendix B). Along the same lines, one of the major methodological problems associated with client satisfaction research is the nonresponse rate of individuals sent questionnaires after they leave treat-

---

Recommendations: Adherence

17. If you are unsure about clients' understanding of the treatment plan, have them specify what they are supposed to do or have them demonstrate the behavior to you. Use role-reversal techniques.

Recommendations: Adherence

18. Match the treatment program to clients' cultural background.

---

ment. Assessing all clients while they are still in therapy eliminates this difficulty. Similarly, the accuracy of information appears to be correlated with the length of time since the client was in the program, so assessing satisfaction long after a client is terminated is not suggested.

The following are some recommendations for conducting client satisfaction assessments:

1. If possible, assess satisfaction with every client.
2. Start this process after the first treatment session.
3. Use open-ended questions in addition to or instead of rating scales.
4. Client satisfaction is multidimensional, so various aspects of treatment (e.g., therapist, treatment, and setting variables), should be evaluated.
5. Consider having someone other than the therapist conduct these assessments to reduce response bias.
6. Formulate questions so that they address both satisfaction and dissatisfaction of services.

Treatment Variables

Treatment Complexity

Studies consistently show that more complex treatment regimens result in less adherence (Haynes, 1976, 1979; Becker & Maiman, 1980; DiMatteo & DiNicola, 1982; Meichenbaum & Turk, 1987). Clients are more likely to follow one general set of procedures as opposed to multiple ones within a complex program. The problem with complex treatment procedures seems to be one of informational overload, where the client fails to process the information or does so incorrectly. This is further compounded because clients are often reluctant to ask questions even when they are confused. This is especially true with professionals who seem very busy or have a high status.

Generally, the more change that is required of the client, the less compliance there will be. Clients are also less likely to comply with treatment procedures that take up too much time or are too disruptive to their normal life-styles. Treatment procedures that cause severe physical side effects (such as medications) are less likely to be followed, but mild side effects do not contribute significantly to nonadherence. Adherence also tends to decrease over time, so that the longer clients are in treatment, the less they are likely to adhere. This would tend to affect persons with chronic conditions or those who need to make permanent changes in their lives (Meichenbaum & Turk, 1987). In this case, procedures that can be made a permanent part of the patient's life-style are more likely to be followed in the long term than those that are seen as only temporary (e.g., new eating habits as opposed to a diet). Procedures that have an immediate impact are more likely to be adopted, especially when the symptoms are obvious and are reduced by following the treatment program. There is some evidence to suggest that clients who attend therapy more consistently are more likely to comply with treatment, but results have been mixed. However, many studies show that compliance to treatment increases if the client adheres to other aspects of the treatment regimen (Haynes, Taylor, & Sacket, 1979).

Treatment Setting

The treatment setting is a variable that does not receive a lot of attention in compliance studies, but it is an important issue. Inpatient treatment settings usually ensure greater compliance with treatment procedures while the patient is at the setting (because of the milieu, greater supervision, etc.), but they also result in less internalization of these behaviors. Clients often stop engaging in them when no one is watching over their shoulder. This is true, for example, with medication usage. Another advantage of the inpatient setting is that clients have more frequent contact with the therapist. Some studies show frequent client–therapist contact increases adherence; at least in the initial stages of the treatment program, this would be advisable for outpatient therapy as well.

Adherence increases when the patient sees the same therapist each time, which is not always the case in some outpatient clinics or some inpatient settings where the patient is moved from ward to ward. Adherence seems to increase when the treatment is done in the natural setting, as opposed to the office or clinic, but of course this may be costly or

> **Recommendations: Adherence**
> 19. Determine if there are any side effects associated with treatment or improvement—for example, weight gain associated with smoking cessation or changes in family dynamics. If so, these may need to be considered.
>
> ---
>
> **Recommendations: Adherence**
> 20. Try to identify any secondary gains that may be contributing to the disorder, and attempt to deal with these.

difficult. It also increases when the client has a lot of supervision such as home visits or phone contacts, and when compliance is supervised or reinforced by family or other social factors. Adherence also appears to increase when all of the staff in a given setting (e.g. secretaries, janitors, etc.) have a good attitude toward the client.

Variables Related to the Disorder

Although there has not been a great deal of research in this area, a number of studies have found a relationship between diagnosis and compliance. For example, clients with schizophrenia, paranoia, personality disorders, or high levels of anxiety appear to be less compliant than other clients (Blackwell, 1976; Haynes, 1979). Other disorders where noncompliance tends to be high are drug and alcohol abuse, eating disorders, posttraumatic stress disorder (PTSD), phobias, and psychotic disorders. Similarly, the more symptoms clients report or the more severe the disorder is, the less compliant they are likely to be. Adherence is less likely to occur in disorders that impair judgment or cognitive processes (schizophrenia, depression, organic disorders, etc.), and it is also less likely to occur with clients who feel hopeless and helpless.

Client–Therapist Relationship

The type and quality of the relationship the therapist forms with clients is probably the most important factor related to compliance. I previously discussed the importance of client satisfaction as it relates to compliance. Studies have been consistent in finding that one of the major source of client satisfaction (and dissatisfaction) is the client–therapist relationship (Hanson, 1986). Since I will devote an entire chapter to general relationship issues, I will cover the topic only briefly in this section.

Szasz and Hollender (1956) suggest that patient–physician interactions should vary depending on the characteristics of the disorder. They offer three general models: (1) the active–passive model; (2) the guidance–cooperation model; and (3) the mutual participation model. The first model is most effective when the physician needs to be active and patients need to be passive—for example, patients in a coma or after a severe automobile injury. The second is appropriate when the patient has an acute illness such as an infection or broken bone. In this case, the physician offers advice and suggestions for the patient to follow. The third is most useful in controlling disorders that are long term or chronic. Here success depends on a high degree of patient responsibility. The mutual participation model is most appropriate for the majority of psychotherapy interventions and also consistent with the general philosophy of this book. This approach should lead to the greatest level of treatment adherence.

Many variables affect the character of the client–therapist relationship. In addition to a caring attitude, empathy, genuineness, acceptance of the client, and similar therapist qualities, the following specific characteristics seem most important:

1. Te clients' perception of the openness and friendliness of the therapist
2. The clients' perception that they are treated with respect
3. The clients' perception that they are actively involved in the treatment plan
4. The degree to which patients feel their expectations are being met in therapy
5. The degree to which the therapist can motivate patients
6. The degree to which the patients feel they can trust the therapist
7. The clients' satisfaction with the therapist and the treatment
8. The therapist's attitude toward clients
9. The type and quality of communication between client and therapist.

Some factors that lead to poor client–therapist relationships are related to the activities of the therapist. The following is a list of behaviors to avoid. Although most of these are probably obvious, they bear repeating:

1. Acting unfriendly, distant, or bored; being too formal or too impersonal
2. Showing clients that you are too busy for them—for example, by constantly looking at your watch, by taking frequent interruptions from

---

Recommendations: Adherence

21. Consider the patient's occupation, family, and other time commitments. Does the client have enough time to adhere to the treatment plan?

Recommendations: Adherence

22. Consider the client's family or other social systems. Will these people support the program or will they interfere? Try to enlist the help of family or friends when appropriate, but clear this with clients first.

---

phone calls or from your secrtary, or by keeping clients waiting a long time

3. Talking "down" to clients or assuming they have no knowledge of their disorder or of mental health
4. Using too much psychological jargon
5. Cutting clients off when they are making statements or giving opinions
6. Not allowing enough time for questions
7. Focusing primarily on clients' symptoms or disorder and ignoring their personal qualities
8. Treating clients as if they are inferior
9. Not providing sufficient feedback to clients or providing largely negative feedback
10. Providing too little social support
11. Asking very personal questions of clients before a sufficient relationship is established—for example, asking about intimate sexual behaviors or information that appears unrelated to the symptoms or disorder without an appropriate explanation
12. Challenging clients' belief systems before a relationship has been formed

To foster the relationship, it helps to get clients to verbalize what they would like to accomplish and allow them to participate actively in treatment decisions. The following types of questions may assist in this process:

- What do they think their problem is, and how was it caused?
- How severe is the problem, and how do they think it will turn out?

- What do they expect to get out of treatment; what kinds of things have they tried on their own to deal with the problem and what were the results of these efforts?
- What has helped in the past?
- What kinds of things would prevent them from following the treatment recommendations or from making improvements?
- What else should you know about them at this time?
- What other information do they think you need to obtain?

In general, it helps to let clients know ahead of time that some of the methods that you will try will work, but others will fail. Point out that we often learn a great deal from our failures. Make sure they understand the rationale behind your methods, and what outcomes to expect. Ask them how effective they think your methods will be and if the treatment method is too hard to follow.

Other suggestions for improving treatment adherence that are related to the client–therapist relationship are given by Brody (1980). He suggests that compliance can be improved by following four steps. The first involves developing a good working alliance by making clients feel that their contributions are valued and appreciated and by showing interest in them. The second step involves finding out clients' expectations and goals of treatment. Brody maintains that clients typically do not volunteer this information and it needs to be elicited. The third step includes education about clients' disorders and symptoms and discussion of various treatment approaches. This also includes the expected costs and benefits of therapy and the therapist's recommendations. The final step involves getting clients' suggestions and preferences and negotiating the final course of action. Brody suggests that clients have the right to refuse any intervention that they believe is not in their best interest, but the therapist also has the right to refuse suggestions for interventions that he or she think are inappropriate.

Social-Environmental Issues

As Voth and Orth (1973) point out, some of the most significant intrapsychic transformations in therapy often result from environmental changes. Despite the importance of factors such as cultural influences, clients' social systems, and immediate day-to-day situational factors on the development, treatment, and relapse of psychological disorders, this area received relatively little attention until recently. This is especially true in terms of how these factors influence the process of psychotherapy. For example, Cummings and Nehemkis (1986) suggest

---

Recommendations: Adherence

23. Consider environmental factors that may be contributing to clients' conditions. These include factors associated with where clients live and work, the need for social services or job training, and similar concerns.

Recommendations: Adherence

24. When designing a treatment program, consider clients' attitudes, values, or life goals. Ask yourself how these may interfere with the plan.

---

that social institutions such as Workmen's Compensation or the Social Security Disability program often promote noncompliance because individuals will lose their benefits if they improve. The same is true for various veterans' benefits. At a conscious or unconscious level, the large increase in chronic pain syndromes in our country is more than likely influenced by such programs, yet these factors are often not addressed in therapy.

The following section takes a brief look at some of these issues and they will be further explored in Chapter 8.

Social Support

This is a complex interactional process that includes material aid, feedback, emotional support, and a potential buffer that may reduce stress, helplessness and hopelessness, in clients. As with many of the other topic areas that I have reviewed thus far, there are a number of methodological problems that reduce the utility of research findings in this area. These include different definitions for the term, difficulty in selecting the dependent variable to be measured, and deciding how social support can be manipulated (see Levy, 1983, 1986, for a review). As a result, much of the research has been inconsistent and inconclusive.

Despite these problems, there has been increasing awareness of the importance of social support, especially coming from the client's family, in improving compliance behaviors (Becker & Maiman, 1980; Cummings, Becker, & Maile, 1980; Gottlieb, 1981; DiMatteo & DiNicola, 1982; Levy, 1983, 1986; Bankoff & Howard, 1992). For example, Haynes, Taylor, and Sacket (1979) report that 15 out of 21 studies found significant positive effects of family support on compliance. These authors found similar results with other social factors, such as the influence of friends or interpersonal relations. Cross and Warren (1984) found that clients who had a strong social network or received help from their spouses and friends were more likely to continue in psychotherapy. Social support also has been found to be useful in fostering compliance in treatment programs such as weight reduction, alcoholism, drug abuse, smoking, taking medications, and other areas of health care (Meichenbaum & Turk, 1987). In a similar manner, peer groups or support groups such as Alcoholics Anonymous have also been found to be useful for enhancing compliance (DiMatteo & DiNicola, 1982). Finally, many studies report the importance of family and social influence in initiating treatment for those who need it. The manner in which social networks can influence and improve compliance are given in Table 4-2

Clients' social networks also may interfere with compliance—for example, in the case of clients who are being treated for drug or alcohol abuse and who have untreated significant others with the same problem. Other examples are clients who come from dysfunctional families; clients who are socially isolated; situations where other family members have a serious psychological or physical disorder; families whose members disagree or are unsupportive of the treatment plan or of the treat-

---

TABLE 4-2   How Clients' Social Networks Can Influence Compliance

Clients' social networks can be used in the following ways:

1. To reinforce, encourage, or assist in compliant behaviors of client and to provide moral support and feedback concerning the changes that are being made
2. To contract with the therapist to supervise or in some cases implement the treatment plan (for both adults and children)
3. To provide negative feedback to client for noncompliance
4. To prompt or remind clients to follow the treatment plan
5. To provide the therapist with information concerning possible factors that may interfere or prevent client compliance
6. To offer recommendations to improve compliance
7. To assist with data collection
8. To make environmental changes that support compliance (buying special foods for clients on diets, joining them in certain activities, etc.)
9. Support clients in times of crisis and act as a buffer to reduce environmental stress
10. To encourage clients to attend therapy and ensure that they do not drop out
11. To remind clients to take medications
12. To have positive expectations for treatment effectiveness
13. To provide support services such as transportation or baby-sitting

---

Recommendations: Adherence
25. Consider your own possible role in clients' resistive behaviors.

Recommendations: Adherence
26. In difficult treatment situations, introduce the individual to a previously successful client with a similar disorder who perhaps can share information on how he or she was able to change.

---

ment in general; families who find the treatment threatening or intrusive; and clients who come from cultures with strong folk methods for dealing with disorders. Social factors should not be ignored when you are trying to pinpoint the cause of noncompliance. Bankoff and Howard (1992) indicate that the three most important nonprofessional support networks for clients are parents, friends, and romantic partners. These persons can help or hinder the psychotherapeutic process in various ways, and the authors suggest that these social systems be evaluated in terms of their influence and importance for achieving effective therapy.

Cost of Treatment

One of the conditions necessary for compliance is that clients be able to afford the treatment regimen. Obviously, this factor alone does not ensure that compliance will occur. The question, then, is to what extent cost influences treatment adherence, including initiating therapy. Results of previous studies of these issues have not been consistent. Although clients sometimes cite lack of financial resources as a reason for noncompliance, one study found that supplying free medications to outpatients with schizophrenia did not increase their compliance rate (Cody & Robinson, 1977). On the other hand, Brand, Smith, and Brand (1977) found that the cost of medication was a significant factor in noncompliance in their study. Similarly, Stefl and Prosperi (1985) found that over 40 percent of a group of individuals who were assessed to need mental health treatment cited cost as a major reason for not utilizing services. Watts, Scheffler, and Jewell (1986) found that income level correlated positively with outpatient mental health visits. Dorken, VandenBos, Henke, Cummings, and Pallak (1993) report that insurance coverage significantly increases the use ot mental health services. However, other studies looking at the correlation between income and compliance have found positive, negative, and no relationship between the two factors (DiMatteo & DiNicola, 1982; Haynes, Taylor, & Sackett, 1979).

Along the same lines, there has been a long and unresolved debate about whether psychotherapy fees affect outcome. Some studies suggest that fees enhance the effectiveness of therapy (e.g., Nash & Cavenar, 1976), while others find no relationship (Tulipan, 1983). This issue becomes more important as third-party payments become widespread in psychotherapy services, but recent studies continue to show inconsistent results (e.g., Conoley & Bonner, 1991; Yoken & Berman, 1987).

Despite these inconsistencies, most studies suggest that cost does influence the *decision* to make use of psychotherapy and that insurance coverage increases potential usage. An implicit finding here is that, without coverage, individuals may be hesitant to begin or continue in therapy because they have little idea of what the total cost of treatment will be. This may be one reason that dropout rates are reduced when clients know ahead of time that therapy will be time-limited. More research clearly needs to be done in this area.

A number of other social–environmental issues are relevant for both compliance and psychotherapy in general. For example, as will be further discussed in Chapter 8, many clients require services that do not fit the traditional individually focused, in-office routine. They may need a place to live or a job. Although these needs may be inconsistent with the traditional roles of psychotherapists, the emotional problems of many clients are directly linked to such problems. Similarly, many psychological disorders are related to factors such as racism, crime, broken homes, and so on. In the long run, it would make sense for therapists to become at least somewhat involved with changes at the macro level, as opposed to working only with individuals. For example, I would be willing to bet that laws requiring the use of safety belts or motorcycle helmets have had much more of an impact in reducing brain injuries than all the therapists working with these disorders put together. Yet despite all the attention given to interventions such as primary prevention, they continue to be underutilized. Social forces operating on therapists probably have a lot to do with this. Insurance companies will not pay them for lobbying, for helping clients find jobs, or for trying to prevent emotional problems from developing in the first place. In the long run, however, I believe that until our profession comes to grips with these types of issues, we will continue to fight an uphill battle.

Communication Variables

As DiMatteo and DiNicola (1982) point out, it is surprising how many clients leave their treatment sessions with little idea of what they are

---

Recommendations: Adherence
27. If nothing seems to work, consult another therapist or seek support from other professionals.

Recommendations: Adherence
28. Be flexible in changing the treatment plan or target behavior when appropriate.

---

supposed to do. Most studies have been consistent in finding that the crucial information that the client must have concerns the treatment regimen rather than the disorder (Kasl, 1975; Becker, 1979; Kirscht & Rosenstock, 1979; Dunbar & Agras, 1980; Meichenbaum & Turk, 1987). Schorr and Rodin (1982) suggest that the therapist should also convey information that increases clients' feelings of control and self-efficacy. Knowing what to do does not necessarily mean that clients will be compliant, but it is an essential first step.

Faulty communication in psychotherapy has a number of origins, including the client, the therapist and interaction between the two. Clients often forget what they have been told about the treatment regimen (Becker & Maiman, 1980; DiNicola & DiMatteo, 1982; Hanson, 1986). For example, Ley (1979) reports that clients forget about half of the information their therapists give them. This may be due to poor memory or concentration; to psychological symptoms such as anxiety, psychosis, or defensiveness; or to intellectual limitations, but it tends to occur with all clients. Anderson (1979) found no differences between men and women in the amount of treatment information that was recalled, and no correlation with social class. Also, this study found only a small difference between clients who were subjectively rated as having a high level of intelligence as compared to those with average or low ratings.

A related problem is that clients do not understand the information given to them. Often they are reluctant to ask clarifying questions of their therapists. For example, Stiles, Putnam, Wolf, and James (1979) found that clients' question-related verbalizations took up only about 7 percent of the interaction time between themselves and their therapists, and similar results were found by Bain (1976).

A frequently cited study by Cassata (1978, p. 498) summarizes communication research as it relates to information given in treatment, and subsequent research has been generally consistent with these findings. Table 4-3 provides a summary.

TABLE 4-3   Research Findings Concerning Communication in Treatment

1. Clients forget much of what the therapist tells them.
2. Instructions and advice are more likely to be forgotten than other information.
3. The more clients are told, the more they will forget.
4. Clients will remember (a) what they are told first; and (b) what they consider most important.
5. More intelligent clients do not remember a great deal more than less intelligent clients.
6. Older clients (except those over 70) remember about as much as younger ones.
7. Moderately anxious clients recall more of what they are told than do highly anxious or clients who have little or no anxiety.
8. The more therapy-related knowledge a client has, the more he or she will recall.
9. Combining both verbal and written instructions appears to improve comprehension.

Potential communication problems related to the therapist or client–therapist interchange include not giving enough information, not exploring clients' expectations for treatment, not communicating at clients' level of understanding, and the manner in which information is conveyed. For example, studies show that therapists tend to overestimate the amount of information that they actually give (Kasl, 1975). Second, it appears that satisfaction with the type and amount of information given by the therapist (as well as satisfaction with treatment as a whole) is related to the harmony between clients' expectations and actual services (DiMatteo & DiNicola, 1982). Similarly, Hanson (1986) suggests that client–therapist differences such as social status, education, or ethnic background may influence the therapist's perceptions of the client—for example, what the therapist thinks the client expects and the amount or type of information that is conveyed. In this case, fewer explanations are given to clients who are perceived as less knowledgeable. He also reports that the style of presentation is important. Therapists who are very formal or authoritarian may intimidate clients and make it less likely that they will ask for clarifying information. Finally, he suggests that the therapist should avoid using scientific or psychological jargon or vocabulary that may be confusing or unfamiliar to the client.

It is also important for the therapist to make sure the client understands the treatment information that is given. Turk, Salovey, and Litt (1986) recommend using a role-reversal procedure in which the clients pretend they are the expert and explain the regimen to a novice (the therapist). The authors maintain that this technique serves three functions:

Recommendations: Adherence

29. Explore how important the proposed behavior change is to clients (as opposed to family members or other persons who may want them to change). Try to choose goals that clients (not others) truly want.

Recommendations: Adherence

30. Monitor client satisfaction regularly throughout treatment and make adjustments as necessary.

---

1. It allows the therapist to gauge clients' understanding of the regimen as well as any misconceptions.
2. It allows the client to integrate the information that is given.
3. The role reversal allows client to generate arguments for engaging in the regimen that may help convince themselves of its merits (p. 59).

Fear-Arousing Communication

A related area that has received some attention is the use of fear-arousing communication to improve compliance—for example, telling client they are likely to get cancer unless they stop smoking cigarettes. Although the results of studies in this area are somewhat inconsistent, Sutton (1982, p. 323) summarizes the major effects of fear-arousing communication:

1. Increases in fear are associated with an increase in the acceptance of the conveyed information and behavior changes.
2. Increases in the perception of efficacy of the recommended action increases the likelihood that the action will be adopted.
3. Providing specific instructions about how to perform the recommended action leads to a higher rate of adherence.

Despite these seemingly positive findings, fear-arousing communication still is not clearly understood. Because outcome with the use of these procedures is affected by clients' personal characteristics and thus is not easily predicted, I would caution therapists against the use of such procedures except in extreme cases.

It is clear that client–therapist communication is a crucial component of treatment compliance. DiMatteo and DiNicola offer some advantages and positive effects of adequate communication between client and therapist:

1. It appears to increase the likelihood of compliance.
2. It increases clients' satisfaction with treatment.
3. It reduces the dropout rate
4. It improves the client–therapist relationship.
5. It is likely to improve outcome.

The following suggestions may improve this communication process:

1. Select the information you give to clients carefully. The fewer the instructions, the more likely they are to be remembered and followed.
2. Tailor the directions to fit clients' vocabulary, educational level, socio-economic background, and current functioning level. Try to make the information personally relevant, not general.
3. If written instructions are to be given, remember that 25 to 50 percent of clients (and of psychotherapists) never read what they are given. Make sure the reading materials match the client's reading ability.
4. Be clear, concrete, and specific (avoid generalities). Use short sentences and avoid scientific jargon.
5. It is better to give short bits of information at each meeting, if possible, as opposed to a lot of information all at once.
6. Give the most important instructions first. These are more likely to be remembered.
7. Indicate the possible side effects of the treatment program and the consequences for not following it, but be careful that this does not produce excessive anxiety in the client.
8. Whenever possible, give treatment instructions at the beginning of the session rather than the end. Indicate the treatment objectives and the rationale for recommendations.
9. Try to organize your information into separate categories and then discuss each category separately. Clients are more likely to remember information presented in this manner.
10. Make sure clients are listening and processing the information you give them. Ask questions or have them rephrase instructions.
11. Repeat important points when possible.
12. Use concrete examples, modeling, analogies, acronyms, or videotapes to help clients understand and remember.
13. Emphasize how important it is to follow the treatment directions, and reinforce clients' self-confidence that they can achieve the goals. However, don't oversell the program.
14. Try not to challenge clients' conception of their disorder (at least in the early stages of therapy).
15. If possible, allow patients to call you if they have a question or run into problems.

Recommendations: Adherence

31. Find out what clients are already doing that appears to be helping their condition, and use this in the treatment plan.

Recommendations: Adherence

32. Address both maintenance and possible relapse in the treatment plan.

---

16. Because clients are often reluctant to ask questions, you may have to elicit these from them. Make sure you leave enough time for questions.
17. Give clients the option of recording the instructions or the entire session.
18. In some cases, videotapes giving information about the psychological disorder may be useful.
19. Encourage clients to write down any questions or problems they have between sessions and bring them to the following appointment.
20. Use role reversal to make sure clients understand the information that was given.
21. Probe into clients' concerns, goals, and expectations. Elicit their suggestions and be willing to negotiate.

Social Influence

This section presents some general techniques and procedures that can be used to improve compliance in therapy. Those who are already familiar with these approaches may skip to the summary.

Social influence can be defined as a change in a person's cognitions, behaviors, or attitudes as a result of the actions of another person or group. Kelman (1961) describes the three stages of this process as compliance, identification, and internalization.

Compliance occurs when an individual changes his or her behavior in order to obtain a favorable reaction from another person or group. This effect is strongest when the influencing source is present and when there is pressure on the client to comply. For example, suppose that just before leaving the session, a client assures you that he will carry out the treatment program, but he then goes home and does nothing.

Identification occurs when someone adopts an attitude or behavior because another person or persons whom he or she admires display that attitude or behavior. For example, your client decides to stop smoking when you do.

Internalization occurs when a person adopts a behavior or attitude because he or she believes it will be useful or beneficial or because it is consistent with the person's own value system. For example, your client faithfully carries out your treatment regimen because he or she strongly believe in the program.

Although therapists tend to group these three sources of influence under the general term of *compliance,* most studies indicate that the strongest of the three, and the one therapists should strive for, is internalization (see Janis, 1983). Internalization tends to lead to self-attributed behavior change, which appears to be longer lasting than behavior change attributable to external factors such as the therapist (Kopel & Arkowitz, 1975). Internalization can be increased by encouraging clients to use the central route of information processing, and by making information personally relevant (see Stoltenberg, Leach, & Bratt, 1989, for detailed description of this process).

Related to social influence is the concept of social power. *Social power* can be defined as the ability to influence the behavior of others. French and Raven (1959) have proposed five types or bases of social power. The first type is reward power. This is based on the other person's perception that you have the ability to provide rewards for him or her. For example, a therapist may attempt to use social reinforcement to increase compliance. A second type, called coercive power, is based on the other person's perception of your ability to punish him or her. Both of these are similar in that your power to influence is limited to the behaviors you can reward or punish. In addition, the effectiveness of these two power bases in influencing others is a function of the strength of the rewards or punishments and the perceived probability that they will in fact occur. In other words, if you seldom use reinforcement or punishment, your reward or coercive power is likely to be weak. In addition, to be effective, reward and coercive power require constant or at least high levels of surveillance.

A third type of social power is referent power. This is based on the other person's desire to be similar to you because they like and admire you (e.g., identification). Unlike reward or coercive power, the strength of referent power is not dependent on observation and is not limited to a small number of behaviors. Religious or cult leaders are examples of referent power. Generally speaking, this is the strongest type of social power and influences the widest range of behaviors. A fourth category, called legitimate power, is based on some appointed or elected position of authority. Military, political, or corporate officers are examples. This type of power is restricted by the boundaries of the source's authority (e.g., your supervisor's influence is restricted to job-related behaviors) and by the observer's adherence to laws or values that establish the influencer's position. Again, observation is not required for influence. The last type, called expert power, is based on the perception that you have some spe-

---

Recommendations: Adherence

33. Find out clients' expectations for therapy during the first session, and match your procedures accordingly.

Recommendations: Adherence

34. Spend as much time assessing clients' strengths as you do assessing symptoms or weaknesses, and use these in the treatment plan.

---

cial knowledge that is useful to the other person. The strength of this source varies in terms of how much perceived expertise you have and is limited to behaviors that are relevant to such knowledge. As with referent and legitimate power, observation is not a necessary condition of expert power. Some writers also add a sixth category, informational power, but this is a subtype of expert power.

In looking at how these types of social power affect social influence (as defined by Kelman), Leet-Pellegrini and Rubin (1974) found that reward power is most likely to lead to identification and that coercive and informational power are most likely to lead to internalization. However, the time frame of the study was short and the subjects were college students, so generalization of these results to a psychotherapy process is difficult. Unlike the study above, Rodin and Janis (1979) and Janis (1983) indicate that referent power is probably the one least used by therapists to influence clients yet it is the one most likely to lead to internalization. On the basis of a number of clinical studies, these authors offer a number of suggestions for building and retaining referent power in interactions with clients. These include developing a strong relationship, showing that you have a genuine interest in clients, showing that you regard them as worthwhile individuals, encouraging clients to make self-disclosures, giving positive feedback, eliciting commitment to the course of action, and making arrangements for future communication after formal termination so that procedures are maintained. Janis (1983) gives a full description of this process. Interested readers should also see Heppner and Claiborn (1989), who have conducted a comprehensive review of social influence research and its implications for therapy.

Self-Management and Behavioral Techniques

Davidson (1982) suggests that both internalization and treatment adherence are more likely to occur with the use of self-management training. A number of other authors have also suggested the use of self-man-agement or behavioral techniques to help ensure maintenance. Such programs are fully described by Kanfer and Goldstein (1991) and by Meichenbaum and Turk (1987). I will review some of these procedures next.

Kanfer and Galick-Buys (1991) offer the framework of this approach. First, it assumes that behavior is due to three sources of influence: the immediate environment, the person's biological system, and the person's cognitive system (pp. 307–308). The rationale for this approach is as follows:

1. Many behaviors are accessible only by clients and therefore their cooperation as observers, reporters and change agents is essential.
2. Upon entering therapy, clients' motivation for significant change is often low, and thus their acceptance of the goals and procedures is necessary. For this reason, the treatment procedure is developed through negotiations and joint decisions.
3. Clients should learn generalizable coping strategies that will help them handle future problems (p. 306).

The general aims of this program are to help clients develop more effective behaviors and cognitions and either to change their stress-inducing environment or to learn to cope with it. Because this topic area has been described in detail elsewhere (DiMatteo & DiNicola, 1982; Meichenbaum & Turk, 1987; Dunbar & Agras, 1980; Epstein & Masek, 1978; Shelton & Levy, 1981; Epstein & Cluss, 1982; Kanfer & Goldstein, 1991), I will give only a brief review here.

Self-Monitoring

Treatment adherence may be enhanced by teaching clients various self-monitoring techniques, such as keeping a diary or specifically recording various thoughts, feelings, or behaviors. Self-monitoring may be useful in a number of ways. Baseline data may be used to increase clients' motivation for change, and graphs can be developed to monitor progress (Kanfer & Gaelick-Buys, 1991). Some programs have used self-monitoring to screen out individuals before treatment begins. For example, if clients are not motivated to comply with baseline recording, they are not accepted into therapy (Brownell & Foreyt, 1985).

Dunbar and Agras (1980) offer some guidelines for using self-monitoring, including: (1) specifically training the client in self-monitoring; (2) using simple recording forms; (3) reinforcing client's accuracy rather than treatment improvement; (4) recording behaviors that are easy to observe and measure; (5) recording "positive" rather than "negative" behaviors; and (6) asking clients to record behaviors as they occur rather than at the end of the day or the week.

Behavioral Contracting

Behavioral contracting has been widely used to increase compliance behaviors (Meichenbaum & Turk, 1987). Turk, Salovey, and Litt (1986) offer some advantages of this method:

1. It involves clients in planning the treatment regimen and gives them responsibility for its outcome.
2. Since the plan is written, it cannot be forgotten.
3. The client gives public commitment to the treatment plan.
4. The contract clearly specifies goals, expectations, and reinforcements for clients.

Contracts can be made by individuals with themselves (without influences from others), between client and therapist, or between client and other members of their support group. Mahoney and Thoresen (1974) maintain that, to be successful, contracts must be fair, terms must be clear, and they should generally reward positive behaviors rather than punish inappropriate ones.

Kanfer and Gaelick-Buys (1991, p. 330) suggest that the following seven elements be considered in all contracts:

1. There should be a clear and detailed description of the required behavior.
2. Time limits for the goals of the contract should be set.
3. The contract should specify positive reinforcements for reaching goals.
4. Aversive consequences for not fulfilling the contract should be considered.
5. Additional positive reinforcers should be specified and used if clients exceed the demands of the contract.
6. The contract should specify how responses will be observed, measured, and recorded, as well as a procedure for regular client feedback covering the duration of the contract.
7. Delivery of reinforcement should follow the response as soon as possible.

Despite the widespread and successful use of behavioral contracting, it has been criticized for producing only short-term results. Often, behavior or treatment effects are not maintained after the contract is terminated. Of course, this problem is not limited to the use of behavioral contracts, and it has no simple solution. Procedures such as self-monitoring, moving from extrinsic to intrinsic reinforcers, helping clients accept personal responsibility for self-care (Turk, Salovey, & Litt, 1986), relapse prevention, and some of the social influence techniques described earlier that lead to internalization may help in this regard (see also Davidson, 1982). Some of the recommendations in this chapter also address this issue.

Reinforcement and Response Cost

Meichenbaum and Turk (1987) summarize various ways that reinforcement and response cost procedures can be used to increase compliance. Some therapists reinforce their clients for adherence by reducing their fees. Others fine patients for nonadherence or refuse to see them after a number of repeated warnings. Another technique is to have patients write out a number of money orders to organizations that they despise (KKK, American Nazi Party, etc.) and then to send the money only if serious nonadherence occurs. Tangible reinforcers such as lottery tickets have been used to reinforce keeping appointments or adherence in the initial stages of therapy. Some programs require that clients make cash deposits at the beginning of therapy, which are returned or forfeited in response to adherence or nonadherence. Of course, some therapists may object to the use of such procedures in trying to influence clients' behavior, and their use may have an impact on the client–therapist relationship. Therefore, use of these techniques should be carefully evaluated.

Relapse Prevention

This technique was originally designed to be used with addictive behaviors but has been utilized with other disorders as well. It uses a cognitive-behavioral model to teach individuals how to anticipate and deal with relapse. A major assumption of this program is that clients have made a voluntary decision to change their behavior (Marlatt, 1982). Marlatt and associates (Marlatt, 1982; Marlatt & Gordon, 1985; see also Chiauzzi, 1991) summarize the steps of response prevention. The first step involves teaching clients how to recognize high-risk situations that may lead to relapse. Previous studies have identified three categories of such situations: (1) negative emotional states (anger, boredom, anxiety, depression, frustration, etc.), (2) interpersonal conflict (marriage or employer conflicts, arguments, etc.), and (3) social pressure (family or peers who engage in target behaviors or direct pressure from others to engage in target behaviors). Many "triggers" for clients can be found in these categories. Another way to help identify high-risk situations is to have clients use a self-monitoring procedure to determine patterns with the highest frequency of target behaviors. As an alternative, they may use "relapse fantasies" where clients imagine potential relapse episodes that may occur in the future.

The second step in the process involves using these identified high-risk situations as cues to engage in actions that are incompatible with the target behaviors. For example, clients can avoid high-risk situations or can rely on coping skills to get through the situation without a relapse. Relaxation procedures and relapse rehearsals may be used for this purpose.

The third step in the process is called *positive outcome expectancies*. Here the goal is to prevent clients from giving in to immediate gratification (e.g., the reversing consequence gradient described earlier). Techniques found to be useful for this are education concerning possible immediate and long-term consequences of engaging in the target behavior, and the use of a decision matrix (see Marlatt & Gordon, 1985, p. 58), which should help reinforce the positive aspects of maintaining desired behavior changes. Also included in this step is cognitive training designed to help prevent a one-time loss of control from developing into a full-blown relapse.

The final step of the program is the *programmed relapse*, in which clients engage in the target behavior through a preplanned arrangement and under the therapist's supervision. Although the relapse prevention program may not be suitable for all clients or disorders, it offers a much needed intervention to help ensure the maintenance of treatment effects.

Paradoxical Interventions

Paradoxical interventions have been used to increase compliance or reduce resistance in clients. Although this label covers a wide assortment of interventions, they all attempt to reduce or eliminate clients' symptoms by directly or indirectly encouraging these symptoms (Betts & Remer, 1993). These techniques come primarily from communication/systems-oriented therapists, but various paradoxical-related methods can be found in psychoanalysis ("joining the resistance"), behavior therapy (symptom scheduling, flooding), Gestalt, and other orientations (Ascher, 1989; Seltzer, 1986).

Haley (1987, pp. 80–84) summarizes the general stages of paradoxical interventions as follows:

1. A relationship designed to bring about change must be established.
2. The problem must be clearly defined.
3. Exact goals must be specified.
4. A plan to deal with the problem (implicit or explicit) must be offered.
5. The current authority on the problem must be disqualified. By this, Haley means that there is usually someone in the target person's family who is in charge of "curing" the client of the problem but is probably instrumental in maintaining it. The situation must be set up so this person or the family does not become upset when the problem disappears.
6. The paradoxical directive must be given.
7. The therapist should observe the results and continue to encourage the problem behavior.
8. As clients make changes and improve, the therapist should not take credit for it. For example, Haley suggests that the therapist should be puzzled by the improvement.

The following are brief descriptions of some of the more popular paradoxical techniques. Reframing (which is similar to but not exactly the same as positive connotation; see Seltzer, 1986) involves changing the meaning of a problem, event, or situation or the way these are classified (e.g., changing their frame of reference). For example, what was once viewed as negative can be seen as positive (I suppose Freud knew about reframing when he suggested resistance is a sign of progress). To be effective, reframing must cause clients to see the problem differently than they did before and in a way that is consistent with their way of thinking or their view of the world. One of the ways reframing can be done is to try to find the positive aspects of a problem. For example, a married couple's constant arguments and fighting can be reframed as a sign of commitment in the sense that at least they are still together (LaCave & Black, 1989). As a last resort, one of my colleagues labeled a client's chronic problem with impotency as a way to protect his wife from a painful pregnancy. To everyone's surprise, this provided the impetus for change.

What seems to make reframing effective is that its aftermath is irreversible. That is, you cannot easily return to your previous viewpoint of the problem once this technique is used. To paraphrase Gregory Bateson, you can never sleep with the same partner twice for the first time. A number of studies have demonstrated the usefulness of reframing with clients who are mildly or moderately depressed, and it appears to be useful for other disorders as well (Dowd & Milne, 1986; Swoboda, Dowd, & Wise, 1990).

Restraining is a technique in which the therapist discourages or prohibits clients from changing or suggests that change occur very slowly. It is an especially useful technique with clients who are highly reactant because the only way to resist the therapist is to change. For example, you might instruct clients who are noncompliant that changing their behavior will be very difficult and that they may want to proceed even more slowly than usual. Thus, clients who have some type of sexual dysfunction are instructed not to have sex except under prescribed conditions. A typical result in this case is a "miraculous" cure.

Restraining is also reported to be useful with clients who procrastinate. Variations of this technique include emphasizing all the negative aspects of change, relapse prediction, and relapse prescription. The last two are useful when clients have improved very rapidly or are apprehensive about maintaining their progress. Relapse prescription is the last step of the relapse prevention program described earlier.

Symptom prescription involves instructing or encouraging clients to maintain or exaggerate their problem behaviors or symptoms. The advantage of this technique is that if clients are successful, they learn that their symptoms are controllable rather than autonomous, and therefore they can potentially eliminate them whenever they desire. On the other hand, if clients are reactant, they must reduce or eliminate their symptoms in order to go against the therapist. An example of this technique is to instruct a child with various phobias to develop new phobias each week and report them to the therapist.

A procedure that is related to symptom prescription is symptom modification, whereby clients are instructed to change their problem or symptom in some way. For example, you might have clients engage in the problem behavior at a time other than when it typically occurs (e.g., the minute they get up in the morning). Another variant is symptom exaggeration, wherein you ask that the symptoms be magnified or increased. In this case, you might instruct an obsessive-compulsive person to take six hours to get ready for work as opposed to his or her typical four.

A technique that was developed by Selvini-Palazzoli and her colleagues is called declaring hopelessness (Selvini-Palazzoli, Cecchin, Prata, & Boscolo, 1978). In this case, the therapist admits his or her failure and incompetence in being able to help clients or families and suggests treatment termination. This technique is typically used as a last-ditch effort with clients who are extremely resistant to change. The only way to help some such clients may be by declaring that change is impossible. Of course, the ulterior motive here is to shock the client into seriously attempting some plan of action.

An interesting case study of this approach is given by Weeks and L'Abate (1982). It involves a couple seemingly going nowhere in therapy. "In a depressed tone of voice, we expressed our feeling of helplessness and hopelessness about the situation. We painted a very grim picture of the couple's past, present, and future. Finally, we said it would be a disservice to them if we continued to see them" (p. 132). After a few minutes, the wife, who up until that time had been very quiet and nonassertive, became angry. She declared that things were not as bad as the therapist had made them sound and that she wanted to continue with therapy. During the next week, significant improvements were made.

Watzalawick, Weakland, and Fisch (1974, p. 154) describe a reframing technique called the Devil's Pact, which appears to be useful with extremely cautious clients who procrastinate with some important behavior. The procedure seems to be especially useful for those who delay taking some necessary action and thus have a sense of urgency and yet desire to reduce any risk of failure. Clients are told that there is a plan that will allow them to reach their goal successfully. They are assured that they are capable of carrying it out and that it will not harm them or be too expensive. However, because they are likely to turn it down if it is disclosed, the plan will be divulged only if they agree to carry it out, no matter how difficult, inconvenient, or unreasonable it may seem. Further, they are told to think about it and return the next week with their decision (the implication is that if they refuse to do it, there is no need to return). In this case, if clients refuse to go along with the plan, they are, in a sense, saying that they can solve their own problems or that their problems really are not very serious. They have no more excuses for looking for the "right" therapist or for an "effective" plan. If they agree to the plan, they have made a commitment to carrying it out and are thus more likely to do so (in addition to ending the "yes, but that won't work" game). In either case, by making a decision, clients have already taken the "risk" that they have tried so long to avoid, and thus the problem is put into a different frame.

The use of paradoxical intentions has been found to be successful with a wide variety of populations and disorders (Romig & Gruenke, 1991; DeBord, 1989). These techniques have been found to be at least as effective as traditional psychotherapy methods and may actually be more effective with severe symptoms or in maintaining therapeutic effects (Shoham-Salomon & Rosenthal, 1987). Despite their usefulness, these approaches have been criticized as being overly manipulative, deceptive, and perhaps unethical (Brown & Slee, 1986). In addition, there has been some concern that their use might undermine the client–therapist relationship or decrease the therapist's attractiveness, expertness, or trustworthiness. Although most research suggests that this does not occur (see Betts & Remer, 1993), some therapists may be uncomfortable with their use or prefer to use them only as a last resort. Weeks and L'Abate (1982) suggest that before using paradoxical techniques, you should give your clients some simple and direct homework assignments. If these are completed as assigned, paradoxical techniques will probably not be needed. However, if clients forget, change the assignment, or are noncompliant, then paradoxical techniques may be useful. To learn more aboaut these techniques, see Ascher (1989); Seltzer (1986); Bergman (1985); Weeks and L'Abate (1982); Selvini-Palazzoli, Cecchin, Prata, and Boscolo (1978); Dowd and Milne (1986); de Shazer (1988); or Watzalawick, Weakland, and Fisch (1974).

Summary

Table 4-4, based on the material reviewed previously, provides a summary of the major reasons that clients do not adhere to treatment recommendations.

TABLE 4-4   Major Factors Associated with Treatment Nonadherence

1. Clients do not understand the treatment program.
2. Clients forget the treatment procedure.
3. Clients do not like the therapist or there is a poor client–therapist relationship.
4. Clients lack the required skills or information to carry out part or all of the plan.
5. Clients disagree with the plan or are not satisfied with treatment.
6. Clients feel that they have had little or no input into the treatment program.
7. Clients' attitudes or belief system interfere with carrying out the program. For example, clients do not believe they have the ability to be successful or do not believe they have a problem.
8. Clients' symptoms or sensory impairments interfere with compliance (anxiety, depression, hopelessness, psychosis, problems with memory, etc.), or clients have other disorders (e.g., drug or alcohol abuse) that interfere with the program.
9. Clients' families, environments, or social systems interfere with, are not supportive of, or prevent them from being compliant.
10. Clients give in to immediate gratification, despite long-term consequences or potential improvement.
11. Clients perceive the "costs" of treatment to outweigh its benefits.
12. The treatment plan is too difficult to carry out, too aversive, too time-consuming, or too disruptive to clients' life-styles.
13. Treatment takes much longer than clients expect or desire.
14. Clients are engaging in self-handicapping behaviors.
15. The therapist fails to supervise the treatment program properly or to make appropriate adjustments to the plan.
16. Clients' symptoms are maintained by strong secondary gains and/or they feel comfortable maintaining the "sick role."

(Continued)

TABLE 4-3   *(Continued)*

17. Clients prefer to leave the outcome of their psychological disorder to fate or to a supreme being.
18. Clients do not want to change, are not ready for change, or are not convinced that change is important or necessary. Or clients may have progressed in therapy to a point where they are uncomfortable (for whatever reasons) with further potential progress.
19. Clients have an ulterior motive for being in therapy.
20. The treatment plan is ineffective and/or clients have multiple problems and the wrong one is being addressed.

Ford (1992) suggests that behaviors that allow a person either to reach a desired goal or to move closer toward reaching that goal will be intrinsically reinforcing and thus will become part of the person's natural behavioral repertoire. I believe that clients' motivation to complete a treatment plan can be partially evaluated using this concept. For example, if clients are noncompliant, a number of possibilities exist:

1. The program is not moving clients toward their goals.
2. Progress is too slow (or they have the perception that it is ineffective or too slow).
3. Clients do not want to reach that goal.
4. Clients perceive that the goal is not achievable.
5. Clients have another goal that is more important at a particular point in time.
6. The goal is unrealistic or too difficult.
7. Something is preventing clients from engaging in the appropriate behaviors that will lead toward the goal.

This list above seems to place the bulk of the burden of noncompliance on factors related to the clients, but many of these behaviors are in fact due to poor or inappropriate treatment techniques used by the therapist, or perhaps to a poor relationship between client and therapist. As de Shazer and colleagues have often pointed out, clients' resistant behavior is their best solution to their problems until a better one is found. Therefore, it is necessary to identify the major reason(s) for noncompliant behavior (there may be more than one) before trying to address it.

The following are the general techniques that can be used to enhance compliance behaviors or prevent noncompliance that were reviewed in this chapter: (1) behavior management techniques, (2) paradoxical interventions, (3) relapse prevention techniques, and (4) client satisfaction assessments with appropriate follow-up. A number of specific recommendations were also presented.

Client–Therapist Interactions, Part I

Overview

The idea of a psychotherapist functioning primarily as a detached transmitter of information and implementer of interventions has become less popular recently. It is obvious that the personal characteristics of both clients and therapists can have a profound effect on psychotherapy process and outcome. In Chapter 4, I reviewed some of the client- and therapist-related variables that lead to or reduce adherence in psychotherapy. In this chapter, I will begin to explore how the *interactions* between the client and the therapist can effect various aspects of therapy. As I have pointed out throughout this book, we should not necessarily blame the client for being resistant. Often, clients appear resistive because they are not getting what they want or need from therapy. For example, the urge to self-disclose can be derailed by a therapist who appears distant, unfriendly, cold, or uninterested. Unfortunately, clients' views have been relatively ignored until recently. Following this reasoning, I will begin with a brief description of the needs, expectations, and fears that typical clients have while attending therapy. From there, I will explore some of the factors associated with "difficult" clients. In the last section I will cover the topic of dealing with anger.

Client Needs

From clients' perspectives, there are many treatment factors that promote progress in therapy and reduce the likelihood of dropping out. Howe

(1993) discusses a number of these in a book devoted entirely to what clients have to say about their experiences in psychotherapy. One of the most important reported components is the perception of the therapist as a warm and friendly person. This includes coming across as "real" or natural, as opposed to someone who simply knows and uses a number of therapeutic techniques. Therapists who are too abstract or technical tend to increase rather than reduce the anxiety level of new clients, and this also appears to have a negative effect on self-disclosure. In addition, clients tend to view such therapists as cold and uncaring. Similarly, it is important to note that the positive attitudes a therapist has toward clients (such as interest and caring) must be communicated. In other words, the more uncertainty clients have about the therapist's attitude toward them, the less likely they are to change (see Strupp, Fox, & Lessler, 1969).

Other treatment conditions that clients want include liking and being liked by the therapist, having a sense of mutual trust, and perceiving that the therapist will be there to support and encourage them (Howe, 1993; see also Wright & Davis, 1994). Similar factors were identified by Strupp, Fox, and Lessler (1969) as the sine qua non for successful psychotherapy (p. 17). Along the same lines, Goldberg (1986, p. 123) summarizes the qualities that practitioners should have for successful therapy: interest in others, self-awareness, humility, courage, capacity for intimacy, curiosity, humor, optimism, flexibility, problem-solving ability, and creativity. Whether a therapist needs to have these qualities or interpersonal skills prior to professional training in order to achieve the effects described here, or whether they can be learned, is unclear. However, these conditions seem to be necessary for the client–therapist relationship to develop and for improvement to occur.

Another important factor reported by Howe's clients is acceptance, which is the cornerstone of person-centered therapy. This concept generally boils down to avoiding judgments about clients, regardless of their qualities or previous behaviors. Of course, this is often easier said than done. For example, I worked with several clients who had killed their young children. In these situations, it was very difficult for me to come across in an accepting manner (see Lietaer, 1984, for further discussion of this issue). Therapists have to be careful in this area because, taken to its extreme, a blanket expression of acceptance is just as unnatural (and ungenuine) as Freud's notion of total neutrality. It is a good example of a concept that is sometimes much easier to accept in theory than in practice.

On the other hand, when used appropriately, acceptance appears to be a very powerful technique. From clients' perspectives, it includes the sense that they can express their thoughts and feelings without fear. This is one factor that differentiates psychotherapy from just talking with a friend. As I described in Chapter 3, self-disclosure brings with it

---

Recommendations: Treatment Interactions
1. Therapists should fully explore clients' expectations for therapy as well as their fears concerning the treatment process at the beginning of therapy.

Recommendations: Treatment Interactions
2. In addition to being technically competent, clients want their therapists to come across in a warm, caring, and human manner rather than detached. Yet, at the same time, this must be genuine.

---

the risk of exposing our weaknesses and flaws and making ourselves vulnerable to others. Psychotherapy offers the opportunity to divulge information in an environment that is theoretically safe and that eliminates the chance that the information will be revealed to persons whom we do not want to include. This in turn contributes to clients' sense of security. In the ideal therapeutic setting, clients can say whatever they want without risking ridicule and without being rejected.

Another characteristic that clients want from therapy is empathy—the feeling that someone understands their feelings and experiences. This does not simply refer to clarification or reflection of feelings but, rather is more similar to how Rogers originally conceptualized the term (see, Rogers, 1951, pp. 28–29). It is an attempt to comprehend clients as they perceive themselves—in other words, trying to understand clients' worlds without confounding our own thoughts, biases, and feelings into this interpretation. When successful, the therapist should be able to experience the world in a manner similar to the client at that particular moment. This might take some time to develop fully.

Maluccio (1979) summarizes the positive therapist qualities that clients feel are related to meeting this need, including a therapist with whom it is easy to communicate; who has the ability to put clients at ease, who shows genuine concern and interest about clients, who is tuned in to clients' needs and feelings, who is a good listener, who makes clients feel comfortable, who understands clients, and who gives clients enough time to talk about themselves.

The relationship between these therapist qualities and client resistance are confirmed by a study by Miller and Wells (1990), who point out that one way to reduce resistance in clients is by increasing the attractiveness of the therapist. This is consistent with social psychology research showing that we are more easily influenced and persuaded by people that we like. By increasing the qualities of therapists that make them more trustworthy and attractive, resistance is likely to decrease. In a similar vein, Sloane, Staples, Cristol, Yorkston, and Whipple (1975) found that about 70 percent of clients who had successful treatment believed that the personal characteristics of their therapist contributed significantly to their improvement. These included the therapist's personality, his or her ability to help clients understand and face their problems, the therapist's being an easy person to talk to, and his or her ability to provide encouragement.

Clients' needs as identified earlier are also consistent with studies that differentiate client experiences that either help or hinder therapy. For example, McLeod (1990) summarizes several studies in which clients identify the factors that were most helpful from their treatment. These included increasing clients' ability to solve problems, having someone to talk to who is interested in them, having someone who offers encouragement and reassurance, having someone who understands them, having someone who instills hope, and achieving self-understanding. The main factors identified by clients as hindering therapy were: being silent or being afraid to talk about certain areas, not cooperating with the therapist; not being able to make a connection with the therapist; and perceiving that the therapist used the wrong interventions or said things that were inconsistent with the clients' feelings. McLeod suggests that clients generally view the *process* of therapy (having someone to talk to, being able to trust the therapist, etc.), as being more important than the techniques used. These studies also indicated a consensus from clients that they wanted more specific advice and recommendations from therapy than they actually received.

Client Expectations

As I previously described, one of the important factors affecting treatment outcome is the consistency between clients' expectations and the services they actually receive. Thus, it is important that the therapist have an idea of what clients expect from therapy. Oldfield (1983, p. 46) describes a large-scale study carried out in England that surveyed client expectations for therapy (see also France, 1988, for similar information). Oldfield found that responses fell into four major groups: (1) a change in feelings, (2) achievement of greater self-understanding, (3) regaining an ability to cope with life, and (4) an improvement in relationships. Responses dealing with a change in feelings usually referred to a reduction of distress or relief from symptoms such as depression and anxiety.

Clients' responses related to understanding typically were associated with greater self-awareness and an increased ability to comprehend the

---

Recommendations: Treatment Interactions
3. Many clients appear to want and need more direct and active treatment approaches. These should be offered when appropriate.

Recommendations: Treatment Interactions
4. Both new and experienced therapists should consider the use of supervision to help deal with difficult clients.

---

causes of their problems. Regaining the ability to cope with life revolved around "getting back to normal." Factors included learning to cope with their problems, increasing their self-esteem, getting back to work, and similar outcomes. The fourth area, improving relationships, usually had to do with getting along with people in general or improving affiliations with parents or partners.

In the same study, Oldfield asked clients how they expected treatment to help them. These responses were grouped into five areas: (1) not sure or uncertain, (2) having someone to talk to, (3) gaining insight into their problems, (4) getting specific advice, and (5) receiving support. The factors that clients reported as most helpful in therapy were therapist characteristics such as showing true concern, trustworthiness, being a good listener, and perceived competence. Other positive aspects of therapy included the client–therapist relationship, feeling "safe," being able to admit to flaws and weaknesses without being judged by the therapist, and talking to someone who could remain objective.

In looking at the responses concerning client disappointments with therapy, the main themes centered around not getting enough advice or specific recommendations, being with a therapist who was too "professional," and factors related to therapists' inappropriate use of techniques— for example, dwelling too much on the past or using interventions without clearly explaining their purpose or rationale.

In a related study, Maluccio (1979) reports findings that are very similar to those just listed. His results are based on posttherapy interviews with a random group of clients and therapists. These suggest that first impressions of therapists are very important in terms of forming a relationship or deciding to continue with treatment. For example, it appears that the initial sessions of therapy are the most vivid for clients.

He also reports that although clients were satisfied with having the opportunity to talk with someone, many of them were not sure how this process could help them with solve their problems. Similarly, many clients expected more active interventions from their therapists, such as specific suggestions and advice. Maluccio also found that clients tended to see termination as being due to their own initiative, whereas the therapists viewed it as a mutual decision.

In looking at clients who dropped out of treatment, he found results that are consistent with other studies (see Appendix B). Clients reported the main reasons for leaving therapy as either having achieved their goals or being dissatisfied with services. Interestingly, these clients tended to report more satisfaction with treatment outcome than their counselors did and also had greater confidence about being able to cope with future challenges than their therapists did about them. On the other hand, clients tended to perceive their improvement in therapy as being due to outside influences such as their social network or natural life experiences. Not surprisingly, therapists were inclined to attribute the clients' improvement to factors related to themselves or to other treatment variables.

In discussing the major themes of his findings, Maluccio was impressed most with some of the striking discrepancies between the perceptions of the clients and the therapists. These tended to be the greatest at the beginning and the end of therapy. He states: "In a sense, client and worker start with divergent perspectives, gradually converge as their engagement proceeds, and again move in different directions as it comes to a close" (pp. 184–185). He concludes that much of therapy involves reducing the discrepancy between the clients and therapists in term of goals and expectations and that consistency between these is necessary for successful outcome. Related to this, Maluccio suggests that in addition to the role induction of clients into therapy, we should similarly be concerned with therapists' role induction into clients' ways of thinking and perceiving. I will have more to say about this in Chapter 8.

Client Fears

Often, behaviors that appear to be resistive in nature are based on fears that clients have about undergoing psychotherapy. Pipes and Davenport (1990) explore some of thes most common fears. One is the fear that therapists will attempt to impart their own values to the client. I suppose one can debate whether in fact therapists should impart their values to their clients, but research clearly shows that most clients do not want this to occur. Although I believe it is impossible for therapists to separate their values totally from their therapy, I do believe it is important to be aware of the potential for overdoing this, especially when developing treatment goals and procedures. By having the client become

---

Recommendations: Treatment Interactions
5. When labeling clients as difficult, we should first look to ourselves to see what we are contributing to the process.

Recommendations: Treatment Interactions
6. This may seem obvious, but if a treatment plan is not working, try something new.

---

an integral part of the treatment planning (see Chapter 2), this issue can be largely controlled.

A similar fear is that the therapist will try to get the client to do something against his or her wishes. There is no simple solution to this problem because in fact this does occur. For example, I worked with a nineteen-year-old client who refused to leave her live-in boyfriend despite the fact that he had severely beaten her a number of times. Despite my efforts, it became painfully clear that there was no chance of her leaving him at that point, and that further discussion would be a waste of time. Of course, you do not have to be a psychotherapist to know that you cannot get people to do things they really do not want to do, but the lesson is sometimes difficult to accept. To relieve these fears in clients, it is best to try to convince them that ultimately the changes they will make in therapy will depend on themselves—in other words, that the therapist really has no extraordinary powers to control or make puppets out of them.

Another common fear is that the therapist will reveal to others what transpires in the session. This can be handled by explaining the rules of confidentiality, using pretherapy or role induction training, or using standard consent forms (see Handelsman, 1990). Studies seldom identify this as a client concern at the end of therapy, although the point can be made that individuals who are overly sensitive to this issue either drop up or never begin therapy in the first place.

Another apprehension some clients have is that they will learn something about themselves that they really do not want to know. This tends to be more of a problem for long-term than for brief therapy, but it can occur with any type of intervention. Some professionals see the prospect of self-awareness as the root of most types of treatment resistance, although I have not found this to be true. One way to handle this problem is to explain that this is a common fear and point out that the fact that the client has decided to attend therapy may be a sign that he or she is ready to explore some personal issues. If we know this is a potential problem, we can also be more cautious with such clients or can work at a slower pace.

My general point is that clients' fears can be handled in a number of ways, but we need to know what type of concerns clients have about the psychotherapy process before we can address them. Because clients are unlikely to bring these out in the open spontaneously, we need to question them about these fears when treatment begins. By addressing these issues early in therapy, many dropouts, as well as various forms of resistance, may be avoided.

Implications

There are a number of things we can learn from the client-focused studies described here. First, compared to other aspects of psychotherapy, the client has been relatively ignored from a research standpoint. Judging from the number of studies I was able to find that investigate psychotherapy from the client's point of view, we have a long way to go before we can fully understand what clients expect from therapy and what they find most useful. Although some therapists may disagree about how important this is, the studies I have reviewed throughout this book clearly show a relationship between meeting clients' expectations and factors such as satisfaction, adherence, remaining in therapy, and (directly or indirectly) treatment outcome. Thus, we need to become more aware of clients' values, goals, fears, and expectations when designing a treatment program. Psychotherapy is already largely "consumer-driven." As our population becomes more educated, more sophisticated, and inclined to take more personal responsibility for its own mental and physical health (and to pay more for it individually), this is likely to become even more important.

Another factor that is clear from the studies cited here is that, although treatment techniques are important, most clients find the personal touch more significant. This should come as no surprise, but clients want and need someone who is easy to talk to, whom they can trust, who understands them, and who is interested in their welfare. In short, they want someone who is human. In this regard, I do not think we have to worry too much about being replaced by computers anytime soon. It would not be an overstatement to say that, to a large extent, therapeutic success depends a great deal on the interpersonal skills of the therapist.

A third generalization that I have deduced from these studies and from my own experience is that many clients want more guidance and direction than some therapists are willing to give. Perhaps because of

---

Recommendations: Treatment Interactions

7. To best serve their clients, therapists may at times have to use techniques that are inconsistent with their theoretical orientation.

Recommendations: Dealing with Anger

8. The first step in dealing with angry clients is to identify the source of the anger and to determine whether or not it is justified.

---

the influence of psychoanalysis and client-centered philosophy, some therapists prefer to allow clients to come to their own conclusions or find their own solutions to their problems. Although this is certainly appropriate in some cases, I believe that the majority of individuals who can do this effectively either do not initiate therapy, or if they do, they probably do so to promote self-growth rather than solve major emotional problems. By and large, I believe that clients need to take major responsibility for selecting their goals and changing their own behavior. At the same time, it is the job of the therapist to decide what type of help should be offered, and I think some therapists need to be more active and assertive in this role. As with other aspects of psychotherapy, we need to reach a delicate balance in this area. Table 5-1 summarizes the important aspects clients want from psychotherapy.

TABLE 5-1   What Most Clients Want from Therapy

1. Acceptance
2. A therapist who understands them
3. Security
4. The chance to talk without fear of repercussion
5. A therapist who is warm and friendly
6. A therapist whom clients can trust and rely on in times of need
7. A flexible but structured environment and treatment program
8. A therapist who likes clients
9. A therapist who is encouraging and reassuring
10. At times, specific advice and recommendations
11. Greater self-understanding
12. The ability to cope with clients' problems
13. A therapist who is competent but "human"
14. A therapist who treats clients with respect
15. A therapist who responds to clients as individuals

Difficult Clients

An interesting way to look at what some therapists call difficult clients is suggested by Kottler (1992). He breaks down this concept in several ways. For example, in terms of diagnosis, he suggests that borderline, paranoid, antisocial, and narcissistic personality disorders are among the most difficult to treat. Added to these are individuals with drug and alcohol problems, persistent mental illness such as schizophrenia and other psychotic disorders, suicidal-depressed clients, and those with organic or neurological disorders.

Cutting across diagnoses, Kottler suggests that four categories of clients are typically found to be most difficult to work with by therapists:

1. Clients who are very demanding or have an extreme sense of entitlement—for example, individuals with strong narcissistic tendencies or those who request a lot of extra time and attention.
2. Clients with an excessive need for control, some of it as a reaction to the helplessness associated with being a client, but often due to a characteristic need to be in control.
3. Individuals with strong defense mechanisms, such as persons with borderline personality disorders.
4. Clients who externalize or project all their problems onto others or the outside world, and who tend to be angry or suspicious and typically do not accept responsibility for their problems (if, in fact, they admit to any).

In addition to these categories, other professionals (e.g., Robbins, Beck, Mueller & Mizener, 1988) have included clients who are passive, impulsive, angry, or hostile and those who act out or are violent. Of course, not all clients with these descriptions are difficult, and the degree or intensity of the problems they produce also varies.

Involuntary Clients

In addition to the factors described here, when thinking of difficult clients we probably picture those who are unmotivated or do not really want to be in therapy, or individuals with a negative attitude toward therapy. All these descriptions are frequently true of clients who come to therapy against their will (see Larke, 1985; Ritchie, 1986; Storch & Lane, 1989; Harris & Watkins, 1987; and Rooney, 1992, for a review). The involuntary client can be seen either as the epitome of resistance or, perhaps in a more classical or purer sense, as not resistive at all. I tend to

Recommendations: Dealing with Anger

9. Reflecting anger back to clients is generally not recommended.

Recommendations: Dealing with Anger

10. Having clients ventilate their anger or hostility should be done with caution and only by experienced therapists.

take the latter view and personally find some of these clients refreshing. Often their attitudes toward treatment or the therapist are transparent and, with some notable exceptions (such as combination antisocial/borderline personalities), their outcome is probably not much different than that of traditional clients.

On the other hand, several factors make the treatment of these clients somewhat different than those who are considered voluntary. First, depending on the referral source, it may be hard to satisfy all of the "clients" at the same time. In other words, if clients are referred by the court system or other social agencies, these sources may be looking for a particular outcome. Often, it may differ from what either we or the clients themselves want from therapy. The first step involves clarifying in our own mind, and for clients, the objectives or requirements of the outside constituents. These should be made as concrete as possible. Once this is accomplished, and within the confines of these guidelines, the client should have input into the goals and procedures of therapy.

In a related matter, we need to determine the stage of the change process that these clients are in upon entering therapy. Many of them may be in the contemplation or precontemplation stage of change. Some may not be aware of what changes are feasible. Similarly, some clients may have acknowledged that a problem exists but do not believe that they need any help from others. For these and other reasons, it has been my experience that it is usually not worthwhile to try to produce major changes too quickly with these clients, because they often need a long orientation period. In this sense, many of the techniques described in Chapter 2 that prepare and mobilize clients for therapy should be useful.

A third point worth mentioning is that many of these clients have an uncanny ability to "push our buttons" or get under our skin. For example, they may show extreme or inappropriate levels of anger, hostility, or uncooperativeness. Often it seems they know exactly what to do in order to upset us. Of course, many of these behaviors may be related to the reasons they were referred for treatment in the first place, and contribute to the difficulty of developing a therapeutic relationship. It is not easy to come across as warm and friendly to people we may not like. Similarly, despite all our training, it is difficult to accept negative affect or rejection unemotionally. I believe these type of reactions form the core of our perception of difficult clients in general (not only involuntary ones). In short, our feelings toward our clients have a lot to do with how they make us feel about ourselves.

In a similar vein, Kottler (1992) proposes a difference between client resistance and client difficulty. He suggests that *resistance* tends to be a natural reaction to change, whereas *difficult* clients are particularly annoying and continually frustrating to the therapist. This is an important distinction because it points out that the clients we tend to find the most troublesome are not simply those whose condition does not improve, but those we find unpleasant to work with. For example, some studies have labeled clients with terms such as "entitled" (Boulanger, 1988), "impossible" (Davis, 1984), "abrasive" (Greenberg, 1984), "boring" (Taylor, 1984), or "manipulative" (Hamilton, Decker, & Rumbaut, 1986). However, when one looks at these investigations, it is interesting to note how troublesome it is to separate the clients' condition from the therapists' reaction. In other words, we do not like these types of clients because they prevent us from being successful and, in a sense, from doing our jobs. This reinforces the concept that client difficulty is an interpersonal rather than a client-focused problem. It is very much influenced by the therapist's qualities as well as their subjective perceptions of their clients. It also suggests that we have to be careful when we label a client difficult, because we may reacting to our own frustrations. Similarly, studies have found that therapists are generally more successful with clients whom they like (see Wills, 1982); in some cases, "difficult clients" may be a self-fulfilling prophesy.

This line of thought is also consistent with the findings of Rosenbaum, Horowitz, and Wilner (1986), who investigated a group of psychotherapists and their assessments of difficult clients. As might be expected, they found that therapist perceptions of client difficulty were highly correlated with corresponding levels of self-reported distress. However, they found a much lower correlation between these same therapist perceptions and independent clinical evaluations of the clients. This implies that perceived client difficulty is not related simply to symptom severity but to other factors as well. On the basis of further evaluation of the data, the authors suggest that perceived difficulty is mostly related to client demandingness. Interestingly, they also found a positive correlation between therapists' judgments of difficulty and clients' educational level. Commenting about this unexpected finding, the authors make a good point about effective therapy and educational levels. As they put it, it is "not whether the patient is *educated* but whether the patient is *educable*" (p. 423, emphasis in the original). Although this latter finding is somewhat surprising, it is consistent in that clients with a higher educational level might also be more demanding. Taking the results of the study as a whole, the authors conclude that perceived client difficulty is not due solely to severe symptoms or lack of progress in therapy but, rather, to complex interpersonal dilemmas between client and therapist.

General Implications

When considering the results of the studies reviewed above as a whole, it becomes clear that, when confronted with difficult clients we need to look to ourselves to see what we contribute to the process. Clients whom we view as difficult are often unpredictable or behave in ways that are inconsistent with the client role we expect from them. I do not think it is any accident that most therapists prefer to work with the infamous YAVIS-type (YAVIS = young, attractive, verbal, intelligent, successful) clients, individuals who tend to share similar backgrounds and experiences with the therapist. In many ways, they also think in ways similar to the therapist, so traditional therapeutic techniques tend to be effective. Thus, one reason some clients are difficult is that they force us to change as well. Part of this involves the power struggle in therapy. Clients are often "difficult" because they do not do as we ask or they try to manipulate us. Our indignant reaction to this may be anger, fear, or an irrational retaliation. Interestingly, I believe this power struggle is strongest with clients who resist us the most.

I am *not* suggesting, as others have, that there are no difficult clients, only difficult therapists. I am suggesting that at times we have to take a less defensive approach to this problem. I believe that the backbone of the behavior of many of the clients we find difficult is fear—a fear of dependency, of facing their problems, of changing, and so on. However, I think we should also admit to having our own fears (or at least apprehensions) when working with such clients—fears of not making the right diagnosis, of making clients angry, of not using the right techniques, of looking foolish, of losing our own composure, and so on. Most of these people are not only difficult clients; some may be difficult persons in any setting or with anybody. Sometimes in our haste (perhaps I should say our need) in trying to help them, we become careless. Perhaps because of our awareness of countertranference, we allow them certain liberties that we do not offer to others. For example, we allow them to get away with "little" things, or we become obsessed with "curing" them. The result is often that the difficulty escalates rather than improving. By attempting to take an objective look at how these types of clients affect us, and vice versa, I believe we can become more effective with them.

It seems appropriate to reiterate at this point that psychotherapy is an interactive process. If clients are difficult, it is often for a good reason. Sometimes it is related to us and what we are doing (or not doing) with them. However, rather than looking at "difficult clients" or "difficult therapists," we should look at difficult client–therapist relationships. This not only helps us understand the dynamics of the client, but also gives us some insight into problematic aspects of our own presentation or therapeutic styles.

Another way we can better deal with difficult clients of all types is to increase the amount of advice or supervision we receive from mentors who are more experienced than we are, or to make use of consultations with other therapists—for example, through the use of peer support. Several factors might block this approach. First, some experienced therapists might find such feedback threatening or awkward. Although this type of feedback is generally accepted by therapists trained in psychoanalysis, those who are trained in more contemporary theories may not be as open to it. Second, this type of supervision is not readily available to everyone. It is more a personal matter of whom you know and feel comfortable with discussing your cases. Similarly, although most states now require continuing education for most psychotherapists, supervision is sometimes not accepted as qualifying for these requirements. Third, busy therapists are likely to give such consultations low priority and thus may never find the time to do them. However, I believe that this type of support is very important. State licensing boards and professional organizations should make more of an effort both to provide such services and to accept them for continuing education purposes.

Over the years, many psychotherapists have written about how important it is to increase and maintain the structure in therapy for difficult clients. I agree with this view if the structure relates to consistency rather than rigidity. In other words, especially for the more disturbed clients, it is important to "maintain the frame" of therapy, not allow them to break the basic rules you have set out, and so on. On the other hand, I also believe we need to have an open mind with all clients and be willing to try new things. Therapists often get caught in a sort of therapeutic rut by continuing to do the same things over and over again.

One of the more surprising (and in some ways disturbing) findings I came across in writing this chapter were the results of Kendall, Kipnis, and Otto-Salaj (1992). This study evaluated a large number of questionnaires returned by therapists who were members of either the American

Psychological Association or the Association for the Advance of Behavior Therapy. They found that even when eliminating clients with schizophrenia, mental retardation, and organic impairments or those that were currently hospitalized, therapists reported an average of 11 percent of their caseload as being made up of individuals who were not making any progress. The authors also asked the therapists to divide all of their clients into those with mild versus severe symptoms and found that 63 percent of clients were rated severe. When asked to explain why some of their clients were not progressing, the two most often cited reasons were that these individuals were unable to benefit from therapy or had problems with their level of motivation. Chance factors or the therapist's role were seen as the least likely cause of this lack of progress. The authors point out that therapists tend to take credit when clients do improve but view themselves as the least important factor in client failures. This tendency is not unique to therapists; in the general population, it is called the fundamental attribution error.

Despite the high percentage of clients with severe symptoms, this factor was not reported as a major explanation for their lack of progress. Another notable finding was that even after eliminating clients who had dropped out or were to be referred elsewhere, 60 percent of therapists had no alternative plans for those clients who were not progressing in treatment. Of course, treatment plans or goals should not be changed willy-nilly; but if something is obviously not working, it does not make sense to "stay the course." Part of the problem is that we tend to think of treatment goals in absolute rather than relative terms. But the "perfect" solution to a client's problem at the beginning of therapy may not be so perfect in the middle or late stages. Psychotherapy is a change process; as people undergo changes, their situation, problems, or solutions may change. It is important to keep in mind that therapists often have to change as well.

Finally, we have to accept that sometimes neither we nor anyone else will be able to help certain clients at a particular point in time. All therapists, from Freud to Rogers (and thousands in between), have what they might consider "treatment failures." I believe this term is a misnomer. Although some clients may not make any obvious or significant changes, at the very least, we can learn a lot from them, and thereby increase our ability to help others in the future. Clients, too, may benefit from therapy in ways that are not obvious to us, or it may take some time for the changes to take effect. As Marston (1984) points out, practitioners seem to be affected more by their failures than by their successes. As difficult it may be, we cannot let these perceived failures damage our self-esteem or sense of competency.

Angry Clients

I chose to discuss the topic of anger in this section for several reasons. First, although I have no empirical evidence for it, I believe that the type of people who are attracted to the profession of psychotherapy may have more of a problem confronting anger than the general population. Readers who disagree might at least concede that psychotherapists have more problems dealing with anger than with other emotions. For this reason, we may find angry clients particularly difficult to work with (the studies I have described seem to support this last statement). For example, this may be one reason that therapists tend not to enjoy working with people with various personality disorders (borderline, narcissistic, etc.), who often display inappropriate anger or hostility.

Second, over the years, anger has not received nearly as much research or professional attention as other emotions, such as anxiety or depression (Deffenbacher & Stark, 1992). One problem associated with anger is that whereas anxiety and depression are clearly recognized as psychological disturbances (at least in their moderate or extreme form), the same is not always true for anger. Perhaps for these reasons, the treatment procedures for anger are not as well developed as those for other emotions. Another possibility is that anger may simply be more difficult to treat because, typically, the therapeutic goal is not to eliminate it totally but, rather, to control it and use it appropriately.

Two topics associated with anger seem to be most relevant for psychotherapists. The first is anger directed at the therapist, and the second is its treatment. Concerning anger directed toward the therapist, we all know that clients (or anyone else) become angry for a number of reasons. For example, Averill (1982) gave a large group of subjects a questionnaire concerning the motives or goals of anger. The questions most frequently endorsed by these subjects (in order) were: (1) to assert independence or improve self-image; (2) to get back or gain revenge on the instigator; and (3) to bring about a change in the behavior of the instigator. (Averill, 1982, p. 177). Consistent with these findings, clients undergoing psychotherapy are often frustrated, have a poor self-image, or feel helpless and controlled; thus, it is not surprising that so many of them get angry during the course of therapy. Anger and fear seem to be closely linked emotions, and when clients feel vulnerable they often lash out at us. It is also important to note here that a client's anger is not always expressed directly. In other words, clients may express it by coming to the session late, not paying their fee, calling you in the middle of the night, and so on. However, it is the direct personal assault on us or on our competence that causes the most problems. As many of us have painfully learned, many clients are experts in detecting and exposing our weaknesses. In short, angry clients tend to promote angry therapists.

Over the years, professionals have given a number of suggestions on how to deal with clients' anger. The first step is to evaluate the source of the anger. Is it due to the treatment plan; to something you have done; to resistance, transference, frustration, displacement, or the client's personality traits; or to other reasons? In some cases, anger may be masking depression or grief or may serve other defensive functions (see Cerney & Buskirk, 1991). Obviously, the most appropriate intervention will vary depending on this factor. Related to this is an evaluation of whether the anger is "justified" in the current situation. In some cases, the client may have valid reasons for being angry with you; in others, it is clearly inappropriate. If a client has a good reason for being angry with you, it is probably best to admit to your mistake and go on from there. For example, you might have made a wrong interpretation or done something to annoy the client. By not reacting in a defensive manner, you are letting clients know that you value their opinions and that they are an integral part of the treatment process. You are also taking away a potentially destructive tool that they can use to manipulate and control you.

Of course, sometimes clients' expressions of anger may be in a gray area between valid and inappropriate. For example, clients may have a good reason for being angry at you, but the intensity of the anger may be much greater than is justified. Or there may be a clear reason for their anger, but a case can be made for your position as well. In these situations, it is best to be open, honest, firm (but not antagonistic), and again nondefensive.

Some therapists suggest that when clients make you angry, you should express this anger back at them. Although there may be isolated instances where this is appropriate, I generally believe that this is not good advice (see Fremont & Anderson, 1986, for a review). I agree with Pipes and Davenport (1990), who suggest that the minimum conditions for expressing anger toward clients are when: (1) you honestly believe the anger will be therapeutic for the client and (2) your anger is not related to countertransference issues (p. 22). I would add a third condition, which is that your relationship with the client is secure. Even with these conditions, expressing anger back to the individual should be done only with great caution.

Obviously, it is much easier to read or write about dealing with angry clients than actually to confront one and debate what to do. Since we often learn by doing, new or inexperienced therapists should consider role playing with their supervisor how to react to angry clients. However, because every situation is different, it is often necessary to use common sense. Most times it is best to listen and try to figure out what the client is trying to achieve through his or her anger. For example, anger sometimes signifies resistance or an attempt to change the subject or the course of the session. If this is the case, it may indicate that clients are not ready for what you are trying to do and you need to take a step back. As with resistance in general, we can often learn something about clients' defense systems or interpersonal styles when they become angry, and we should take advantage of this situation. Anger should also be evaluated in terms of the stage of our relationship with clients. For example, toward the end of therapy, it may be that clients have reached a level where they feel more comfortable expressing their emotions to us. In many cases, this should be viewed as a positive sign.

We also need to make a distinction between infrequent and chronic anger in clients. Everyone has a bad day once in a while so there are times when client anger really does not have any special significance other than that the person is annoyed for some reason. With clients who are chronically angry at you, it is best to set limits with them at the start of therapy (usually you can distinguish this type early on). Explain exactly what will and will not be tolerated in therapy, and what the consequences will be if these limits are broken (e.g., ending the session, having a "cooling off" period, etc.). Some therapists prefer to terminate therapy with clients who are chronically angry or hostile, but I have mixed feelings about this. By doing this, you are in a sense reinforcing clients' anger and hostility. They have learned once again that they can get their own way through intimidation. If clients are frequently angry in therapy, it is a good bet that this is they way they deal with people in general and that their anger needs to be formally addressed in therapy. This is the topic of the next section.

In terms of treatment, the first well-controlled study of anger was done by Novaco in 1975. Novaco maintains that anger has a number of consequences for humans, some of which are positive and some negative. For example, anger energizes or intensifies our behavior (e.g., slamming doors, yelling). It disrupts our thinking and concentration and makes us more likely to engage in impulsive behaviors. It serves as a protective function; for example, it can lead to physical aggression or displace anxiety and project the conflict outward. Sullivan, (1956) claims that "anger blunts the feeling of personal insecurity." Anger allows us to express or communicate negative feelings to others, and it prompts certain behaviors or actions (aggression or coping responses).

Novaco's proposed treatment program includes a cognitive stress inoculation procedure based on Meichenbaum's (1977) model for treating anxiety, in conjunction with relaxation training. Specifically, clients are taught to focus on the particular aspects of provocations that trigger anger and on the thoughts or feelings that accompany the provocations.

Novaco's general premise is that one's response to anger is influenced by two factors: emotional arousal and cognitive activity. He believes that anger results from self-statements that are made in provocative situations, which then influence and, in turn, are influenced by emotional arousal. These self-statements include unreasonable expectations of others and a need for retaliation. Such statements might include: "Who the hell does he think he is?" "He can't get away with that." "He can't do that to me." Treatment includes becoming aware of and modifying these self-statements. Overall, Novaco's treatment procedure appears to be very effective, and many subsequent studies have been based on it (see Rokach, 1987; Deffenbacher & Stark, 1992). However, as with any other form of treatment, the big issue is getting clients to generalize what they learn outside of therapy.

In addition to the program described here, anger has been treated with methods such as anxiety management training (e.g., Suinn, 1990), social skills training (e.g., Eisler & Frederiksen, 1980), and problem-solving therapy (e.g., D'Zurilla, 1986). All of these treatment methods have been found to be effective in controlling anger (Moon & Eisler, 1983; DiGiuseppe, Tafrate, & Eckhardt, 1994), and the interested reader is referred to these sources.

Before leaving the topic of anger, I would like to make some comments about encouraging clients to ventilate their hostile or angry feelings. This is a widely used therapeutic process that has its roots in psychoanalysis and the idea of catharsis. Despite its wide use, there is no strong empirical evidence (at least that I can find) of its effectiveness. I am not suggesting here that clients should not get in touch with and express their feelings, but I believe that this is often overused and at times may cause more harm than good. I would particularly suggest that inexperienced therapists not make use of this technique and that it be avoided in brief therapy as well.

Summary

This chapter has explored a number of issues related to clients and therapists in psychotherapy. The point was made that clients' views, needs, and expectations have been generally ignored from a research standpoint until relatively recently. Most of the aspects that clients report as being important in therapy have to do with the personal characteristics of the practitioner. Probably more important than techniques, the interpersonal qualities of the therapist appear to be the backbone of successful treatment.

This chapter also reviewed the importance of therapists addressing the expectations and fears that clients bring to therapy. Because many of these will not be divulged voluntarily, they may need to be elicited. In addition, some clients appear to want a more direct and active treatment approach than is offered by some theoretical orientations.

The topic of anger was briefly reviewed. It was recommended that the factors responsible for clients' anger be evaluated before trying to deal with it. A number of techniques for treating anger were offered.

6

Client–Therapist Interactions,
Part II: The Relationship

Overview

As I have tried to point out throughout this book, much of the resistance that occurs in therapy can be reduced by forming a negotiating partnership with clients. However, this requires that therapists be willing to explore and share their own thoughts and feelings in treatment and, at a different level, that therapists also be willing to grow and change. Some of the traditional psychotherapeutic techniques that favor total objectivity or neutrality may actually produce some, if not much, of the resistance found in treatment. At the same time, for psychotherapy to be successful, therapists must be willing to give up a certain amount of their power and mystique, which some practitioners may not be willing to do. This chapter will explore some of these issues as well as other factors associated with a therapeutic relationship.

Transference

It is difficult to discuss the role of relationships in psychotherapy without talking about transference. As I wrote in Chapter 1, Freud has had a tremendous impact on the field of psychotherapy. In addition to resistance, he introduced the idea of transference, one of the major components of psychoanalytic theory. According to Freud, it is through understanding the transference neurosis that the analyst is able to overcome resistance and successfully treat the patient. Over the years, this concept has dominated psychoanalytic practice and has influenced virtually all other forms of treatment as well. However, therapists from other orientations have responded in disparate ways to Freud's emphasis on transference. Some therapists discount its importance, and others may see it simply as generalization of previous learning experiences.

As psychoanalytic theory has gradually declined over the years, some people have dismissed Freud's ideas in their entirety. One might argue that there are some good reasons for this. Freud's theory tends to be sexist, pessimistic, and difficult to evaluate objectively. However, this "throwing away the baby with the bath water" is unfortunate because many of Freud's ideas, including that of transference, are very useful. As an example, consider the following quote: *"Transference is a fiction, invented and maintained by the therapist to protect himself from the consequences of his own behavior"* (Shlien, 1984, p. 153; emphasis in the original). Although I do not completely disagree with this statement, I find it a bit extreme. The same can be said of the original definition of transference. Although Freud changed the meaning of this term somewhat over the years, it basically implied that all of the feelings that clients have toward their therapists are due not to current interactions but rather to significant conflicts and relationships of the past. Some of Freud's followers tried to moderate this view, but his original concept has remained largely intact. Whether this idea of transference was directly related to Breurer's unpleasant experiences with Anna O, or whether it was a convenient way of protecting the therapist from affective involvement with the client, is unclear. However, to completely absolve the role of the therapist seems a bit fanatical. If a client is angry at me, it does not seem reasonable to blame it all on the past.

The fact that therapy produces strong emotions between client and therapist should come as no surprise. The conditions of psychotherapy make it almost inevitable that this should occur. Actually, someone might just as easily explain what we term transference as a misattribution of arousal (Valins, 1970). For example, according to Schachter and Singer's (1962) two-factor theory of emotions, when people are not sure of the true source of their arousal, they will look for or make up viable explanations for it. In ambiguous circumstances, which are common in certain therapy situations, clients may attribute their physiological arousal levels to feelings or emotions they have toward the therapist. Similarly, under these conditions, as Schachter and Singer's famous study showed, clients are extremely vulnerable to accepting any explanations for their arousal that are consistent with other cues in the environment. Thus they may be easily influenced by suggestions or countertransference signs of the therapist.

Recommendations: Relationship
1. Regardless of your theoretical orientation, consider possible transference issues of treatment.

Recommendations: Relationship
2. Become aware of and make use of countertransference feelings rather than trying to deny or overcome them.

In a related fashion, as Freud discovered, certain psychotherapeutic techniques promote transference. For example, psychoanalytic therapists, with their focus on past experiences, neutrality, limited use of self-disclosure, and technique of "mirroring," might produce more transference than cognitive-behavioral therapists. In other words, the obvious lack of emotional feedback from the therapist might invoke reactions in the client such as anger, fear, or confusion. In a similar mode, because of the therapist's neutral stance, clients may make their own interpretations of how the therapist feels toward them and behave accordingly. In this case, certain types of "transference" may be a direct consequence of the procedures used and may not always be related to past experiences. This suggests that there are a number of ways that transference can be interpreted or studied.

On the other hand, it seems just as unreasonable to argue that previous relationships have no influence on the feelings that clients have towards us. Consider the following example: A male therapist tells a female client that the reason she may not want to get married is because of a fear of commitment. The client gets angry and replies, "You sound just like my father!" The naive therapist ignores the possible signs of transference and continues to work with her fear of commitment. Taking an extreme position about transference in either direction tends to reduce the therapist's effectiveness. Those who totally ignore the effects of transference risk having clients drop out of therapy, or not fully understanding the origin of some of their resistance. Sometimes transference can occur even before a therapist says anything, such as when his or her name or appearance reminds a client of previous relationships and invokes a reaction. On the other hand, if one takes a orthodox view of the original concept, the problem lies almost entirely within the client, which is precisely why I believe there should be some modification of that perspective. As Eastern philosophers have argued for so many years, what we need is a middle ground.

Countertransference

Some of my arguments about the extremist positions held on transference are true for countertransference as well. This topic was virtually ignored by both Freud and his followers for many years (see Tansey & Burke, 1989). In its original conception, countertransference was seen mainly as a response to the client's transference. It was something that was undesirable and needed to be overcome. More recently, its meaning has generalized to all the feelings therapists have toward their clients, but it still maintains a negative connotation.

The interpretation of countertransference that I favor is consistent with Natterson's (1991) model of intersubjectivity. As he points out, countertransference is not a dangerous reaction to the client but, rather, a natural consequence of the therapeutic encounter. Natterson maintains that the therapist's thoughts, fantasies, and desires cannot (and should not) be isolated from the therapeutic process. Rather, psychotherapy as a whole is a dynamic interchange between client and therapist that cannot be totally broken down into separate parts.

Natterson suggests that viewing psychotherapy in a holistic manner leads to several advantages. First, the self-monitoring function becomes a essential element of the therapeutic process; second, "the futile and simplistic search for a neat linear understanding of the therapeutic process can be set aside" (p. 228). The countertransference that results from interacting with clients is not only inevitable but can also be a source of valuable information. For example, the feelings that clients stir up in us are usually the same ones they produce in others. In this case, countertransference allows us to have a indirect glimpse into their interpersonal effect on people outside the therapy setting. This type of information can be useful both for further understanding the client and for setting up treatment goals.

The Dilemma of Objectivity

Freud's theory has been criticized as being untestable and unscientific. Ironically, although there is some truth to this criticism, Freud's concepts of transference, resistance, and countertransference were part of his effort to make the process of psychotherapy consistent with the physical sciences. By making his theory and therapy model almost entirely intrapsychic, Freud was attempting to make sure that patients were treated in a totally objective and uncontaminated manner. It was almost as if therapists should have no separate existence of their own. In fact, Freud warned analysts to set aside all their feelings when providing treat-

---

Recommendations: Relationship
3. Consider the relationship from the client's point of view.

Recommendations: Relationship
4. Try to make the therapy process as collaborative and egalitarian as possible.

---

ment and, in effect, to become a *tabula rasa*. As many writers have pointed out, Freud often did not practice his own advice, but his legacy has influenced psychotherapy to the present day.

The idea of the study of humans and their behaviors as a totally objective science was further emphasized by behaviorists, who took an even more extreme position. In a pure sense, however, such objectivity is not possible. Everything clients tell us is filtered through our own thoughts, values, and experiences. To pretend that we can be totally objective with our clients reminds me of the Laurel and Hardy movie where Oliver asks Stan to read a letter but not to listen to its contents: It simply cannot be done. Even if we were vigilant about it, the involuntary frowns, gestures, and tones of our voice will still give us away. Like or not, psychotherapy virtually always involves values, judgments, and some form of directiveness.

This dilemma of objectivity is possibly exemplified by our current struggles with the scientist-practitioner model. Many therapists like to see themselves as objective scientists, and much of the research explored in this book is a good example of this. However, many of them ultimately fall short of this ideal. Perhaps this is why most practicing clinicians carry out few investigations of their own (of course, time is another major factor) or why many therapists ignore research studies. I believe most clinicians would agree that psychotherapy for the most part is not research-driven.

I am not suggesting that research is not useful or that we abandon the scientific model, only that its basic premises and tools sometimes fall short in investigating many of the properties of psychotherapy. I think everyone would agree that psychotherapy is a *process*. Yet, it is often treated as a static event in terms of research. If we have twenty clients in our practice, we typically play twenty different roles. Which of these represents the "real" therapist is difficult to determine. Our various relationships with different clients are unique, and each of these exchanges influences us almost as much as we influence them. Thus, the "control factor," a necessary condition in science, becomes similar to looking at the popular optical illusion of the pretty young women or the witch: It is all in the way you look at it. As Natterson suggests, psychotherapy is not a simple linear process, and most current research strategies simply do not evaluate adequately the interactiveness of this process.

Similarly, many of the changes that psychotherapy produces may not be obvious immediately after therapy ends. Therefore, outcome studies may not be fully evaluating the effectiveness of therapy. Some changes that originate in therapy may take many months or years to blossom fully, but current research methods generally do not address these changes. Looking at psychotherapy as an complex multirelational process, rather than a totally objective endeavor, can set us on the right track to solve some of these inconsistencies (see DeVoge & Beck, 1978, for an excellent review of a similar issue). However, this may be a long and rocky journey to make. Many of the traditional assumptions of the objectivity of psychotherapy are so ingrained in our beliefs and ways of doing things that it may be very difficult, if not impossible to change. For example, despite Carl Rogers's gallant efforts, psychotherapy almost by definition remains an unequal relationship. A client comes to therapy with a problem, and the therapist is assumed to know how best to treat that problem. In the practical sense, outcome studies are based on the assumption that clients change or do not change in "appropriate" ways. In a truly egalitarian model, however, there are no appropriate ways. If, after undergoing therapy, clients decide that they want to continue smoking, it should not be seen as a treatment failure. Many people, including myself, would have difficulty supporting such an approach. Similarly, I cannot fully accept the proposed balanced relationship of postmodern practice (see Friedman, 1993, for a review of these approaches). It seems to me that the fact that clients pay for our services prevents psychotherapy from ever being a truly equal enterprise, but this may simply be a bias on my part. However, I do fully support the idea that therapy is a collaborative venture and that we should make it as egalitarian as possible. For example, I believe both client and therapist have the right to refuse to participate in any aspect of treatment that they feel is inappropriate. Nevertheless, as our culture (and that of the rest of the world) continues to move toward more personal freedom and autonomy, the field of psychotherapy at some point must deal more fully with these issues.

Client–Therapist Interactions

In the approach to psychotherapy that I am advocating in this book, the most important aspect is the client–therapist relationship (of course, this

Recommendations: Relationship
5. Match your relationship style to the needs of the client.

Recommendations: Relationship
6. Consider ways to find out more about your clients before they begin therapy. For example, consider having them submit a detailed autobiography.

is not a new idea; see Frank, 1961; Orlinsky, Grawe, & Parks, 1994). The necessity of a therapeutic relationship between client and therapist is currently accepted by almost everyone in the field. However, the form and function that this takes vary depending on the professional orientation of the therapist. Behaviorists tend to downplay the importance of this factor while concentrating on technical procedures. Humanistically oriented therapists probably emphasize the importance of relationships more than those with other orientations. Psychoanalytically oriented workers fall somewhere in between.

The overwhelming weight of evidence suggests that a relationship in and of itself is not sufficient to help all clients accomplish their goals in therapy. It is obvious that clients must first accept responsibility for their condition and then work to make appropriate changes. An interesting analogy that one of my colleagues pointed out is that if a person is trying to learn to play a new instrument but only talks to the music teacher for an hour per week, he or she will not get very far. On the other hand, it is also clear that some people can and do make significant changes on their own without the help of others. However, I believe that a relationship can be a strong therapeutic tool that can be used to magnify the effects of other interventions in therapy. For example, it tends to increase clients' satisfaction with treatment and makes adherence more likely. It also increases the likelihood of client self-disclosure and that clients will listen and be receptive to what the therapist says. Given that the other techniques and interventions used in treatment are effective, I believe a strong relationship can speed up the therapy process and lead to stronger and more lasting therapeutic gains. Again, this is not a new idea. For example, Mahoney and Norcross (1993) make a similar point: *"therapeutic techniques and therapeutic relationships are not (and cannot be) mutually exclusive: they are inherently interrelated and interdependent"* (p. 423; emphasis in the original).

As I implied in the previous chapter, many client behaviors that might be assumed to be resistant in nature can be reduced by a strong therapeutic relationship. Being a therapist, however, places us in a unique position in relation to our clients, and many of the factors that are important in promoting attractiveness in other associations need to be treated in a very delicate manner in psychotherapy. In other words, we are more than mere acquaintances with most of our clients, but not really friends. On the other hand, some clients share with us aspects of themselves that they have never revealed to others. This, of course, makes psychotherapy a process that differs from any other human encounter. It is one of the few (if not only) relationships that is designed from the beginning to be both intimate and short-lived. Second, it typically centers on a problem or problems of only one of the participants. Thus, it is not a symmetrical relationship as are most friendships, and the only real obligation clients have is to pay their fee. However, as I will describe, it is the real relationship between client and therapist that ignites the therapy process.

The effectiveness of the client–therapist relationship seems to be a function of at least five factors:

1. Clients' personal characteristics, including personality factors, values, expectations, previous therapy experience, and so on, as well as clients symptoms or psychological disorders (relationship building with clients who have a severe personality or psychotic disorder will be different than with other individuals; see the next chapter)
2. The personal characteristics of the therapist
3. The competence and expertise of the therapist
4. The match between client and therapist
5. Factors outside of therapy, including clients' personal social systems and the overall culture and society

The many ways that the characteristics of clients affect therapy have already been discussed in this book and will not be repeated here. However, I would like to take another brief look at the therapist in relation to factors 2 and 3 listed here before considering matching and external conditions.

The Therapist

As I have already discussed, one of the most important variables for effective psychotherapy is client satisfaction. Obviously, it is not possible to build a relationship with someone who is not there, and in some ways, clients' ultimate expression of dissatisfaction with the therapist is dropping out of treatment. Of course, clients drop out for all sorts of reasons (see Appendix B). These include a lack of motivation or resolution of their crisis. I believe that many drop out because they are unsatisfied

Recommendations: Relationship

7. Try to demystify clients' symptoms and the process of psychotherapy in general.

Recommendations: Relationship

8. Address the issue of termination at the beginning of therapy. Find out from clients how they will know treatment is completed.

---

either with their treatment or with other therapist characteristics. For example, in a dated but still relevant investigation, Levinson, McMurray, Podell, and Weiner (1978) studied a sample of private practice clients who dropped out of therapy. They found that most did so because of a combination of factors, but the common reasons for dropping out centered around dissatisfaction with client–therapist interactions or treatment. Likewise, summarizing the common mistakes that therapists make that may lead to premature termination, Kottler and Blau (1989, p. 140) cite the following: (1) failure to identify clients' real problems or reason for coming to therapy; (2) setting unrealistic goals or goals that conflict with clients' values; (3) being too passive in therapy; (4) failure to develop an adequate relationship with the client; (5) using ineffective interventions; (6) not communicating care, respect, or acceptance to the client; (7) excessive self-disclosure; and (8) appearing too "technical."

As these results imply, it is difficult to separate therapists' interpersonal skills totally from their professional competency. However, a number of studies have tried to identify the most important therapist-related characteristics for successful therapy (see Seligman, 1990; Orlinsky & Howard, 1986; Beutler, Crago, & Arimendi, 1986, for a review). Some studies have looked at the professional training and competence of the therapist and various treatment effects. Unfortunately, this is a complex topic, and most of the research in this area is contradictory and inconclusive (Durlak, 1979; Berman & Norton, 1985; Svartberg & Stiles, 1992). Although it is clear that therapists must have some level of professional competence, research conclusions are fuzzy at best. Many unanswered questions, such as how competence and interpersonal skills interact (Thompson & Hill, 1993), or even simpler ones such as how competence should be measured, remain. Perhaps some of the research looking at the use of manual-guided training for professionals (Binder & Strupp, 1993; Waltz, Addis, Koerner, & Jacobson, 1993) will shed more light on this topic

On the other hand, there tends to be more research consistency between the personal or therapeutic qualities of the therapist and treatment effectiveness. For example, Seligman (1986, p. 49) summarizes a number of studies suggesting that the following characteristics correlate positively with outcome: therapist acceptance of clients' beliefs and values; treatment emphasis on client support rather than insight or interpretation; moderate amounts of self-disclosure from therapist; demonstrated interest in the client; therapist credibility and confidence; ability to engage clients and keep them on task; ability to identify relevant concerns and motivate clients to make positive changes. In a similar vein, Strupp, Fox, and Lessler (1969) give a composite representation of an effective therapist as "a friend who is warm and natural, is not averse to giving direct advice, who speaks one's language, makes sense, and rarely arouses intense anger" (p. 117). These findings are consistent with what clients have to say about their therapy, which was reviewed in the last chapter, and highlight the importance of relationship-building processes for reducing dropouts and improving outcome.

Client–Therapist Matching

The basic idea behind client–therapist matching is that some pairings work better than others. This concept has a long and varied history and has been influenced greatly by Sullivan's interpersonal theory (Sullivan, 1965; Kiesler, 1982), Leary's theory of personality (1957), the writings of Bateson and his colleagues (Bateson, 1979; Haley, 1963), and more recent developments (e.g., Tracey, 1993). It covers a wide area, which includes matching client and therapist on such factors as gender, race, social class, values, or personality to the idea that effective intervention requires the therapist to have experienced some of the same dysfunctional behaviors of their clients (this is true in some substance abuse programs and is a concept I do not fully support).

Gender matching of client and therapist seems to be more effective in certain conditions, such as working with adolescents or in cases of rape. Clients also seem to respond to treatment more readily when they work with a therapist of the gender that they request. The correlation between facilitating a relationship and matching variables such as age, ethnicity, or socioeconomic class is inconclusive, but there is some support for client–therapist matching in these areas as well. On the other hand, the overall findings of the extensive research done with client–therapist matching lack any firm conclusions (see Berzins, 1977; Abramowitz, Berger, & Weary, 1982, for dated but still relevant reviews).

Given these results and all the pragmatic problems involved in attempting to match clients and therapists, I hardly see it as worth the

---

Recommendations: Relationship

9. Schedule follow-up sessions during the termination phase
of the relationship.

Recommendations: Relationship

10. Be aware of the different stages of the therapeutic relationship, and
vary your behaviors and techniques accordingly.

---

effort at this time. Although there is some support for matching in certain treatment conditions, on an individual basis it is virtually impossible to predict beforehand who will work well together. However, in many cases, both therapist and client will know early on in therapy if they will be able to "hit it off" with each other. If they cannot, there are no simple solutions. Ideally, it would make sense for the therapist to terminate the therapy, but a number of ethical or pragmatic factors may prevent this from occurring. Another problem is deciding how long to wait before terminating an unsuccessful relationship. Often, however, clients are one step ahead of us in this regard—they drop out. (One potential problem with managed care is that clients' ability to choose or change therapists may be reduced, but that, of course, is another matter.)

In summary, simple client–therapist matching should be given some consideration when feasible or when a client asks to work with someone who has certain qualities or characteristics. If the idea of psychotherapy practices "without walls" ever becomes more popular, then this approach would be much more practical. On the other hand, I believe our research time and efforts would be better served with potentially more fruitful topics. Even in a total mismatch, there are a number of things the therapist can do to develop a more compatible relationship. I will explore some of these relationship-enhancing techniques in a later section. Greater use of pretherapy orientation or role induction training would serve a similar function as simple matching in that it might allow client and therapist to be on a more harmonious basis in terms of expectations. It would also reduce the ambiguity of psychotherapy, which may be one reason that working with someone who shares similarities with the client (e.g., matching) is less threatening and perhaps more effective.

Treatment Matching

An area that is related to the matching concept but appears to offer more potential benefits for psychotherapy is the idea of matching the therapist's therapeutic and relational style to clients' individual characteristics. This technique has been given a number of labels, including treatment matching, prescriptionism, and eclecticism, among others (Norcross, 1993), but it basically involves therapist altering their interpersonal and treatment style to fit the needs of clients. Beutler and Consoli (1993) suggest that treatment decisions should be based on four interactive and interrelated levels: (1) predisposing client variables, (2) treatment contexts, (3) relationship variables, and (4) specific strategies and techniques (pp. 417–418). Beutler and Clarkin (1990, Chapter 2) break the first level down further into three general classes: (1) diagnostic dimensions, (2) personal characteristics and (3) environmental circumstances. All these relate to attributes clients have when entering therapy. These authors tend to downplay the significance of diagnosis, but acknowledge its importance for issues such as medications or hospitalization. On the other hand, individual characteristics such as problem severity, ability to relate to others, personality and attitudinal styles are weighted heavily when selecting treatment interventions. For example, the authors discuss the relationship between clients' initial expectations for therapy and motivation. By assessing what clients expect from therapy and more closely matching this to what actually occurs, clients are likely to be more cooperative, and outcomes should improve. In addition, clients' environmental influences, which include family and social systems or work environments, may also influence the type of therapy or therapist and the duration or intensity of treatment. In some cases the family unit may need to be treated, or greater emphasis may be placed on social support systems.

The second level in this model involves the treatment context and includes the setting, type of interventions, frequency of meetings, and duration. The various options include a psychosocial versus a medical model, individual, group, or family therapy, hospitalization, brief versus long-term therapy, or whether treatment is needed at all. These decisions should be based on the goals of treatment, the problem to be addressed and its course, clients' characteristics and preferences, the efficiency and efficacy of treatment, and the qualities of the therapist.

The third level involves the broad area of relationship variables. In this context, the authors discuss the role of initially matching clients to specific therapists, the use of pretherapy training, and procedures that can facilitate the therapeutic alliance. Similar to what I have stated above, the authors support the idea that simple client similarity is not sufficient to foster a strong relationship in therapy and that change often is built on different (though not necessarily conflicting) viewpoints and perspectives. Along the same lines, the persuasive qualities of the therapist and interpersonal influence techniques (e.g., interpersoanl attraction, perceived expertness, and trustworthiness) that can be used with diverse client populations are emphasized. In addition, the initial qualities of the client should be considered when deciding on the type of therapy to be used. For example, clients with characteristics that are associated with premature terminations may be assigned time-limited or very brief types of therapy.

Finally, in the last phase, intervention techniques are selected based on the complexity of clients' problems, their overall personality characteristics, their style of relating and coping, their stage of change, and progress made in therapy. This stage also considers clients' motivational levels, overcomes obstacles as they occur, and actively attempts to reduce or prevent relapse. As in this treatment model in general, the focus is to modify the process and procedures as necessary during the course of treatment. Table 6-1 summarizes the steps just described.

Obviously, this is a very brief portrayal of this treatment approach, and interested readers should consult the detailed description offered by Beutler and colleagues. However, the treatment model proposed here fits very well with the approach to resistance that I have been advocating in this book. It accepts the interrelational aspects of psychotherapy, promotes a flexible approach by the therapist that changes depending on

---

TABLE 6-1   Treatment-Matching Decisions

I. Client variables:
   a. Diagnosis
   b. Personal characteristics
   c. Environmental circumstances

II. Treatment contexts:
   a. Individual
   b. Group
   c. Family therapy
   d. Hospitalization
   e. Brief versus long-term therapy
   f. No therapy
   g. Referral

III. Relationship variables:
   a. Role induction and pretherapy training
   b. Use of social power bases
   c. Client–therapist matching

IV. Treatment strategies:
   a. Treatment progress
   b. Client feedback
   c. Stage of change
   d. Relapse prevention

the progression of treatment, and attempts to consolidate the relational and technical aspects of therapy. In the next section, I will use some of the ideas presented here and others to describe how relationships can be enhanced in psychotherapy.

Stages of the Relationship

As the client–therapist relationship unfolds in treatment, it goes through a number of levels or stages corresponding to the general ongoing treatment process. At each stage, a number of things can be done to enhance the relationship and make therapy more effective. As the relationship grows, both client and therapist adjust their behaviors accordingly. Of course, as with other classifications based on stages, they tend to overlap and repeat themselves so that boundaries or time limits are difficult to pinpoint exactly. It is important to note that unlike other such descriptions, the premise here is that both client and therapist are moving through these levels and both are influencing each other (although perhaps not at the same level of intensity). It appears that, to be successful, psychotherapy requires mutual liking, trust, and respect between client and therapist. Although for the most part relationship development remains largely under the control of the therapist, the efforts of clients should not be totally ignored. As Harold Searles has pointed out (e.g., 1977), clients often fulfill therapists' needs so that therapists can more effectively treat the clients in return. The following are some typical stages through which clients and therapists move.

Stage 1: Exploration

At this level, each person is trying to learn about the other and to make an initial (though not final) determination of whether they can work together. Most evidence suggests that the first few sessions are important for establishing a strong bond and avoiding dropouts. In the beginning much of this process is based on first impressions about each other and on preestablished expectations (including expectations the therapist has about the client). The therapist is being evaluated from both a personal and a professional stance, and it is important to come across positively in both areas. At least in the first few sessions, however, the personal characteristics of the therapist (e.g., coming across as warm, caring, etc.) may be more important than perceived professional competency (e.g., see Horvath & Luborsky, 1993). Finally, clients are also exploring what this particular therapy (and therapist) will entail for them. On the basis of these factors, several suggestions are recommended for this stage:

1. Pretherapy or role induction training should be used so that client expectations are more consistent with what they actually experience in treatment.
2. At times, therapists may want to find out more about clients before therapy actually begins so that they can better prepare for the first session. A technique that can be used is to have clients write an autobiography outlining the most important aspects of their lives, social structure, and interests, and submit it before therapy begins. Although this may involve some time outside the therapy session, it may prove to be more cost-effective than gathering this information during actual treatment.
3. The therapist may also want to get an idea of the books clients have read recently related to treatment or disorders. This might provide some clues to their expectations or even help explain some of the symptoms they present.
4. Client satisfaction measures should be used early in treatment (e.g., after the first session) while there is still time to make appropriate changes. Some of the problems that clients have with therapists can then be addressed. Similarly, common sense suggests that the therapist should not engage in negative attitudes, anger, criticism of clients, "talking down," or belittlement.
5. The therapist should begin to demystify problems or symptoms for clients so that these are reduced to a level where clients feel more capable of controlling them rather than appearing insurmountable. In other words, clients usually come to therapy because they have certain skill deficits or do not know how to handle their problems, and it the job of the therapist to teach them what we know in simple, ordinary language.
6. Along the same lines, the therapist should try to convince clients that they have the ability to make their problems or conditions understandable to them, which serves both to decrease initial anxiety and to increase the client's self-efficacy.

Stage 2: Identifying Personality Patterns and Tolerance

In this stage, both persons are attempting to identify each other's stable patterns or traits and to gauge tolerance levels. For the therapist assessing clients, these would include personality traits, values, coping abilities, social roles, and similar signs. This can be done both formally and informally. (It appears, however, that many therapists have dramatically reduced their use of formal testing and assessment procedures and depend mainly on subjective findings, which may not always be appropriate). After these have been identified, they can be matched with appropriate relational styles and treatment procedures. For example, the use of self-monitoring (self-management) techniques or what Lazarus (1993) refers to as an "authentic chameleon" can be used whenever possible in order to increase the therapist's attraction level for the client. The goal here is not so much to match the treatment to clients' disorders, but, rather, to match the treatment to clients' unique qualities. Although some therapists may view the use of possibly self-ingratiating techniques as dishonest or nonauthentic, it is important to keep in mind that their purpose is eventually to help the client, and in this sense I believe they are warranted. Some of these techniques are fully described in the references given in the "treatment-matching" section.

Another important pattern to be identified is how clients relate to others. This should be fairly easy to gauge because the type of relationship clients have outside of therapy is typically mirrored in the one they have with the therapist. This offers some advantages because many of the problems clients bring to therapy are associated with poor relationships with others, and therefore, as their relationship style with the therapist is modified, their outside relationships should also change, and one hopes improve. In this case, the client's outside relationships may be potentially used as markers for outcome. In addition, the client's intra-therapy relationship style offers some indication of what changes may be needed.

Clients undergo a reciprocal process at this stage and are looking for consistent patterns relating to the therapist and therapy. It is important for the therapist to be consistent, concrete, predictable, logical, and reliable (which may be some of the traits the client is lacking). Some studies suggest that meeting at the same time and day each week offers benefits for the relationship and for the general therapy as well. In addition, it is important for the therapist to speak in a language that clients will understand. In some cases, this may mean that the therapist will need to learn more about clients' culture to change their own style of communication. I will talk more about this in Chapter 8.

Stage 3: Commitment

If the relationship reaches this stage, there is a good chance it will be successful. At this level, both parties make a commitment to cooperate and work with each other. This is what is often called the therapeutic or working alliance. The most important aspect here is that both client and therapist agree on what the focus of therapy will be, and come to an agreement on targeted problems, causes, and solutions. In this case, many of the procedures recommended in Chapter 2 (motivation) will be relevant, but a strong bond between client and therapist is also necessary.

Stage 4: Growth or Stagnation

Typically, this is the phase of the relationship that lasts the longest. It can probably be broken down into several other components, but it is generally the stage where changes are introduced and progress may be made. At some point, however, client progress often levels off before increasing again. Aside from the beginning of the relationship, this is the point at which there is likely to be conflict and resistance, and thus many of the techniques and recommendations described in Chapter 4 (adherence) should be relevant. As clients struggle with making changes and experience the discomfort and difficulty most meaningful changes require, they are likely to become temporarily demoralized, dependent, angry, ambivalent, or hopeless. Consequently, the strength of the relationship also tends to plateau at this point. Therefore, at this stage it is important for the therapist to be very supportive and to listen actively to what clients have to say. Depending on the course of this phase, clients may regress or relapse, or a new problem may be identified. In this case, some of the previous stages may need to be repeated, or goals may need to be reevaluated. Also, aside from the first few sessions, this is the stage at which the client is most likely to drop out. This may not always be inappropriate: Some clients may reach their own goals or may decide further changes are not warranted. Likewise, in certain instances, it may be necessary for the therapist to terminate treatment temporarily or to refer the client elsewhere—for example, if many sessions pass without any significant progress. It is very important for the therapist to be creative, remain flexible and be willing to make changes in the treatment plan or goals as needed. Along the same lines, there are times when clients may not be able to make any additional significant changes (at least at that point). In these cases, the role of the therapist may simply be to help clients accept themselves as they are.

Stage 5: Termination

At this level, the goals of therapy have been accomplished or the client has reached a level of maximum benefit. This is a very important stage of the relationship because it may have a major effect on whether the changes made in therapy are likely to continue. As most therapists know, termination can be difficult for both client and practitioner. Some clients (especially those with more severe symptoms) may have a relapse or begin to act out. Those who have formed a stronger therapeutic bond with the therapist are likely to have more intense reactions than others. Similarly, the therapist may be the one who is reluctant to "let go." Thus, it is important to address a number of issues here.

1. Termination should be considered from the beginning of therapy. In some cases, a set number of sessions can be agreed on (of course, outside agencies may do this for us). Similarly, it is important for clients to indicate to the therapist how they will know when they no longer have to attend, and then to use this as the marker for termination.
2. The potential for relapse should be addressed (see Chapter 4).
3. The door should be held open for follow-up sessions if necessary. Some of these may simply be telephone contacts or one-session "booster" meetings.
4. The therapist should formally schedule follow-up evaluations at this stage, for several reasons. First, most therapists will probably agree that what is most important is what happens after therapy has ended, and this allows some feedback in this regard. Second, scheduling follow-up evaluations reinforces the notion that you really do care about your client as a person. Third, if clients know there will be a follow-up, they may be more likely to maintain their changes. Finally, it serves as a prompt to the therapist to engage in this procedure before losing track of clients. Table 6-2 summarizes all the steps outlined here.

TABLE 6-2 Stages of the Therapeutic Relationship

I. Exploration—Techniques that can be used to improve the relationship:
   a. Pretherapy training or role induction
   b. Finding out more about clients before therapy begins
   c. Using client satisfaction surveys early on in treatment
   d. Demystifying the therapy process
   e. Making use of therapist self-disclosures

II. Identifying stable patterns of both client and therapist:
   a. Considering clients' intratherapy and outside relationship patterns
   b. Being consistent, concrete, predictable, logical, and reliable

III. Commitment:
   a. Honestly accepting clients' values, opinions, feedback, and suggestions
   b. Developing a reciprocal working alliance

IV. Growth or stagnation:
   a. Being prepared for relapse or for client dropping out of therapy

(Continued)

TABLE 6.2   *(Continued)*

    b. Being aware of your own anger, frustration, and other feelings toward the client

    c. Emphasizing listening, support, flexibility, and encouragement

V. Termination:

    a. Being prepared to let go

    b. Addressing relapse

    c. Scheduling follow-up sessions

Summary

This chapter has discussed various factors related to the therapeutic relationship, including the concepts of transference and countertransference. A number of variables related to developing a relationship were considered, including the characteristics of the therapist and client–therapist matching. Generally, the therapist's interpersonal skills appear to be more important than technical aspects in terms of client attrition and treatment outcome. A brief description of treatment matching was also given. Finally, five potential stages of a therapeutic relationship were outlined, along with specific suggestions for each level.

Working with Seriously Mentally Ill Clients

Overview

A group of clients who tend to be the most resistant to treatment are those with chronic mental disorders (see Bachrach, 1988). The most often accepted criteria for chronic mental illness hinge on four general factors: (1) diagnosis (e.g., schizophrenia or major depression), (2) duration of the disorder (typically a minimum of two or three years). (3) disability (impaired functioning in activities of daily living), and (4) prior psychiatric hospitalization. Many professionals exclude organic mental disorders and mental retardation from this definition. Both of these disorders are considered irreversible, and in both cases the *underlying* condition is, in a sense, not treatable, so the idea of chronicity seems to be tied to disorders we think we can treat.

People with chronic mental illness usually have a history of either a long-term stay at a state psychiatric hospital or multiple admissions to community psychiatric units. They often lack supportive social networks or close friends, and they tend to have very poor interpersonal skills. They are also often shy, awkward, passive, dependent, unmotivated, occasionally aggressive, and sometimes frightening to the general public (see Bachrach, 1982).

Before the large-scale use of psychotropic drugs and the community mental health movement, most individuals with major psychiatric disorders ended up in state hospitals, where they often spent many years or perhaps their whole lives. However, as a result of deinstitutionalization

---

Recommendations: Persistent Disorders
1. Psychotherapy and psychopharmacology should be used together so that each can complement the other.

Recommendations: Persistent Disorders
2. Treatment should be broad-based and centered around the therapeutic relationship.

---

and the fact that many states have closed a number of their state hospitals, many of these individuals have returned to the community. Unfortunately, many are on the streets as homeless persons. In general, community treatment of the chronically mentally ill leaves a lot to be desired.

Over the years, a number of labels that have been used to describe these types of individuals including, *chronic mentally ill, treatment failures, tough patients, long term patients, severely mentally ill, severely impaired, very poor outcome patients, treatment refractory patients, persistent mentally ill,* and a few others. All of these classifications communicate the difficulty of working with such clients. Rather than simply blaming these clients for being resistant to treatment, however, we should be taking a closer look at the services being offered, which in many cases may be inappropriate or ineffective. I will not address the important issue of who is going to pay for the treatment of such clients or whether such therapy is cost-effective. I do not have an adequate answer for either question. I would suggest that if every mental health professional in the country took on such a client on a pro bono basis, a great deal of suffering, inpatient hospitalizations, and even some suicides could be prevented. Figure 7-1 summarizes the main points of this chapter.

Rationale

The rationale behind this chapter centers on two issues. First, although the basic psychotherapy techniques used with these types of clients are similar to those used with others (e.g., caring, empathy, developing a trusting relationship), there are also some important differences, which I will outline. Second, I was able to find literally hundreds of articles dealing with chronic mental illness and issues surrounding psychotropic drugs, but very few that focused on the use of psychotherapy. There seems to be a clear bias in relating the treatment resistance of persistent men-

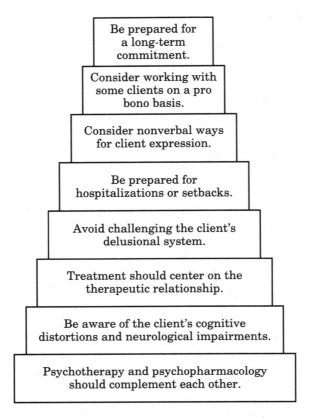

Be prepared for
a long-term
commitment.

Consider working with
some clients on a pro
bono basis.

Consider nonverbal ways
for client expression.

Be prepared for
hospitalizations or setbacks.

Avoid challenging the client's
delusional system.

Treatment should center on the
therapeutic relationship.

Be aware of the client's cognitive
distortions and neurological impairments.

Psychotherapy and psychopharmacology
should complement each other.

FIGURE 7-1   Steps for Working with Persistent Mental Disorders

tal illness to the failure of somatic types of therapy. Thus, the role of psychotherapy has been deemphasized.

I believe that this general bias against the use of psychotherapy stems from a number of sources. First, psychotherapists in private practice, either by design or by circumstance, tend not to work with such clients, and this has resulted in less professional attention to this area. Second, previous research suggests that psychotherapy does not make a significant contribution to the treatment of such populations. For example, the May study (May, 1968) concluded that psychotherapy used alone is much less effective than medications used alone (specifically with schizophrenic disorders), and therefore is not cost-effective. Other studies (e.g., Mueser & Berenbaum, 1990) report that some types of psychotherapy may actually be deleterious for certain chronic conditions. Along with this, there has been increasing evidence that disorders such as schizophrenia, ma-

---

Recommendations: Persistent Disorders

3. Try to separate clients' stable personality traits from behaviors that are due primarily to their underlying condition.

Recommendations: Persistent Disorders

4. Take into account clients' cognitive distortions or neurological deficits that often accompany these types of disorders.

---

jor depression, bipolar disorder, and other chronic conditions may result from genetically transmitted brain dysfunctions. The false implication here is that these conditions do not respond to psychological interventions. All of these forces have lessened the role of psychotherapy with individuals who have chronic impairments. Unfortunately, the focal point tends to be whether to use psychotherapy *or* medications, rather than how each can complement the other, which I believe is a much more useful approach. For example, a schizophrenic disorder does not preclude the client from having other concerns, such as depression, loneliness, or simple problems in living that can best be dealt with through psychotherapy.

The point I will make in this chapter is that psychotherapy not only is feasible with persons with persistent mental illness, but also can be very effective (see also Hargrove & Spaulding, 1988; Coursey, 1989). The approach I am about to describe is not the only one that can be used for such clients. Social skills training, cognitive, behavioral, and family therapy have all been found to be useful with this group (Glynn & Mueser, 1986; Bellack & Mueser, 1986; Green, 1993; Breslin, 1992; Bellack & Mueser, 1993). What follows is largely based on the experience of myself and my colleagues (DiGiacomo, Cullari, Kelley, & Krohn, 1994; Cullari, 1994) working with a large group of individuals with persistent mental illness for over a decade.

General Guidelines

Client Characteristics

If we eliminate organic brain disorders and mental retardation, clients with persistent mental illness seem to fall mostly within a small number of primary diagnoses. These include schizophrenia and other psychotic disorders, affective disorders (primarily major depression and bipolar disorders), personality disorders (primarily borderline or mixed types), posttraumatic stress disorders, and various combinations of these. In addition to the primary diagnosis, such clients often have problems with drug and alcohol abuse.

The single largest diagnostic group is made up of schizophrenic disorders (representing about 60 to 70 percent of treatment-resistant clients across various settings). In my own experience, this group can be broken down into two subgroups. The first is made up of persons who are under age 30 and who often have substance abuse problems in addition to schizophrenia. These clients tend to have a history of aggressive, antisocial behaviors or petty criminal offenses. They typically have relatively short but multiple inpatient psychiatric hospitalizations. They often relapse soon after discharge (usually as a result of treatment noncompliance) and thus make up a large percentage of the so-called revolving-door patients. As a group, these clients are very difficult to work with and generally respond poorly to psychotherapy.

The second group of clients with schizophrenic disorders are somewhat older. They have relatively few inpatient admissions, but their stays are significantly longer (typically over a year). Most of these clients are psychotic, but they tend to present a mixture of positive and negative symptoms (see Carpenter, Heinrichs, & Wagman, 1988; Andreasen & Carpenter, 1993, for a review of this concept). They also tend to have other problems, which may or may not be related to their schizophrenic condition, such as an underlying personality disorder, acting out or aggressive behaviors, poor social skills, intrusive or obnoxious behaviors, inappropriate sexual habits, and other social deficiencies. As compared to the first group, these patients may actually be somewhat easier to work with in psychotherapy, but progress is very slow.

Although it is difficult to generalize with this group of clients, the following variables seem to be the best predictors of a positive response to psychotherapy: (1) shorter durations of previous hospitalizations, (2) less family history of mental disorders, (3) relatively normal premorbid adjustment, (4) some signs and symptoms of affective disorders, (5) previous history of positive social relationships (e.g., marriage, steady boyfriends/girlfriends, etc.), (6) higher IQ, (7) absence of significant neurological impairments, and (8) no history of psychotic assaultiveness.

Treatment Orientation

Because these individuals present so many varied symptoms and problems, I would generally recommend an eclectic approach, as opposed to any one specific orientation. Therapists will have to make use of basic

---

Recommendations: Persistent Disorders

5. Because of the long-term nature of treatment, it is very important for client and therapist to be compatible and feel comfortable working with each other.

Recommendations: Persistent Disorders

6. At times, it may take six months or longer for a working alliance to be established and at least a year before any significant gains are observable.

Rogerian relationship-building methods, behavior modification, modeling, cognitive therapy, and other techniques. However, insight-oriented therapy, interpretations, or a confrontational style should be avoided. The psychotherapy should be supportive in nature, with the use of a lot of suggestions, advice, and reassurance. Therapists should keep in mind that treatment typically will be long term and open ended. Some clients may require some support for their whole lives.

Most of these clients will be taking some type of psychotropic medication, so a close working relationship with whomever is prescribing these drugs is necessary. The prescribing physician is likely to see such clients infrequently and only for short periods of time, so the therapist will be in a unique position to help monitor the effectiveness of such drugs. As Coursey (1989) suggests, neuroleptics and psychotherapy play complementary, not opposing, roles. By maintaining frequent communication with the physician and reporting the client's condition, the lowest effective dose of medications can be maintained and side effects can be reduced. For example, some of the client's symptoms, such as extreme restlessness (akathesia) may be drug-induced. In addition, it is difficult, if not impossible, to make progress with anyone who is grossly psychotic, so medication monitoring is crucial to success. Such clients typically need a myriad of other services as well, so it is also necessary to maintain frequent contact with their case managers, and at times the therapist may need to become more involved with out-of-office treatment (I'll talk more about this in Chapter 8).

Assessment

The assessment of persons with chronic mental conditions will be somewhat different than with typical clients. Because of the biological nature of many of these disorders, there may be a need for a greater emphasis on diagnosis, especially with younger clients or those who have not previously been treated. The reason is that persons with schizophrenia, major depression, bipolar, organic, or borderline personality disorders may all at some point present similar symptoms. However, both the type of psychotherapy and the most effective drug treatment for each of these subgroups may be vastly different. Similarly, therapists should not automatically accept clients' established diagnoses as valid because these are often inaccurate (see Lipman & Simon, 1985).

Second, when dealing with clients of this type, it is important to separate symptoms associated with the disorder itself from those that are due to the underlying personality. If clients are fairly well stabilized on medications, they may still display peculiar or bizarre behaviors, which may in fact be part of their personalities. If so, medications will have no effect on them, but you may be able to change them through other means (through your relationship, behavior therapy, etc.). Of course, it is often difficult to separate the two. As you get to know them, clients may provide much useful information about themselves. Another procedure that may help (if it is available) is to review clients' first psychiatric hospitalization. This often gives a good picture of clients' premorbid personalities, whereas repeat hospitalizations tend to focus mainly on psychotic symptoms. Other good sources of information are clients' families or childhood friends. These persons may add important aspects of clients' histories that are missing, such as childhood traumas, history of head injuries, drug and alcohol use, and how they functioned when younger. In addition to further understanding their personality, this information is useful for making differential diagnoses and for developing realistic goals for these individuals.

Third, many of these clients have various cognitive and neuropsychological deficits, including problems with memory, information processing, attention span, concentration, impulse control, and others that are often associated with mild brain damage. If possible, clients should be given or referred for a neuropsychological assessment. In a similar vein, many clients with persistent mental disorders have a number of cognitive distortions that appear to affect their ideas or behaviors. These have been described elsewhere by Beck (1976) and Perris (1989) and are summarized in Table 7-1. The most common include the following:

1. *Arbitrary inference:* This occurs when a person comes to a conclusion about a specific situation with little or no support.
2. *Magnification:* This involves grossly overestimating the importance of an event or a state of affairs.
3. *Dichotomous or polarized thinking:* This is similar to the concept of

---

Recommendations: Persistent Disorders

7. Treatment goals should focus on improving self-esteem, increasing clients' social network, and promoting independence.

Recommendations: Persistent Disorders

8. Start with modest goals; work on only one change at a time, and build on clients' strengths.

---

splitting, and refers to processing information in absolute (either–or) as opposed to relative or in-between modes.

4. *Personalization:* This involves a tendency to relate everything that happens to oneself. Ideas of reference are a good example.
5. *Premature assignment of meaning:* This refers to reaching a conclusion about an experience without considering it as a whole—for example, assuming someone dislikes you if he or she does not sit next to you.
6. *Concrete thinking:* I can offer a personal example of this. Many years ago, I had an office on a ward of a state hospital with a sign on the door that said "Please Knock." Almost daily, someone would see the sign, knock on the door, and then quickly proceed with whatever it was he or she were doing.

Of course, members of the general public may have these distortions at times, but probably not to the same degree as individuals with persistent mental impairments. A number of cognitive interventions have been developed to treat these difficulties, and the interested reader is referred to these sources (Beck, 1976; Perris, 1989; Green, 1993; Flesher, 1990).

TABLE 7-1   Common Cognitive Distortions and Examples

---

1. *Arbitrary inference:* Coming to conclusions with little or no support
2. *Magnification:* Overestimating the importance of an event
3. *Dichotomous thinking:* "Splitting" and absolute thinking
4. *Personalization:* Tendency to relate everything to oneself
5. *Premature assignment of meaning:* Overreacting to someone's irrelevant behavior
6. *Concrete thinking:* Taking what someone says at face value

---

The Relationship

As was suggested in the previous chapter, one of the most important aspects of treating all clients is establishing a strong relationship with them. This is especially true with clients who have persistent mental disorders. As in all relationships, the willingness of each partner to engage in behaviors that will please the other is perhaps the most important aspect of the alliance. Because the underlying mental disorder imposes so many limitations on these types of clients, most of the significant behavior changes will result from this process.

Sometimes a strong bond cannot be established because of client–therapist incompatibility. This is a much more important issue with these types of clients because you are likely to be working with only a small number of them and because you may be meeting with them regularly for months or even years. Therefore, it is crucial that you feel comfortable working with clients, and vice versa. Some of the "matching" research conducted by Gunderson (e.g., 1978) may be useful in this regard, as well as the treatment matching procedures presented in the last chapter. Usually, however, after a few sessions it is relatively easy for the therapist to determine if he or she will be able to work with a client, and vice versa. For example, incompatibility may be marked by feeling uneasy when working with the client, becoming bored, daydreaming, not paying attention to what the person is saying, dreading the treatment sessions, hoping the client does not show up, and similar factors. If this occurs, depending on the circumstances, it may be best to terminate the treatment. However, it is important to note that it may take up to six months of regular meetings before a workable alliance can be developed with many chronic clients. If a relationship has not developed by this time, it becomes less likely that it will, and there is an increased chance of clients dropping out or of therapist burnout.

Goals and Process of Treatment

With virtually all clients having chronic mental disorders, four broad long-term goals will need to be set: (1) increasing clients' self-esteem; (2) increasing and improving the quality of clients' social interactions with others; (3) increasing clients' ability to function independently, and at times (4) modifying cognitive processes and their belief system or clients' ways of perceiving and relating to their environment. These will have to be broken down into many small steps, with gradual changes made through the use of modeling, environmental manipulations, cognitive procedures, and a supportive relationship. In making these changes, previous experience has shown that it is more effective to build on the

---

Recommendations: Persistent Disorders

9. Avoid the use of time-limited, formal contracts with clients.

Recommendations: Persistent Disorders

10. Try to meet at the same time and on the same day each week. Avoid missed sessions and give clients plenty of notice before your vacation or other scheduled leaves.

---

strengths these clients already have in these areas rather than trying to develop totally new repertoires. In addition, no attempt should be made to change clients' behavior until a strong alliance has been developed. It is generally best to work on only one goal at a time and to start with something you are reasonably sure can be accomplished.

Therapists may note that, in the beginning stages of therapy, clients may become overly dependent on them. Although the long-term goal is to promote autonomy, dependence in the early stages may actually be therapeutic. One reason is that this dependence tends to promote identification with the therapist. In a sense, the therapist is filling in gaps in the client's personality or abilities. In this case, it is not unusual to find the client imitating the therapist's style of dress or other mannerisms. This can be a strong therapeutic tool if used appropriately, and, in the long term, many of the client's problem behaviors or cognitions may be modified through this process. Of course, the therapist needs to use some caution here, because having others dependent on him or her can be addictive and potentially used to satisfy his or her own personal needs. Similarly, as the relationship grows, this dependence sometimes results in clients becoming very angry at the therapist. Part of this is probably due to clients' increasing awareness of personal shortcomings compared with the therapist. As the relationship proceeds further and clients improve, both their dependency and their anger tend to decrease. However, it is not unusual for clients to want to drop out of therapy for a time. If this occurs, they may need a short break before they feel they are able to continue with treatment.

Depending on clients' condition, it may take a year or more to see any "objective" or measurable improvements in their functioning level, although you will probably see more subtle changes earlier than this. Be patient. Do not expect to see any immediate or dramatic results. By definition, these persons have had a mental illness for many years, and it will take a while before they make any noticeable improvements.

Treatment Contracts

The issue of treatment contracts becomes complicated when working with these individuals. In general, time-limited, detailed, or written contracts are not recommended, for several reasons. First, many of these clients are psychotic and may have various neuropsychological impairments. From an ethical point of view, there is some question as to whether they are competent to engage in this type of arrangement. Second, if clients do not fulfill their part of the contract (which is often the case), they can interpret this as another instance where they have failed. This may further damage their already fragile self-esteem. Third, it may be difficult to come up with consequences that clients do not consider overly punitive or that do not interfere with the therapeutic relationship. So in general, it is likely that formal contracts with these clients will do more harm than good. This is not to say that you should not have any treatment goals, but even here, the goals should be informal, flexible, and not time-limited.

Therapeutic Framework

As with all clients, the framework of the relationship should be explained during the first session. With some individuals, you will need to set limits in terms of behaviors that will and will not be tolerated during your meetings (e.g., sleeping, lying on the floor, general appearance). Some clients may try to test your loyalty early on, either by breaking rules or in other ways. For example, they may ask to see you more often or ask you to do something for them that is out of the ordinary. The way to handle these situations depends on the specific conditions involved, but generally it is better to be rigid about following the therapy framework once it is set. Note that I am speaking specifically about the frame here. The treatment process itself should be flexible and compatible with clients' needs and progression.

To make progress with these clients, it is generally necessary to meet at least once per week, and this will have to continue for an extended period of time. Some clients will not be able to tolerate the typical fifty-minute hour so the length of the meetings may vary. If possible, the day and time of the meetings should remain constant. This is not to say that you cannot have any flexibility, but once a routine is established it is sometimes difficult for these clients to deal with change. For the same reason, cancelled sessions are to be avoided in order to prevent possible feelings of abandonment. Likewise, if you are going to be absent for any length of time (such as a vacation), it is usually necessary to prepare them well in advance in order to prevent a relapse. If you have any doubts

> **Recommendations: Persistent Disorders**
> 11. Be willing to self-disclose and share various aspects of your life with clients.
>
> ---
>
> **Recommendations: Persistent Disorders**
> 12. Teach clients to recognize prodromal signs of psychotic breaks. Do not treat hospitalizations as therapeutic failures.

about being able to meet with these people on a regular basis, it may be best not to start treatment at all, because many of them have been abandoned repeatedly in the past.

Working with Schizophrenic Disorders

Many years ago, Whitehorn and Betz (1954) conducted studies in an attempt to determine the type of therapists who work best with schizophrenics. They came up with Type A and Type B therapists, who were identified by their responses on what was then called the Strong Vocational Interest Blank. They found that Type A persons, who had personality characteristics such as "open," "outgoing" and "optimistic," obtained better outcomes with schizophrenics than did Type B therapists, who tended to be more introverted, more authoritarian, and less disclosing. Type B therapists tended to have poor outcomes with schizophrenics but better outcomes with neurotics. Over the years, hundreds of studies have been done in an attempt to replicate the Whitehorn and Betz results, but few people have been able to do so (see Razin, 1977, for a review). My own experience with a large group of clients with schizophrenia and their therapists shows that these authors were at least partially right. In our treatment program, the general approach we have taken is, first, to accept only volunteer therapists with certain characteristics that we have found work best with these clients, and then to have each client and therapist agree to work with each other after a period of interaction. The personality characteristics of therapists who seem to work best with people with schizophrenic disorders include being open minded, flexible, active, enthusiastic, optimistic, talkative, nonconfrontational, and willing to accept outside support. Therapists should also have a warm, outgoing personality; an ability to spend time with even the most disturbed or withdrawn client; an ability to tolerate frustration and disappointment; a willingness to self-disclose, and an ability to express themselves concretely. These characteristics are important because, perhaps more than with other clients, the therapist will often rely on his or her own personality or intuitive ability to augment other psychotherapy techniques. Similarly, clients with schizophrenic disorders not only need a therapist, they need someone to be their friend. However, working with such clients is very difficult and can easily lead to burnout. It is likely that only therapists with some of the basic qualities outlined here and with a strong commitment and need for helping these types of individuals will be successful.

Most clients with schizophrenia lack a close personal association with anyone, and the willingness of the therapist to self-disclose seems to be especially important in developing such a relationship. Part of the reason for this social isolation is related to various symptoms of the disorder, such as withdrawn, paranoid or autistic behaviors. However, while medications can often reduce or control many of the symptoms of schizophrenia, such as delusions and hallucinations, drugs alone usually are not sufficient to eliminate this detachment or fear of the world. To a large extent, the purpose of the therapeutic relationship is to help these persons reach out and trust others. By relating with a therapist, they are taking a step toward relating to others. For some clients, it has been many years since they have been able to do this.

When working with schizophrenic disorders, it is important that you take responsibility for the conversation during your meetings, and avoid any long periods of silence. Many of these clients require extra time to process information, so be sure to give them enough time to respond after a question (e.g., 10 to 30 seconds). With a very quiet or withdrawn person, you will have to work at keeping a conversation going. You may have to talk literally for the entire session or perhaps even read something to the client until a mutual conversation can be built up. The behavioral technique of successive approximations (shaping) appears to be useful for doing this, with attention being used as a reinforcer. It is also important to model appropriate verbal behaviors by offering your own thoughts, feelings, or awareness.

Until an adequate relationship has been established, it may be necessary to avoid any "hot" topics with your client. As a rule of thumb, if you are talking about something and your client's eyes start to glaze over or the client seems inattentive, he or she may not be ready for that issue yet. Often clients will attend to internal stimuli as a way of avoiding the topic of discussion. In the beginning, it is best to keep the conversation low-key, informal, and nonthreatening. As the relationship takes hold, you will be able to introduce some topics without increasing clients' anxiety. However, this may take a while.

It is not unusual to find that clients remain lucid when they are with you even if they are very delusional elsewhere. However, if clients start

---

Recommendations: Persistent Disorders
13. Do not try to convince clients that their delusions are not real.

Recommendations: Persistent Disorders
14. After a strong relationship has been established, try to get at the underlying meaning of some of the client's delusional thinking.

---

to hallucinate or become delusional during your meetings, there are several ways to handle it. The easiest way is through redirection. You may have to change the topic to one that you know is less threatening, or to something that the client really likes to talk about. This usually brings clients back to "reality." Generally, if these persons are kept busy or involved with something, they are less likely to hear voices or to become delusional. Avoiding long silent periods also helps.

Persons with schizophrenic disorders tend to be highly emotionally committed to their delusions. Explaining that their voices are not real or trying to refute their delusional thinking or beliefs is *not* recommended. Generally, these clients perceive this challenge as a personal attack, and it is unlikely that you can really convince them of your point of view. Similarly, it is not useful to argue about what is or is not real. Overall, experience has shown that reality-testing methods tend to cause more harm than good. Reality is very subjective; to your clients, their voices and delusions *are* real. Sometimes, however, it is useful to say something like, "I see that a little differently than you," and describe your own beliefs without implying that the client is wrong. You may also tell clients about any unusual thoughts or feelings you have had at certain times and how you have dealt with them. Similarly, reframing delusional ideas into very concrete concepts appears to be very useful. For example, suggesting to clients that when other people raise their voices to clients, it does not necessarily mean that these people hate them or want to harm them, but that sometimes people talk loudly simply to get their point across or to be helpful. Once clients begin to trust you, they may start to question their delusions or at least be less rigid about them. The point is to chip away at these ideas rather than confronting them all at one time.

At times, with very psychotic clients, you can "contract" with them to limit the amount of time they may respond to the hallucinations, and then gradually reduce this length of time. In other words, allow them to talk about delusions or hallucinations openly and without comment for about ten minutes per session, and then gradually reduce this to five minutes, one minute, and so on. At the very least, this helps make the meetings less disruptive. A similar method is to contract with clients to discuss certain delusions with you and no one else, or to engage in certain behaviors only when they are alone. If they are cooperative, this often results in less agitation in their lives and reduces the chance that these ideas will be reinforced or strengthened by others. Some therapists have tried to reduce delusions by allowing the individual to talk about nothing else except delusions for the entire session (a flooding procedure). In my own experience, this is not really effective and I do not recommend it.

As your relationship grows stronger, you might explore the hallucinations or delusions in order to help clarify their purpose or meaning. One way of doing this is by relating them to the person's life experiences or perceptions. For example, one of our previously employed clients complained about being tired all the time because she had a job working all night (which was not true). In this case, it was helpful to explore her feelings of worthlessness and of not making any contributions to anyone. Arieti (1974, p. 572) gives a similar example of a patient who had an olfactory hallucination of a bad odor emanating from his body. He suggests that the hallucination symbolizes what the person felt about himself—in this case, that he had a rotten personality. According to Arieti, this substitution results from the process of concretization, which occurs when anxiety-producing abstract ideas are reduced to concrete representations such as delusions and hallucinations. These, in turn, are more easily comprehended and assimilated by persons with schizophrenic disorders. The important point here for psychotherapy is that, rather than coming from nowhere, hallucinations and delusions are based on past or current sensory and perceptual experiences, which can therefore be explored.

Although schizophrenic symptoms are very disruptive, they do offer (subjectively) a less threatening way for clients to deal with the outside world, and a means to preserve their sense of self. This is probably why these clients are often resistant to treatment and sometimes prefer to retreat back to their illness. They may almost long for their symptoms to return, just as individuals with bipolar disorders may long for their manic episodes. For some clients, delusions are all they have. Try not to take them away unless or until they have something to replace them. For the most part, the goal of treatment should be to manage delusional thinking rather than to eradicate it, and to reduce destructive acting out behaviors based on these beliefs.

Fred Frese, a psychologist who himself suffers from a schizophrenic disorder, recently wrote a paper that describes twelve steps of coping with schizophrenia (Frese, 1993), which may be useful to practitioners

---

Recommendations: Persistent Disorders

15. Consider having clients express themselves through music, art, or poetry.

---

who work with such clients. Frese suggests that persons with this disorder frequently talk to themselves in an effort to replay previously injurious interpersonal exchanges. Although they may seem to be responding to internal voices, they are actually developing strategies for possible future encounters. One way to deal with these behaviors is by suggesting to clients that they engage in them only in private.

Similarly, Frese suggests that the underlying disorder tends to create a number of social communication deficits. For example, schizophrenics tend not to look at others to whom they are talking. As I suggested earlier, they often need more time to process information and respond to questions. Such behaviors might strain interpersonal exchanges, including those with the therapist, unless he or she is aware of these tendencies. Frese also suggests that persons with schizophrenia should be encouraged to express themselves in a "nonrational" manner—for example, through music, dance, art, or poetry. Such activities offer a way to handle pressures or stresses without reverting to verbal processes that may be more difficult for them.

Conclusions

Psychotherapy is not a cure for schizophrenia, but it appears to be a useful intervention (see Ruocchio, 1989). Nevertheless, progress will be very slow, and it is a good idea to keep a detailed written log that can be used to monitor changes over time. This may help reduce the feelings of frustration and hopelessness that sometimes result from working with this group. It also may help to review the case frequently with an objective observer or an experienced senior mentor who may help separate the forest from the trees. Remaining humble and having a good sense of humor also goes a long way.

As with other client groups, one problem area that will be encountered is treatment adherence. Some of the recommendations given in Chapter 4 may be useful. However, even if clients cooperate with treatment and continue to take their medications, you should expect that they will have some relapses. These may occur at certain times of the year (e.g., Christmas), but many times there is no pattern to them. Often inpatient treatment will be needed, but as Coursey (1989) points out, rehospitalization should not be viewed as a therapeutic failure. Frequently, these relapses are due to the progression of the schizophrenic process itself. However, part of the therapy should include making clients aware of various prodromal signs, such as difficulties with sleep or increasing delusional ideas, which often precede a psychotic break. Timely interventions can sometimes reduce the severity of these episodes. It is also very important to be supportive at these times. If not, you will probably lose the level of trust you have built up to that point. Finally, after a psychotic break, it will often take about six months to a year before clients will be able to start to progress again. Within this time period, the therapist should not pressure clients or expect too much from them.

Borderline Personality Disorders

Another very difficult group of clients to work with are those with borderline personality disorders. They have a number of characteristics that can easily frustrate the most experienced therapist. These include dependency issues, poor impulse control, manipulativeness, excessive attention seeking, acting out, suicidal gestures, self-abusive behaviors, inappropriate anger, and splitting. The latter has been viewed in a number of ways but generally refers to the tendency to see things in absolute rather than relative terms. For example, a person is either "good" or "bad," but there is nothing in between.

The characteristics described as useful for therapists of clients with schizophrenia should also be effective with clients with borderline disorders. Overall, therapists should be predictable, reliable, and nonthreatening (basically, everything the borderline personality usually is not). Therapist characteristics that tend to interfere with treatment include passivity, dependency, and submissiveness. Again, an eclectic approach is recommended, within a consistent therapeutic framework. Because of the acting-out behaviors, group therapy is not recommended (at least in the early stages of treatment) because these individuals may be difficult to control in this setting. They also tend to disturb other group members with their histrionic behaviors. Many clients with borderline personality disorders also have other impairments that need to be addressed. For example, some clients may become psychotic at times, especially under stress. Thus, they may need to be treated with psychoactive medications. Similarly, such clients often have problems with depression or substance abuse.

One reason that borderline clients are difficult to work with is that they often become extremely dependent on the therapist, to the point that daily contacts or telephone calls are common. Part of this is due to their belief that they cannot function independently. When they start to believe they are losing social support, they may become manipulative and self-destructive. Another common response is intense anger, often due to the individual's low frustration tolerance and need for immediate gratification. It is typically based on inappropriate and unexpressed expectations of persons to whom they feel close. Ironically, this anger is often directed to those on whom they feel most dependent, which in turn often drives these individuals away.

There are no hard and fast rules for dealing with the intrusiveness of borderline clients. Some therapists refuse to have any contact with clients between sessions, and others limit contacts to a certain number per day or week. Neither approach is totally satisfactory, but typically some limit setting is necessary. As the clients develop some appropriate social networks outside of therapy, some of these behaviors decrease, but typically it takes a long time for this to occur. My own experience is that some between-session contact is unavoidable. Of course, the therapist will need to use common sense here, and if the intrusiveness becomes extreme it should be brought up and addressed in the treatment sessions.

The primary treatment goal of working with people with borderline personality disorder should be to establish a very strong relationship and then to use it as an avenue to chip away at problem behaviors. Without one, progress will probably not occur. However, it is important to remember that more than most other groups, these clients have a strong fear of getting better because of losing social support. Thus, they tend to improve enough so that the therapy will not be terminated, but are extremely resistive to functioning independently. A useful goal is to shift this support from the therapist to some person in the natural environment. This may be done by helping clients to expand their social support network. Various behavior therapy techniques, such as modeling, desensitization, and role playing, have been found to be useful for this. Social skills training is also recommended. In addition, it is important to help patients become aware of and deal with their extreme egocentric tendencies. The most important point is that, as with clients with schizophrenia, progress will be very slow. It most likely will take years rather than months, and the therapist will need to be very patient.

Another hallmark of borderline patients is their tendency to violate the treatment contract. Often this is an indirect expression of anger toward the therapist. It is important to help clients express this anger directly so it can be dealt with. In doing so, you have to make sure patients understand that you will tolerate this behavior, at least initially. Eventually, however, the client's tendency to overreact needs to be addressed and reduced. Basically, after the treatment ground rules are set, the therapist should be firm in not allowing clients to break them (or not allowing clients to convince the therapist to break them).

Once a strong relationship has been established, it can be used to decrease self-destructive behavior. It may be necessary to contract with the patient to contact you before engaging in such behaviors, but of course these often occur so frequently that it can become very frustrating for the therapist. Persons with this disorder often use suicidal threats and gestures to manipulate others, including the therapist. Although most of these clients never actually kill themselves, some do, so the threats do have to be taken seriously. Because these behaviors are, again, often expressions of anger, as therapy progresses clients should be taught how to express their feelings appropriately so that the likelihood of self-destructive behaviors can be decreased. Most of the techniques discussed in Chapter 5 for dealing with anger should also be useful. In addition, clients often need to be taught the skill of independent decision making. Problem-solving training and cognitive techniques have been found to be helpful here. The patients' tendencies toward impulsive behaviors also have to addressed and reduced. Systematic desensitization has been shown to be useful in this regard.

Toward the end of therapy, the patient's anxiety and fear of being alone need to be addressed. Biofeedback has been found to be effective in helping patients deal with anxiety, but sometimes its use has produced a paradoxical decompensation. Patients' fears of being alone should decrease as their social network develops and their self-destructive behavior comes under control, but it may have to be treated directly with such techniques as systematic desensitization.

Finally, patients need to be weaned from therapy. Timing is very important here because terminating therapy too soon may lead to a suicide gesture or other inappropriate behavior. If all these goals have been reached, this process should be easier, but a relapse should be expected.

Recently, Linehan (1993a, 1993b) has developed a comprehensive program to treat patients with borderline personality disorders. Her approach is called *dialectical behavior therapy* (DBT) and shares some commonalities with cognitive and behavior therapy. Her basic procedures involve four components: (1) a focus on the acceptance of clients and their behavior; (2) an emphasis on treating therapy-interfering behaviors; (3) an emphasis on the therapeutic relationship; and (4) a focus on dialectical processes.

The focus on accepting and validating clients and their behavior is, of course similar to ideas fostered by client-centered therapists. However, Linehan's approach is different in that she requires a balance between acceptance and change. In other words, the emphasis is on teaching clients that their behavior makes sense and is understandable within their own context, but that some of their behaviors are dysfunctional and need to be modified. The goal is get clients to a point at which they can trust their own emotional reactions or interpretation of events before attempting to change their behavior.

Therapy-interfering behaviors include those that can be classified as resistive in nature—for example, not coming to treatment, coming late, engaging in aversive behaviors, avoiding difficult topics, and so on. Linehan advocates that these behaviors not be ignored but be dealt with directly in the treatment sessions. Along the same lines, she recommends that lack of progress in therapy should be used as grounds for treatment termination. In other words, if clients do not make any progress, treatment is terminated at the end of the contract period. The problem here is that borderline patients progress very slowly, so it is often difficult to know when treatment termination is appropriate. As with many other treatment procedures, this is an art that cannot be precisely described. However, as with my recommendations earlier, Linehan suggests that therapist supervision is crucial for helping to make this decision.

Linehan's views on the therapeutic relationship are very similar to mine and thus will not be repeated. Suffice to say that she feels it is a necessary part of treatment, and, to a large extent, it *is* the treatment. Linehan emphasizes that therapists should not be manipulative or defensive, and that they should not assume that what is learned in therapy will generalize unless this issue is specifically addressed.

The fourth component, which is Linehan's focus on dialectics, is what makes her approach unique. She describes this as having three general characteristics. The first is the emphasis on interrelatedness and wholeness. In this respect, it shares many similarities with the systems approach. For example, it makes use of paradoxical interventions and ideas consistent with Eastern philosophies (e.g., Zen Buddhism).

The second characteristic is called the principle of polarity. This is also consistent with Eastern thought in that it advocates an integration of opposing forces. In other words, all reality is seen as comprising polar opposites. This influence can be seen in Linehan's approach to validating a client's behavior; within the client's dysfunctional behavior, one can also find function. Similarly, although most clients with a borderline personality have many inappropriate behaviors, they have within themselves the potential to change. This idea is most clearly symbolized by the Chinese concepts of yin and yang.

The third attribute of dialectics is the idea of reality as having an interconnected, nonreductionist, and oppositional nature. This suggests a dynamic rather than static representation of change. In other words, as the client changes, so do the therapy and the therapist. This, of course, is very similar to some of the points I have been making throughout this book. In this respect, it is difficult to separate the client from the therapist or the therapy from the outside social system.

This has been a brief summary of Linehan's approach, but it is compatible with the approach I have been advocating. Interested readers are urged to read Linehan's original works.

Summary

This chapter has reviewed the use of psychotherapy with clients who have persistent mental disorders. Specific techniques and recommendations were given for treating individuals with schizophrenic and borderline personality disorders. The most important characteristics of treatment with this group of clients are that it will be long term and will center on the therapeutic relationship. Insight-oriented, neutral, or confrontational psychotherapy styles should be avoided. It is also important for the therapist to be open to and actively seek out peer support or consultation when working with these clients. The suggestion was made that all therapists take on one such client on a pro bono basis.

Working with clients with schizophrenia or borderline personality disorders is time-consuming, frustrating, and often aversive. It is thus important for therapists to have a support system of their own that they can use for consultation and guidance.

8

The Role of Cultural
Influences on Resistance
and Psychotherapy

Overview

As I stated in Chapter 1, psychotherapy cannot be done in a vacuum. No matter how much we try to be objective, we cannot escape our social environment. This chapter looks at cultural and environmental factors that affect the process of psychotherapy and how these relate to the perception of resistance. Specifically, this chapter will review (1) how social/cultural factors influence the notion of mental illness, treatment process, and outcome; (2) how culturally diverse clients may potentially react to psychotherapy; and (3) the impact of cultural differences on how the client and therapist relate to each other.

While reading this chapter, keep in mind that when I describe a culture, I am using global terms. Obviously, the behavior of an individual may conform or differ from the dominant norms, and many clients are bicultural. Thus, both within-group and between-group differences should be considered. As I have tried to emphasis throughout this book, it is important to treat each client as an individual and to avoid stereotypes or making over-generalizations. In a similar vein, clients will differ in terms of their level of Western culture assimilation and ethnic identity (for example, see Kitano, 1989). Minority group members with a high degree of acculturation generally tend to have values similar to the dominant culture. However, psychotherapeutic techniques may need to vary depending on where the person stands in this dimension (see Sue & Sue, 1990, Chapter 5, for a review).

Having some general knowledge about clients' cultural backgrounds may help us better understand them and their behavior. Further, it may prevent us from using inappropriate procedures or making erroneous judgments. Having been born in Italy and raised in a traditional southern European manner, I know first-hand how our cultural backgrounds can color our perceptions of the world. At times my family struggled to understand some of the "strange" behavior of Americans. At the same time, it was often difficult and frustrating when the general society expected us to think and act the way everyone else did. With some cultural sensitivity, this should be less likely to occur in the therapeutic environment.

Aside from Chapter 7, many of the recommendations I have made so far are geared largely to mainstream (White, middle-class) clients. As we all know, however, our country is made up of many cultures. As mental health professionals continue to work with diverse populations, it is important to be aware of the traditions and orientations that some clients bring to therapy. Cultural minorities such as African Americans, Hispanics, Native Americans, and Asians make up more than 20 percent of our population, and their number is increasing rapidly. Therefore, virtually all therapists will work with members of these groups at some point.

At the same time, many studies show that such clients underutilize mental health services and that about half of them drop out after the first session (Sue & Sue, 1990). Even while undergoing therapy, many minority group clients may appear to be hesitant or uncooperative during the treatment process, and they may not make significant improvements. However, rather than prematurely blaming these clients, it is important to look at factors that may promote these types of avoidance behaviors. Although the reactions of such clients may be interpreted as resistive in nature, at least part of the problem appears to be related to treatment methods. In other words, certain conventional psychotherapy practices and techniques may be ill suited for some non-traditional clients.

As a simple example, the use of psychoanalysis often requires the client to recall childhood memories. However, my experiences with my relatives living in Italy indicate that they remember very little of their childhood (especially the older individuals). Although it is not clear what factors are responsible for this phenomenon, it has been reported elsewhere as well (see Prince, 1980). If one of these persons were being treated with psychoanalysis, his or her "reluctance" to recall early experiences might be interpreted as a sign of resistance, whereas the tendency appears to be common in nonaffluent societies. This underscores the importance of trying to understand the culture of clients undergoing psychotherapy.

> **Recommendations: Cultural Influences**
> 1. Therapists should be especially careful to avoid stereotypes and overgeneralizations with culturally diverse clients.

The concept of resistance as it relates to the treatment of individuals from different ethnic groups and subcultures has not received much research attention thus far, but it is an issue that I believe must be addressed. As I have maintained throughout this book, resistance is a interactive process, and tailoring therapeutic methods to match clients' needs seems to be especially crucial when working with culturally different populations. Behaviors such as a lack of self-disclosure, a reluctance to reveal psychological distress, an avoidance of direct eye contact, or a loose adherence to schedules or time limits may need to be interpreted and dealt with in a manner different from the one you use when working with traditional White middle-class clients.

When working with any ethnic group, it is important to distinguish low self-disclosure resulting from cultural norms from that employed as a defense or resistance. Similarly, transference or countertransference issues that result when a White therapist works with a Black, Japanese, or Vietnamese person (or vice versa) are potentially different from those for traditional clients. In these situations, both parties may be overly influenced by stereotypes or other misinformation (see Tseng & McDermott, 1981).

I am not suggesting that conventional psychotherapy techniques should never be used with clients of a different cultural background, nor am I recommending that psychotherapists should undo all that they have previously learned in order to be successful with these clients. What I am proposing is that psychotherapists who work with clients from different backgrounds need to flexible. They should accept the idea that individuals from other cultures may have legitimate values that are different from their own and that certain modifications in therapy may be needed. In this case, the therapist must take into account what assumptions both he and the client bring to therapy.

Many of the common approaches used in psychotherapy appear to be universally applied by healers (see Wohl, 1989). These include a strong relationship, sharing a common world view, instilling or increasing clients' expectation of change, giving guidance and direction, using persuasive techniques. However, various cultures may differ in terms of how these processes can be used in an effective manner. For example, clients from some cultural backgrounds may process information differently, have a different type of "sick role," or have a communication style that differs from that of the dominant culture. Some clients will express their emotional problems only through physical complaints, and others may not believe that change is a necessarily a positive occurance. Higginbotham, West, and Forsyth (1988) created the concept of culture accommodation as a means to match appropriate therapy styles to the needs of culturally diverse groups. Part of this chapter will explore this approach.

Though not covered specifically in this chapter, conventional clients who are being treated by foreign-born therapists or those coming from different cultural backgrounds may experience many of the same problems as minority group members. Large mental hospitals throughout the United States employ many foreign-born professionals, and I have often experienced patients being misunderstood or misdiagnosed as a result of language problems or cultural inconsistencies. Thus, the material that follows should be relevant for all therapists working with clients with a different cultural background from their own.

Some readers may note that so far I have ignored the theory of social constructionism. Many of the tenets of that system are extremely relevant to this chapter and, in fact, to this book in general. I agree with many of the assumptions that make up the construction perspective, such as the view that the therapeutic relationship is a dynamic interactive process, and the appreciation for individual differences. At this point, however, I believe this perspective is largely theoretical in nature and it is difficult to translate much of the theory into practical terms. I am taking a back seat to see how this position develops. Those of you who are interested in the implications constructionism may have for psychotherapy are urged to see Owen (1992) or Sexton and Whiston (1994).

For the purposes of this chapter, *culture* will be defined as "a generalized, coherent context of shared symbols and meanings that persons dynamically create and recreate for themselves in the process of social interaction" (Jenkins & Karno, 1992, p. 10). This definition assumes that culture is a complex, ever-changing, and active process in which we filter all of our behaviors and experiences. Included in this definition are the culture's language, beliefs, values, traditions, customs, laws, norms, and scientific paradigms. All of these can have a major impact on our thoughts and behaviors, both inside and out of the therapy room.

Culture and the Concept of Mental Illness

In terms of emotional problems, universalists operate on the principle that all people are essentially the same—in other words, that cultural differences do not significantly alter the symptoms, prevalence, course,

---

Recommendations: Cultural Influences
2. The techniques used in psychotherapy should be adapted to clients' backgrounds and needs.

---

or outcome of mental disorders. This view is especially strong for so-called biological disorders such as major depression or schizophrenia. However, a number of mental health professionals have begun to challenge these assumptions (Kitayama & Markus, 1994; Kleinman, 1988; Draguns, 1980, 1990). The emerging viewpoint is that culture and ideology may have a profound effect on the definition and prevalence of mental disorders found in any society, as well as their direction and outcome.

The developing concept of cultural relativism is not new. Some anthropologists have been writing about it for decades, and Thomas Szasz (e.g., 1970) was making similar arguments many years ago. Szasz, coming from a different perspective from that of the authors cited here, objected to classification systems such as the DSM on the grounds that their primary purpose is to control human behavior. Rather than being natural systems based on biological processes, Szasz argues that these diagnostic systems are relative, largely artificial, and consistent with the ideology that develops them. He sees the primary function of therapists as helping individuals adapt to the values of the society, maintaining the status quo, and indirectly protecting the main concerns of the majority culture.

Anyone who has worked with serious psychological disturbances such as schizophrenia might say that Szasz has gone too far with his assertions. In fact, it is sometimes difficult to draw the line between legitimate and questionable disorders. For example, no one in the twentieth century would have a problem disclaiming the veracity of such so-called disorders as "drapetomania" (the "affliction" of slaves who ran away from their masters), but others such as alcoholism, hyperactivity, chronic pain, or premenstrual syndromes result in much greater controversy. In similar fashion, Szasz's arguments seem especially pertinent when addressing the treatment of racial or ethnic minorities in our country (e.g., see Block, 1981; Good, 1993). There seems to be some clear evidence that, at least in the past, the diagnosis and treatment of these groups was biased and significantly influenced by the desired outcome of some type of social control. In this context, it should be easier to understand why some minority clients are "resistive" to treatment. As Block (1981) points out, having a Black client treated by a White therapist is in some ways analogous to a Jew in 1930s Germany being treated by a German. Thus, I do not believe that mental disorders are myths, but the way they are interpreted and treated is largely influenced by cultural factors.

Though coming from a different perspective than Szasz, Kleinman (1980, 1988) has also written a great deal about the potential effects of culture on the practice of psychotherapy. Like Szasz, he argues that it is difficult to separate the fields of psychotherapy from the culture that determines their boundaries. He states: ". . . practice and teaching and research are part of elaborate social structures where psychiatric knowledge is socially created and its application transacted" (p. 182). He goes on to say that the values of society determine whether a condition is called a disease, crime, sin, or social problem (consider the history of homosexuality, substance abuse, child abuse, etc.). He also points out that diagnostic criteria are permeated with cultural norms and biases. Speaking mainly to psychiatrists, Kleinman urges psychotherapists to take an anthropological view of human conduct and to focus on how cultural values, social norms, styles of communication, families, age, gender, work, and ethnic background can significantly influence behavior.

As implied, the effects of culture and ideology have many implications for the practice of psychotherapy. For example, behaviors that Americans may interpret as highly unusual may not be viewed similarly by other cultures. Likewise, various psychological disorders may be expressed in culturally diverse ways. This might affect the validity and reliability of diagnostic systems such as the DSM-IV (American Psychiatric Association, 1994) for clients who do share the tenets of Western culture (see Kleinman, 1988; Lewis-Fernandez & Kleinman, 1994). In other words, the symptoms and disorders described in the current and previous DSMs are based largely on ideologies and research conducted with European Americans and are not *necessarily* transferable to other cultural groups. Consistent with this view, some syndromes appear to be culture-bound and found only among certain populations. Examples of these include *Pibloktoq* (Alaska Natives), *Amok* (Malaysians), *Koro* (Chinese), *Windigo* (Canadian Indians), *Susto* (South and Central Americans), *and Taijin-kyofusho* (Japanese) (see Kleinman, 1980, 1988; Lonner & Malpass, 1994). Other disorders appear to have different prevalence rates across cultures. For example, there seem to be higher rates of paranoid schizophrenia, agoraphobia, depression, personality disorders (anti-social, borderline, narcissistic), and eating disorders in Western than in non-Western countries. At the same time, anxiety disorders, which are very common in the United States, are rare among the aboriginal people of Australia (Kleinman, 1988).

The likely outcome of disorders such as schizophrenia appears to be more positive in non-Western cultures as well. Speaking of the latter, Kleinman suggests that this effect may be due to cultural expectations

> **Recommendations: Cultural Influences**
> 3. Therapists should attempt to become more aware of the cultural differences some clients bring to therapy and to increase their knowledge of groups with whom they work.

(e.g., poor prognosis of schizophrenia in the West), the West's high value on productivity (work and income), social isolation, or perhaps even the treatment itself. Although some of these findings may be influenced by methodological problems or research design inconsistencies (see Draguns, 1980, 1995, for a thorough discussion of this issue), it would be foolish to disregard them totally. As Draguns (1995) suggests, whereas disorders such as schizophrenia and major depression may be less affected by culture, no disorder is immune its influence.

Even within a culture, various disorders may become more or less prevalent over time. Examples include the apparent decrease of hysterical disorders since Freud's time (which is more pronounced in Western cultures than in developing nations), and the recently increased observation of multiple personality disorder, posttraumatic stress disorder, attention deficit disorder, and chronic pain syndromes in our country. Some people may argue that this is due to improved diagnostic methods and an increased exposure of these disorders, but ideology should not be overlooked. Ellsworth (1994) supports this notion with the following observation: "In the 1950's . . . Americans suffered from paralyzing anxiety; a decade or so later, anxiety was replaced by depression; currently people are visited by a variety of debilitating 'syndromes' caused by past abuses and victimizations" (p. 42).

Beiser (1985) points out that starting in the 1950s, the definitions of mental illness expanded dramatically in our country. Although there may a number of reasons for this, Beiser believes that the increased efficacy of treatment resulting from the use of psychotropic medication had a lot to do with it. In other words, when people are convinced that disruptive behaviors can be treated, they are more likely to define such conduct as an "illness." Individuals coming from different cultures may attribute the same behaviors to demons, personal weaknesses, or fate, or perhaps consider them normal. The expectations for how these "symptoms" should be treated will vary greatly among cultural groups.

I am certainly not advocating the abandonment of diagnostic systems or supporting Szasz's contention that mental illness does not exist. I am merely suggesting that all mental health workers should become more aware of how ideology can influence diagnosis and treatment, and that therapists should become more conscious of their own cultural biases. Our profession has already started to deal with these issues with the changes made in the DSM-IV and various graduate training programs, but we still have a long way to go. The next section further describes cultural influences on psychotherapy.

Individualism versus Interdependence

Psychotherapy as practiced in the United States seems to be heavily influenced by the cultural framework of independence. This perspective, which is common in North America and parts of Europe, views the self as a unique and encapsulated collection of personal attributes (traits, values, etc.), which in turn largely control behavior. The underlying social goals of such a system include detaching oneself from others, avoiding undue outside influences, and maintaining the separation between the observer and the experience (Markus & Kitayama, 1994; see also Landrine, 1992). In an interesting study exploring the sociopolitical nature of psychotherapy, Katz (1975) further describes the major components of this dominant European-American value system. She argues that by ignoring the cultural underpinnings of our profession, psychotherapists may continue to be seen as status quo agents or perpetuators of cultural oppression. Some of her descriptions and their influence on therapy are given in Table 8-1. Although many people may find nothing wrong with these values, it would be a mistake to believe that all cultures share this orientation.

It is not difficult to identify examples of this ethnocentric influence on our field. We can begin with Freud's largely intrapsychic theory of psychoanalysis, move on to the fact that 95 percent of U.S. therapists practice mainly individual therapy (Beutler & Clarkin, 1990), and continue with the scientific methods we use to develop and evaluate our theories. Likewise, traditional psychotherapy, which is based largely on the model of independence described here, emphasizes verbal and emotional self-expression, individual change, diagnostic categories, clear distinctions between mental and physical problems, and long-range goals. However, many of these approaches are not universally accepted.

In contrast to the European American model is that of interdependence (also called *collectivism*) which is common in large parts of Asia, Africa, and South America and in other parts of the world. This view suggests that individual and their behavior should not be viewed as separate from others or from the surrounding social context. In this case, the social goal is to become a harmonious part of various interpersonal relationships, rather than to remain autonomous (Markus & Kitayama, 1994).

```
┌─────────────────────────────────────────────────────────────┐
│            Recommendations: Cultural Influences             │
│   4. Therapists should become aware of any biases they may   │
│      have that might interfere with the treatment process.   │
└─────────────────────────────────────────────────────────────┘
```

Here, the needs and wishes of the collective group are deemed more important than those of the individual. The old Japanese proverb that the "nail that sticks up gets pounded down" reflects this sentiment. The major components of these two social models are described in Table 8-1.

Triandis (1994a) suggests that the more homogeneous a society is, the more collectivist it is able to become (p. 294). In a heterogeneous society like the United States, clear-cut norms are more difficult to define or to be agreed on by the general population, and thus individuals tend to revert to themselves for guidelines. Triandis describes the collectivists as having an "emphasis on the values of society, obedience, duty, in-group harmony, in-group hierarchy, and personalized relationships." By contrast, individualists "favor pleasure, personal achievement, competition, freedom, autonomy, and fair exchange" (p. 292). For individualists, the needs and personal goals of the self are most important, whereas in-group goals are dominant in a culture influenced by interdependence. Triandis (1994b) also suggests that affluence is a major building block of individualism. Affluent people are more likely to behave as they wish, as opposed to being influenced by others. They are also more likely to be mobile, which results in leaving their families and close relatives, which in turn further increases isolation and decreases social influence.

Behaviorally, collectivists tend to interact mostly with in-group members and relatively little with strangers. As a result, they form very close relationships with other in-group members, with whom they share very intimate information. However, they tend not to reveal personal information to people they do not know well. Collectivists prefer private versus public display of emotions, tend to be family- and group-oriented, they are focused on the present, and they do not make clear distinctions between mental and physical disorders.

Individualists interact much more with strangers but tend to form less intimate or close personal relationships. They also tend to spend more time alone and to value their privacy. Collectivists tend to suppress negative communications and to say what others want to hear in order not to hurt their feelings. Their quantity of communication is lower, and, unlike individualists, they tend not to have problems with silence. In addition, collectivists believe that behavior can best be explained by group influences, customs, and norms, whereas individualists tend to empha-

TABLE 8-1 Characteristics of Independence versus Interdependence (Collectivism)

Independence
Rugged individualism
Autonomy and competition are
   highly valued
Individual has primary responsi-
   bility for behavior
Focus on controlling nature
Adherence to rigid time standards
Protestant work ethic
Future-oriented
   (delay of gratification is valued)
Emphasis on scientific method and
   cause-and-effect relationships
Focus on status and power
Self-determination
Oriented toward nuclear family
Concept of a single God
"Left-brain" linear mode of thinking
   and problem solving
Focus on doing things and having
   things
Discomfort with silence

Compatible Treatment Techniques
Focus on individual change
Time-limited appointments
Diagnostic categories
Highly verbal procedures
Emphasis on self-disclosure
Reflective listening
Client-centered approach
Focus on long-term goals
Promotion of insight, personal
   growth, and self-awareness
Emphasis on intrapsychic processes
Little or no physical touching;
   direct eye contact

Interdependence
Should live in harmony with nature
Group and extended-family-
   oriented
Behavior largely controlled by
   cultural norms and customs
Private versus public display of
   feelings
Cooperative and noncompetitive
Present-oriented
Belief in folk or religious explana-
   tions of physical and mental illness
Psychological disorders often ex-
   pressed in somatic modes
Personal goals secondary to those
   of group
Often use indirect or nonverbal
   type of communication
Reduced conceptualization of
   "talking" psychotherapy
"Right-brain," intuitive, creative
   style of thinking and problem
   solving.

Compatible Treatment Techniques
Direct advice and active treatment
   style
Focus on practical and immediate
   needs
Use of pretreatment orientation
Use of therapist self-disclosure
Mutually agreed-on goals
Family or group therapy
Environmental manipulation
Consideration of cultural background
Flexible and eclectic orientation
Reduced emphasis on insight and
   self-awareness
Adjunct and community support
   services

Recommendations: Cultural Influences

5. Clients' level of acculturation may influence which techniques should be used in treatment and thus should be assessed.

---

size internal psychological constructs (Triandis, 1994a). As a result of these different orientations, perceived psychological stressors tend to be intrapersonal ones for individualistic societies and interpersonal for collective cultures.

Triandis (1994b) describes the contrast between collectivists and individualists as one of the most important cultural differences resulting in variations of social behavior. These differences also have many implications for psychotherapy. As a group, White middle-class clients most closely resemble the individualist description given here. Hispanics, Asian Americans, and Native Americans (and perhaps White American women) tend to follow the collectivist style. African Americans are usually bicultural, but their African roots also influence them toward collectivist behaviors. The next section further details these distinctions. Because of space limitations, I will not deal specifically with the treatment of women, children, homosexuals, the elderly, or other groups who also may have different orientations than the therapist. However, much of the material presented here will be relevant for these groups as well.

Working with Diverse Cultures

Recently, a number of professionals (Pedersen, Draguns, Lonner, & Trimble, 1989; Sue & Sue, 1990; Ivey, Ivey, & Simek-Morgan, 1993; Ridley, Mendoza, Kanitz, Angermeier, & Zenk, 1994) have explored potential sources of conflict that may occur when some of the common Western-oriented therapeutic techniques are used with different cultures. The following is a brief summary of this topic. Note that the area of transcultural psychotherapy has only recently gained the attention of mental health professionals, so inconsistencies in research findings are to be expected (e.g., see Folensbee, Draguns, & Danish, 1986; Yau, Sue, & Hayden, 1992). The lack of clear-cut unambiguous procedures that should be used with various cultural groups only underscores the importance of the therapist remaining flexible and open-minded. However, the following techniques seem to cause the most problems with culturally diverse groups.

Insight

This concept comes largely from Freud's theory of psychoanalysis. It maintains that individuals benefit from a thorough exploration and understanding of the causes of their underlying emotional problems. As a result of this process, psychological symptoms should be eliminated. However, many cultures do not subscribe to this point of view. For example, many people in Asia believe it is better not to think about or explore negative feelings or emotions. From their point of view, doing so may actually cause some emotional problems to develop. Similarly, clients coming from lower socioeconomic environments may be much more concerned with reaching concrete or practical goals than with achieving insight (Sue & Sue, 1990).

Self-Disclosure

As everyone knows, our current methods of psychotherapy are dominated by verbal procedures. As I described in Chapter 3, self-disclosure is often seen not only as a method for exploration but also as a process for achieving positive mental health. This idea of openness is, again, not shared by all non-Western cultures. Asian Americans tend to exert pressure on their families not to reveal personal information to outsiders. Similarly, Native Americans and Hispanics tend to share intimate aspects of themselves only with close friends. However, clients coming from these backgrounds tend to form close friendships only after an extended period of time. In this case, their reluctance to open up or reveal personal information to an unknown therapist may be inappropriately perceived as a sign of resistance. Along the same lines, it may take certain clients longer to be able to trust their therapist and establish a workable relationship. For example, because of what is often called "healthy cultural paranoia," African Americans may initially be suspicious or guarded with someone they see as a possible symbol of oppression.

Verbal and Emotional Expressiveness

Similar to the process of self-disclosure, the goal of many types of psychotherapy is to get clients to share their thoughts, feelings, and emotions. Again, some cultures do not see the value of this approach. Many Asian groups believe that a sign of maturity is the ability to control one's feelings and emotions. Although some therapists may view these clients'

Recommendations: Cultural Influences
6. Because of the diversity of clients' needs and individual characteristics, an eclectic therapy approach appears to be more appropriate with culturally different groups.

---

reluctance to open up as a sign of being inhibited, in fact their behavior is consistent with their social norms. Similarly, in a therapeutic setting, such clients may withhold their thoughts or remain silent as a form of respect for the perceived higher status of the therapist. Also, clients coming from a Japanese, Chinese, or Hispanic orientation may have a problem living up to possible treatment expectations of high assertiveness.

Focus on the Individual

As I have noted, most therapy in the United States centers on the individual. Many non-Western cultures do not share the concept of explicit focus on individual rights. Many societies subscribe instead to a notion of "oneness" between themselves and other in-group members, or perhaps even the universe. Often the identity of the individual is intermingled with that of their family or collective society. In this case, clients may not be able to conceive how changing their individual behavior will help them. For example, in China, therapy is often done with the whole family or perhaps with the whole community present (see Kleinman, 1980). Therapists who do not understand the culture of such clients may incorrectly see them as immature, overly dependent on their families, and resistant to change.

Some clients may not understand or accept the notion of mental disorders as distinct from physical ones. Some Asians and Hispanics are likely to express their emotional problems as physical symptoms. They may also expect to receive services similar to those of physicians or perhaps of their priest. All of this points to the importance of therapists becoming somewhat familiar with the culture and values of the diverse clients with whom they work with so that they do not inappropriately blame clients for being uncooperative or resistant to their techniques.

Client-Centered Techniques

Carl Rogers has had a tremendous impact on the process of psychotherapy in the United States and has introduced many valuable ideas and procedures. Nevertheless, although research findings are not totally consistent (e.g., Folensbee, Draguns, & Danish, 1986) Rogers's particular style of client-focused, nondirective therapy may not be suitable for all cultural subgroups. Sue and Sue (1990) suggest that Native Americans, Asian Americans, African Americans, and Hispanic Americans may prefer more active and directive types of therapy. These clients appear to want more practical advice and opinions from the therapist as opposed to the more ambiguous client-centered approach (also see the client-centered approach discussed in Chapter 6). For example, Asian-Americans tend to prefer a structured, direct and practical orientation to therapy. Many Puerto Rican clients expect advice, information, and specific suggestions from psychotherapy (Sue, 1981). Because of these differences in expectations, the highly verbal (client-centered) focus on paraphrasing, reflection of feelings and avoidance of direct influence may confuse or alienate members of some subgroups.

Conventional Goals and Procedures

In working with culturally diverse clients, therapists may need to break away from traditional treatment activities. Because of their life experiences, some clients may have different needs and expectations. For example, common therapeutic procedures such as exploration of a person's past, achieving insight, or working on long-term goals may not always be appropriate. Some minority group clients might see the root of their difficulties as residing within the general society or political system. These clients may not see the need to change themselves but, rather, the need for intervention in the outside world. Along the same lines, the therapist may have to reduce the use of a intrapsychic counseling model and get involved in out-of-the-office interventions. Many clients are concerned primarily with day-to-day survival or other immediate issues. Focusing on long-term goals and behavior changes may not make any sense to them. Part of the high psychotherapy dropout rate may be related to this factor.

As I have already mentioned, psychotherapists who work with culturally diverse clients may need to branch out and focus on practical or environmentally focused changes—for example, helping clients find a job or a safe place to live, or helping them obtain other adjunct services. Consistent with Abraham Maslow's concept of the hierarchy of needs, clients who do not have a safe place to live or enough food for their families may not be willing to spend their time talking about their past or gaining insight about themselves.

Recommendations: Cultural Influences
7. With some culturally diverse groups, the therapist may need to focus more on environmental concerns or offer out-of-the-office services.

Therapist Values

Therapists should be careful not to inappropriately impose their own cultural goals, standards, or values on clients from different backgrounds than their own. For example, while in graduate school, I worked with poor African American children in a community mental health agency. One of the common goals with this group was an attempt to reduce or eliminate fighting behavior. However, we had little concern for how our interventions might have been inappropriate for clients coming from ghetto neighborhoods. In a similar mode, minority clients may feel that therapists are trying to impose value systems on them that they find foreign or inconsistent with their own. What is important here is that we not assume that all of our clients see the world the same way we do.

Along the same lines, Ridley (1984) describes how certain inconspicuous clues given by the therapist may undermine the treatment process. These include subtly racist attitudes or any signs of bias or disapproval of the client's life-style or values. These clues also include unfounded stereotypes or expectations the therapist may have about certain racial groups or minorities. For example, some studies have found that therapists expect clients from various minority groups to be less compliant or motivated or to have more limitations than White clients. Likewise, therapists, who typically belong to the middle class, may hold different expectations for clients within their own social class than they do for those from other classes. Some researchers have labeled these type of therapist actions *cultural countertransference* and the corresponding negative client reactions to these as *pseudotransference* responses (see Ridley, 1984, 1989).

In all likelihood, the factors described here contribute to the high numbers of minority clients who drop out after only one session of therapy, or to the "resistive" behavior of minority clients. However, since these often involve attitudes or behaviors on the part of the therapist that are very subtle or perhaps even unconscious, they may be difficult to address. Sue and Sue (1990) suggest that part of the solution to such problems includes having therapists first become aware of their own cultural heritage and how these attitudes and values shape their behavior; and second how these may then impinge on minority clients or interfere with effective psychotherapy. This type of personal exploration includes the identification of possible racist attitudes or stereotypes that develop simply as a result of living in our culture (see Ponterotto & Pedersen, 1993). It also includes having an open attitude about accepting differences between ourselves and others and not assuming that our values or traditions are necessarily the best. Along the same lines, it involves exploring and learning more about the culture of others.

Characteristics of Culturally Diverse Groups

Consistent with the last statement, the following is a brief description of the general characteristics of several minority groups with whom psychotherapists are likely to work in their practice. Rather than being comprehensive, it is meant to serve simply as an initial introduction to these cultural groups. Again, these are global generalizations, and each client should be treated as an individual. As Sue and Sue (1990, p. 187) appropriately point out, knowledge of a culture should not be used for stereotyping but, rather, to help the therapist become more flexible and generate alternative approaches and solutions. Along the same lines, techniques that are successful with someone from one cultural group (Hispanic) may not be useful with a person from a different one (African American) or even with other individuals within the same group.

The characteristics described next relate primarily to issues surrounding psychotherapy. Much of this section is based on research and publications by Sue and Sue (1990); Bennett (1994); Jenkins (1982); Kleinman (1980); Pedersen, Draguns, Lonner, and Trimble, (1989); Leong (1986); Edward and Edwards (1980); Jones (1985); Beiser (1985); McGoldrick, Pearce, and Giordano (1982); and Paniagua (1995). The interested reader is urged to obtain these and other sources for additional information. General treatment guidelines for multicultural groups are given in Table 8-2. More specific recommendations for particular ethnic groups follow.

Native Americans

American Indians are a very diverse group because this term represents approximately five hundred different tribes in various parts of the country. Because each tribe has its own customs and practices, there is really no single Native American culture (of course, the same thing can be said about a single "White" culture). However, the following are some general themes commonly found among these groups. Native Americans often

> **Recommendations: Cultural Influences**
> 8. For many clients, there is a need to include their family or social groups in the therapy process as opposed to the traditional individual approach.

believe that the tribe or family is more important than the individual. Rather than autonomy and independence, their extended family system fosters interdependence. Because of this collective orientation, they may have problems with the typical individually focused psychotherapy approach, and with techniques such as introspection. Similarly, they value cooperation and generosity and may be reluctant to compete with others. For example, sharing and collaboration are seen as more important than control. In addition, prestige is generally gained through giving rather than accumulating property. Because they are brought up with this perspective, they may not understand why eligibility rules need to be met for certain social services, especially when a need clearly exists.

TABLE 8-2 General Treatment Guidelines for Multicultural Groups

1. Evaluate clients' level of acculturation in the early stages of therapy.
2. Consider working with clients' extended families and using group methods.
3. Generally, therapy should be brief, directive, and problem-oriented.
4. Use pretherapy training if possible.
5. Deal with day-to-day survival issues as necessary.
6. Consider the use of community resources and support groups.
7. Be careful not to falsely interpret a client's passivity, reluctance to speak up, or lack of self-discloser as resistance.
8. Strict adherence to client-centered and psychodynamic models of therapy may be ineffectual with many of these clients.
9. Try to learn as much as possible about clients' culture before starting therapy.
10. Try to be aware of any biases you bring to therapy and avoid imposing your own values onto clients.
11. Try not to challenge clients' native beliefs about mental illness until a secure relationship is established.
12. Be aware that psychological symptoms may be expressed as somatic concerns.
13. Be aware of clients' cultural approach toward concepts such as time, personal space, self-exploration, and disclosure.
14. Be cautious in recommending medications or hospitalization in the first session.
15. Consider using the microskills approach with these clients.

American Indians tend to be present- rather than future-oriented and not overly influenced by clocks and calendars. They may have difficulty with deadlines or be late for sessions. Similarly, they may be uncomfortable with the limits of the traditional fifty-minute hour. Because of this "present-time" orientation, they may question the usefulness of long-term goals. For example, their idea of progress may be different from those of the White culture. In fact, many Native American groups tend not to value progress. The purpose of their community is simply to live, experience positive relationships with others, and engage in special ceremonies. They also believe in the harmony of nature and humans, and they may assume that eventually "something will happen" to solve their problems (an attitude that therapists may interpret as passivity).

As with other minorities, it may take them a while before they feel they can trust a therapist with a different background. Given the past history of how Native Americans have been treated by the U.S. government, this should not be surprising. Perceptions of therapist expertise and signs of respect for the client (nonverbal cues) appear to be very important variables for instilling trust and for successful treatment. For example, if the therapist dresses very casually for a session, this may be seen as a sign of disrespect (see Trimble & Fleming, 1989).

Some Native American clients may have a problem with maintaining eye contact, being assertive, or expressing strong emotional feelings. Traditionally, Indians have been taught not to talk excessively about themselves or to exaggerate their abilities. In fact, it may not be unusual for Native Americans to bring another person to the session in order to speak for them (Edwards & Edwards, 1980). Extended periods of silence are not uncommon with these clients. For example, Beiser (1985) reports an interesting case study of an Native American women being treated for depression after the death of her mother. Despite hospitalization, medications, and psychotherapy, her condition did not improve until an arrangement was made with the tribal elders to hold a traditional ceremony one year after her mother's death. This client had refused to talk about her mother both before and after the ceremony, but this non-verbal community grieving process proved to be the turning point for her condition. Had her treatment team not considered alternative strategies, her condition might not have improved. This example also points out the importance of nonverbal communication among Native Americans.

General Treatment Recommendations

1. Use group therapy or work with the extended family whenever possible.
2. Avoid interrupting clients while they are talking, and avoid confrontations.

> **Recommendations: Cultural Influences**
> 9. Pretherapy orientation and role induction training appears to be especially important with diverse cultural groups.

3. It may take a while before clients are able to trust you and be comfortable with self-disclosure. Avoid asking very personal questions or questions unrelated to the presenting problem. In the initial sessions, avoid taking too many notes.

4. Use problem-oriented, directive approaches.

5. Try to focus on short-term goals and brief therapy.

6. Native Americans may not know what to expect, so pretherapy orientation is important.

7. If possible, try to find historical information about the client's tribe, ceremonies, community reservation, or other background information. This may avoid misdiagnoses and give you a clearer idea of what is "normal" or "abnormal" behavior.

8. Some clients may prefer or feel more comfortable with same-sex therapists.

9. Some clients may prefer or be more responsive in outdoor settings.

10. Some clients may be sensitive about the use of medication, so use caution in bringing up this topic.

Asian Americans

Like Native Americans, the term *Asian American* includes a variety of groups—Chinese, Japanese, Korean, Vietnamese, Laotian, Cambodians, Pacific Islanders, and others—each with its own unique language, customs, and characteristics. There is really no single "Asian" culture. However, these groups share certain characteristics. Psychotherapy may not be a familiar concept to many Asian groups, and they may not be open to the concepts of talking therapy or of self-actualization but may attribute their symptoms to fate or lack of willpower. In fact, their language may lack specific words to describe their emotional feelings. Kleinman (1980, p. 141) points out that part of the process of psychotherapy with Chinese clients may be teaching them how to communicate their internal experiences. In addition, there may be more stigma attached to seeking mental health services with these groups than with middle-class White Americans. Related to this, some Asians may express psychological problems through physical complaints (headaches, fatigue, etc.). For example, Kleinman (1980) suggests that native Chinese rarely complain of anxiety, depression, or similar psychological symptoms but, rather, express these as heart and chest disorders. Thus, they may also expect to receive physical treatment.

Asian American clients may have problems opening up to outsiders or volunteering any information about themselves. Mental illness may be viewed as a failure on the part of the family, and clients may not be willing to admit to any problems. Often, they prefer to rely on their elders rather than on professionals for advice and direction, or to solve problems on their own. Many Asians have strict dichotomies concerning mental illness. They see a person as either "sane" or "crazy," with little in between. Thus, most of this population use mental health services only as a last resort. Like other minority groups, they tend to underutilize such services.

As I mentioned above, many Asians believe that strong feelings should not be expressed overtly but, rather, should be kept under control. Often communication styles are dictated by personal characteristics such as age, gender, occupation, social status, or family background. Also, because they do not want to offend anyone, their style of communication tends to be highly indirect. McGoldrick et al. give as an example two Malaysian mothers of different social classes who supposedly met to discuss the potential marriage of their children. Although the topic of their children's union never entered into the conversation, the fact that the hostess served tea and bananas at the meeting (which is never done in that culture) was a sign that the marriage would be incompatible.

Most Asians believe in the model of interdependence among individuals, rather than independence. They may expect their families or close friends to be involved in the treatment process. Part of this relates to their belief that what they do and how they behave is the product of their interactions with nature and with others, especially family members. Likewise, many of these clients are influenced by philosophies such as Confucianism or Buddhism, which tend to have formal rules and roles for everyone. A number of cases have been described in the literature of well-meaning professionals trying to encourage freedom and independence from their families for young Asian American clients, only to find their efforts further aggravating these clients' symptoms. A more appropriate program would take into consideration the interdependence of such family systems.

General Recommendations

1. Treatment generally should be brief, active, and problem-focused.
2. Avoid asking too many questions, or direct ones, until a fair amount of trust is developed.

> **Recommendations: Cultural Influences**
> 10. For clients who have been exposed to racism or other forms of oppression, the therapist may have to open up first and be willing to self-disclose so that trust can be built up.

3. Use pretherapy orientation and role induction to explain the purpose and process of psychotherapy.
4. Allow clients to develop their own goals when possible.
5. Address survival issues or daily living needs of the client when appropriate.
6. Use an environmentally focused approach as needed, and deal with the present or with short-term goals.
7. Many clients (e.g., those exposed to war in Laos, Vietnam, or Cambodia) may have problems with culture shock or posttraumatic stress disorder (PTSD), and these may need to be addressed separately (see Lefley, 1989).
8. Clients may also be ambivalent about many aspects of their own culture as they try to assimilate American ways, and this may be a source of stress.
9. Some of the problems these clients bring to therapy may be related to conflicts within the family, and these should be totally explored. This may be especially true for new immigrants, where there are likely to be clashes between "old" and "new" values.
10. Many Asian Americans may expect to play a passive role in therapy. This should not be interpreted as a lack of motivation or resistance.
11. Direct confrontation should generally be avoided.
12. The use of family therapy should be considered.
13. Advice and suggestions should be concrete and tangible.
14. Many of these clients prefer a formal as opposed to friendly client–therapist relationship.

African Americans

African Americans are unique in a number of ways. First, they make up the largest single minority group; second, most have not newly immigrated to the United States; third, language barriers are less of a problem than with other cultural groups. Many are either bicultural or hold values similar to those of the majority culture. However, even though most African Americans have lived in the United States for their entire lives, some of their values are still influenced by their African roots. For example, as a general characteristic, they tend to be more group-oriented than independent, and they tend to have a holistic world view.

The extended family is very important to African Americans; in fact, many are directly or indirectly raised by relatives other than their parents. However, therapists should not jump to the conclusion that parents reject their children in these situations. Sometimes these "child-keeping" practices are the only means of survival. These extended family figures should be involved in the therapy whenever possible.

Many African Americans believe in the harmony between humans and nature. They also tend to put a strong emphasis on spirituality, and ministers may be the first to be consulted when emotional problems arise. It is no accident that many African American political leaders are also religious authorities. It is important for therapists to know how important religion is to some African Americans, especially women; in these cases it may be a powerful resource to use. In some cases, these clients may view emotional problems as something that was "meant to be" and thus make little effort to change. In a similar manner, it may be useful to understand some of the religious beliefs that guide client behaviors.

With others of the same race, African Americans tend to be open, responsive, and playful, but they may be guarded or less verbal when interacting with Whites. As a result of long years of racism and oppression, it may take them a long time to really trust White therapists. As a result, they may appear aloof, unresponsive or resistive until a relationship is built. Many African Americans have problems self-disclosing to White therapists. This may be even more pronounced in interracial group therapy. Although African Americans as a group tend to self-disclose less than Whites, much of this type of behavior in therapy appears to be a survival mechanism that results from living in a racist environment. As I mentioned in Chapter 4, self-disclosure leaves one open and vulnerable, and nondisclosure to therapists or others of a different race tends to be a protective rather than a resistive response (see Ridley, 1984). Similarly, many African Americans may appear to display paranoid-like behaviors because of the many years of prejudice and racism. In fact, misdiagnoses of African American clients are common. On the other hand, as Ridley (1984) suggests, some African Americans truly are paranoid, and a careful differential diagnosis needs to be done

African Americans tend to have a neutral (though not necessarily negative) view of mental health services. About half drop out of therapy after the first session, and treatment outcome is often not very positive. Much of this, however, may be due to treatment procedures that many of these clients perceive as inappropriate (Berman, 1979). For example, some African Americans see most of their difficulties as rooted in social or environmental conditions and may not see the usefulness of intrapsychic change or gaining insight. Likewise, they may not understand why the therapist needs to gather a lot of personal information about them. In this case, the rationale for treatment procedures should be fully explained. In addition, the therapist may also need to consider how outside systems such as welfare, the courts, the protective system, or other agencies might affect the treatment plan or the problems these clients bring to therapy.

General Recommendations

1. The first few sessions of therapy may be crucial in terms of preventing dropouts and developing a positive relationship. For example, therapist self-disclosure may help break the ice and increase the likelihood of the client opening up.
2. If applicable, find out how the client feels about working with a therapist from a different race. Try to determine realistically whether the two of you can work together, and make referrals if appropriate.
3. Involve the minister or other church members when applicable.
4. Explore clients' expectations for therapy, and help them develop their own goals.
5. Work with the extended family if possible.
6. Therapy should be direct, problem-oriented, and brief whenever possible.
7. Daily survival issues should be addressed as necessary. At times, the therapist may have to be involved in activities that may be more of a caseworker's function, but these are often necessary. Similarly, consider the use of community resources such as support groups or legal aid.
8. Therapeutic procedures should be individually tailored, flexible, and eclectic (in general, many of the recommendations made in Chapter 6 appear to be applicable to minority group clients).
9. Focus on short-term rather than long-term goals.
10. Totally explain your procedures and your rationale for using them.
11. Make use of pretherapy orientation and try to dispel any myths clients may have about treatment or mental illness.
12. Find out what clients feel about the causes of their problems, and build this into the treatment plan.
13. Similarly, get feedback about the goals and procedures of the intended treatment plan, and make adjustments as necessary.

Hispanic Americans

As with other minorities, the term *Hispanic* refers to a number of different groups—Mexicans, Puerto Ricans, Cubans, South Americans, and so on—whom have different orientations. The following is simply a generalization based on the many Hispanic cultures.

Hispanics tend to focus on family or community relationships as opposed to having an individual orientation. The extended family as well as godparents are extremely important. Likewise, once close friendships are developed, they are frequently long-standing and very intense. Hispanics tend to rely on their families and close friends as resources for problem solving and for coping with emotional problems. Thus, they seek the help of outsiders only reluctantly. When they do seek help, they may be reluctant to discuss certain issues because of loyalty to the family. Within this family structure, males tend to be the primary authority figure, and females often play a submissive role. The traditional family structure and boundaries of authority should be respected during therapy.

Hispanics as a group tend to believe in the harmony between humans and nature. As opposed to many White Americans, they emphasize cooperation rather than competition. Religion may play a strong role in their lives. As a result, some clients may see life events as inevitable or due to fate. They may feel that some problems are meant to be and thus cannot be changed. Likewise, as opposed to White Americans, Hispanics tend to have a somewhat greater external locus of control. On the other hand, the alleged Hispanic inclination toward extreme fatalism and predestination may be exaggerated. Some of these beliefs are based on single case studies or insufficient evidence. Again, therapists are urged to treat each person as an individual and to avoid stereotypes.

Depending on their nationality, some Hispanics may be primarily present-oriented. Thus, they may not be overly concerned about deadlines or time restraints. At times, the therapist may have to be flexible about session lengths. Similarly, these clients may not be overly concerned about long-term future events or goals. Like members of other minority groups, most Hispanics come to therapy only in times of crisis. Thus, they often expect immediate results.

Many Hispanics are unfamiliar with the concept of verbal psychotherapy and may link emotional and physical problems. For example, Puerto Ricans generally do not present symptoms of depression directly but, rather, complain of eating problems, weakness, or exhaustion. Likewise, many Hispanics still believe in a number of folk illnesses such as the *mal ojo* (evil eye) or *mal puesto*. In some cases, the symptoms they present may appear odd or inconsistent with the DSM-IV. Care must be taken to make appropriate diagnoses in these cases. If the therapist suspects that clients believe in spiritism, care should be taken not to challenge their convictions strongly. Similarly, clients' levels of acculturation are important to assess early in treatment.

Treatment Recommendations

1. Group or family therapy may be more effective than individual therapy.

2. Pretherapy orientation should be used to explain the purpose and process of therapy.
3. If appropriate, treatment should be brief, problem-focused, and directive.
4. Be careful to pronounce clients' names correctly.
5. Therapists should help clients express their expectations for treatment and help them develop their own goals.
6. Survival and day-to-day living issues (food, shelter, living in dangerous areas, etc.) may need to be addressed.
7. As with many of the other groups above, the therapist may need to address problems associated with poverty, racism, culture shock, or conflicts of ethnic identity or acculturation.
8. Hispanics tend to have a shorter personal space than most Americans and are not uncomfortable with appropriate physical contact, such as an embrace. These modifications by the therapist may facilitate more trust and openness.
9. In a related manner, therapeutic relationships that are perceived as distant or too professional are not likely to be successful.

With Hispanics, as well as other ethnic groups, the therapist may need to use an interpreter. Though often overlooked, this person can potentially seriously affect the treatment process and thus should be chosen carefully. The therapist should meet with this individual beforehand in order to go over expectations. For nonprofessional interpreters, the therapist should specifically explain what they should and should not say or do, how to avoid biasing responses, and so on. Care should be taken to choose an interpreter who will not offend the client. For example, in some cultures, older males may be embarrassed or unwilling to express themselves to a young person or a person of the opposite sex. Female clients also may have similar problems expressing certain types of information depending on the characteristics of this person. To avoid having to build up the client's trust or sense of security repeatedly during the treatment process, if a suitable interpreter is found, this person should not be changed. My experience has been that the use of family members as interpreters usually does not work very well. Table 8-3 gives some guidelines for using translators in therapy.

The Microskills Approach

In addition to the various recommendations given here, a general set of procedures that can be used with different cultural groups is the microskills approach (Ivey & Authier, 1978; Ivey, Ivey, & Simek-Morgan,

TABLE 8-3   Guidelines for Using Translators in Psychotherapy

1. Avoid the use of family members or friends.
2. Try to use translators who are trained in psychotherapy.
3. Adjust the time of the session to take translations into account.
4. Try to use the same translator each time if possible.
5. Try to allow time before the session for the translator and client to meet and get to know each other.
6. Try to select a translator who speaks the same dialect as the client and shares the clients' cultural background.
7. When using a translator, avoid using technical terms, acronyms, or psychological jargon.
8. Be aware of possible distortions between what the client really means and what is translated, and also of the effect of a translator's presence on the client's self-disclosures.
9. Avoid client–translator mismatches.
10. Try to translate what is said one sentence at a time.

1993). The purpose of this set of techniques is basically to match the therapeutic style of the therapist with the communication style of the client. Although this method was originally based on traditional Western psychotherapy conceptions, it has gradually been revised to take cultural differences into account.

Ivey and his colleagues break down the counseling process into the basic components of attending, listening, and influencing. Each of these is then modified for various client groups. For example, the attending skills used for White middle-class clients may include direct eye contact and a low to moderate emotional tone. However, Native Americans tend to be uncomfortable with direct eye contact, and some cultural groups, such as Hispanics, may prefer a more expressive style than is used with other clients. Similarly, in trying to influence middle-class clients, there may be more of an emphasis on interpretation or self-awareness, whereas in working with some minority group individuals, there may more of a focus on family or cultural issues. The microskills approach emphasizes a flexible orientation and the use of many of the treatment-matching techniques mentioned in the previous chapter.

The following are some of the questions that Ivey and his colleagues feel are important for the therapist to investigate when working with culturally diverse groups:

1. **What is the interactive or relational style of the group?** As I have discussed, the European American system tends to emphasis the individual, whereas many other cultures focus on the family or collective society.

2. How are decisions made, and which persons are likely to influence the client? Again, the European American culture tends to rely on the individual, whereas other cultures are very much influenced by family members or elders.
3. What is the basic family unit? In the United States, we generally consider the nuclear family as the primary unit, but other societies place greater importance on the extended family.
4. What are the general attitudes toward change? Because of the fast pace and constantly evolving nature of our society, many people may be more comfortable with the overall concept of change, whereas some groups may believe that you cannot change fate or that given enough time, problems will work themselves out.
5. What is the general communication style of the culture? White Americans tend to have a straightforward style of communicating, but some ethnic groups may place more emphasis on storytelling or on the use of metaphors.

All of these differences in orientation may require the use of modified treatment strategies, and the authors maintain that the microskills approach can be a very effective system with all cultural groups. Readers are urged to find out more about this treatment method.

Summary

This chapter has looked at the influence of cultural factors on both the concept and treatment of abnormal behaviors. In one sense or another, culture affects both what we consider to be abnormal and how we treat it. Similarly, the ideology of much of Western psychotherapy is based on the notion of individuality. However, this type of social system is not universal and clients coming from a different perspective may have difficulty with some of the traditional Western-oriented therapy procedures. Along these lines, the techniques that appear to cause the most problems with culturally diverse groups were reviewed.

Therapists face the challenge of deciding when behaviors such as a lack of disclosure, a reluctance to form a trusting relationship, or an inability to remember various events is associated with some form of defense and when it is due to a person's cultural background. The latter can influence the type of disorders a client brings to therapy, the corresponding roleclients play in treatment, and what they will be willing to talk about.

This chapter also briefly described the basic characteristics of several ethnic minorities with whom psychotherapists are likely to work in their practice. General recommendations to be used with these groups were given. A brief overview was given of the microskills approach to therapy, which appears to have a number of advantages for working with both cultural minorities and traditional clients.

Appendix A

History of Resistance

Over the years, many professionals have attempted to refine the definition of resistance according to their specific orientation. For example, Mahoney (1991; p. 326) suggests that there are currently five different theories of resistance in psychotherapy: (1) motivated avoidance (psychoanalysis); (2) motivational deficit (behavioral model); (3) ambivalent choice (social learning theory, including self-defeating behaviors and self-destructive behaviors); (4) reactance (cognitive theory); and (5) self-protection (humanist/existential theories).

In a similar vein, Kottler (1992) has organized the various theories of resistance on a continuum ranging from the view that resistance is the therapist's enemy to the view that it is the therapist's friend. His ideas are presented in Table A-1. The sections that follow review most of these different perspectives, but not necessarily in the same order as the table.

Freud and Psychoanalytic Theory

In patient–healer relationships, the concept of treatment resistance dates back to at least Greek and Roman times (Ellis, 1985; DiMatteo & DiNicola, 1982) and probably thousands of years before that. But the first formal theory of resistance in psychotherapy was developed by Freud, who introduced the term in the classic book he wrote with Josef Breurer, *Studies on Hysteria* (Freud, 1895/1955). Freud came up with the concept of resistance through his work with Fraulein Elisabeth Von R. He wrote, "In the course of this difficult work, I began to attach a deeper significance to the resistance offered by the patient in the reproduction of her memories" (Freud, 1895/1955, p. 154). In this early stage of psycho-

TABLE A-1   Theoretical Assumptions of Resistance

Resistance as Enemy

Problem solving: Resistance is the enemy and must be overcome.

Psychoanalytic: Resistance must be interpreted and counteracted.

Behavioral: Resistance is annoying noncompliance with assigned tasks.

Social influence: Resistance is viewed neutrally as a form of communication.

Cognitive-behavioral: Resistance is a natural component of the change process.

Systematic: Resistance is a way to maintain the structural integrity of the family.

Existential: Resistance is a means of legitimate self-expression.

Strategic: Resistance is embraced and paradoxically prescribed.

Resistance as Friend

Source: From *Compassionate Therapy: Working with Difficult Clients,* by J.A. Kottler, 1992, p. 7. Copyright 1992 by Jossey-Bass Inc., Publishers. Used by permission.

analysis, Freud viewed resistance primarily as a force that affected memory and as a nuisance that had to be overcome in order for therapy to be successful.

According to psychoanalytic theory, the basic type of resistance results from repression, an unconscious ego defense mechanism that blocks or diverts highly threatening or anxiety-producing ideas, images, or affect from conscious awareness. Once this material is repressed into the unconscious, a strong counterforce is set up that prevents it from becoming conscious again. This counterforce is called *resistance.* As Freud (1895/1955) stated: "Thus a psychical force . . . had originally driven the pathogenic idea out of association and was now opposing its return to memory" (p. 269). Freud maintained that effective psychotherapy requires that this anxiety producing material reemerge into consciousness. However, the counterforce of resistance attempts to prevent this and therefore blocks therapeutic progress. What motivates resistance is the prevention of unpleasant or even unbearable ideas or emotions. As examples, Freud gave feelings of shame, of low self-esteem, or of being harmed. From the psychoanalytic point of view, the ego unconsciously views recovery as dangerous and perhaps as a threat to its very existence. In this case, the drive behind resistance is protection.

Freud realized that, on an intuitive level, the idea of patients spending a great deal of time, effort, and money while simultaneously struggling against treatment does not make sense. However, he quickly recognized the importance of this approach–avoidance conflict. He wrote, "How improbable such an assertion must sound! Yet it is true; . . . A man who has gone to the dentist because of an unbearable tooth ache will nevertheless try to hold the dentist back when he approaches the sick tooth with a pair of forceps" (Freud, 1916/1963, pp. 286–287).

As Freud made revisions in the theory of psychoanalysis, he gradually altered his concept of resistance as well. For example, in addition to suppressing unacceptable unconscious material, Freud wrote, resistance is also responsible for the distortions that often appear in the patient's free associations. In other words, the anxiety-producing material would be allowed to become conscious, but only in highly disguised forms, similar to the manifest content of dreams. In this sense, Freud viewed resistance as being primarily an intrapsychic protective force that was present at all times. He stated: "Every step of the treatment is accompanied by resistance; every single thought, every mental act of the patient's, must pay toll to the resistance, and represents a compromise between the forces urging a cure and those gathered to oppose it" (1912/1958a, p. 103). Freud considered the concept of resistance so important, that he made it the cornerstone of psychoanalytic theory. In his words, "It may thus be said that the theory of psychoanalysis is an attempt to account for two striking and unexpected facts of observation . . . the facts of transference and of resistance" (Freud, 1914/1957b, p. 16). Furthermore, Freud blamed the use of hypnosis for preventing him from having discovered resistance sooner. Speaking of hypnosis, he says, "it does not permit us, for example, to recognize the *resistance* with which the patient clings to his disease and thus even fights against his own recovery" (1905/1953, p. 261; emphasis in the original). He subsequently writes: "I have been able to say that psychoanalysis proper began when I dispensed with the help of hypnosis" (Freud, 1917/1963, p. 292).

Later in his career, Freud expanded his concept of resistance to include "all the forces that oppose the work of recovery" (1926/1959, p. 223). To separate resistance more clearly from repression, he described five major types of resistance, three of which had their roots in the ego, and the other two in the id and superego (Freud, 1926/1959). Toward the end of his career, Freud also introduced the concept of a "meta" resistance that resists analysis as a whole, as well as the idea of four biologically based resistances (e.g., the interaction of the life and death instincts; Freud, 1937). However, his five original conceptions of resistance have remained the most influential.

More recently, Sandler, Holder, and Dare (1970) have further described and expanded on Freud's original five types of resistances, as follows:

1. *Repression-resistance:* This is the basic type of resistance and relates to the ego's internal adaptation to anxiety, which results in a need to defend itself against impulses, memories or feelings that can potentially cause psychological pain. This is consistent with Freud's concept of the "primary gain" of emotional disorders, since one of the functions of symptoms (similar to repression) is to protect the ego from anxiety-producing material. In this case, the patient avoids thinking or talking about topics that may lead to negative emotions. Sandler, Dare, and Holder (1973) add to this category resistance that results from the threat that psychotherapy poses for the way the individual has learned to adapt to the external world. Thus, potential behavior changes that may affect how an individual responds to his or her environment will be resisted as well. An example is a therapist's attempt to reduce or eliminate certain defense mechanisms.

2. *Transference-resistance:* This involves the conscious and unconscious thoughts and feelings the patient has toward the analyst. Freud considered this type of resistance to be the most powerful. He saw transference as a repetition of past feelings or attitudes that were now experienced by the patient (rather than remembered) and directed toward the therapist. Freud believed this tendency was associated with the "compulsion to repeat." In other words, he believed that individuals have a natural tendency to re-create or relive previous traumatic experiences. When this occurs in a therapy setting, the analyst assumes the roles of the key figures of the patient's past.

In the early stages of psychoanalysis, the concepts of resistance, repression, and transference were virtually synonymous. As time went on, Freud differentiated all of these in his writings. Transference basically means that patients relate to the therapist in ways that are influenced by previous strong relationships (e.g., parents or previous lovers). Freud described it as follows: "What are transferences? . . . a whole series of psychological experiences are revived, not as belonging to the past, but as applying to the person of the physician at the present moment" (1905/1953, p. 116). Later, he wrote, " The patient . . . directs towards the physician a degree of affectionate feelings (mingled, often enough, with hostility) which is based on no real relation between them and which—as is shown by every detail of its emergence—can be traced back to old, wishful fantasies of the patient's which have become unconscious" (1910/1957a, p. 51). In this sense, the conflicts and fantasies that are the core of the patient's psychopathology are repeated in the relationship with the therapist and are thus available to be analyzed and interpreted.

In *Studies on Hysteria,* Freud (1895/1955) wrote about three typical ways in which transference resistance can develop. The first is when the patient feels he or she has been neglected or insulted. The second is when the patient is afraid of becoming too dependent on the therapist or, as Freud put it, "sexually dependent on him" (p. 302). The third is when the patient transfers to the therapist the disturbing ideas that are brought out in therapy (Freud introduced the term *transference* in this discussion). Menninger (1973) suggests that transference resistance is due in part to patients' resentment at not getting what they want from the therapist, and prefers to call it frustration or revenge resistance (p. 108). An example is when a client does not progress in therapy as a way to get back at or punish the therapist.

As Freud originally suggested, Strean (1990) notes that transference occurs in all relationships. He states that our perceptions of the people we meet, as well as the way we respond to them, are greatly affected by our previous experiences. Greenson (1965) agrees with this view but suggests that in order to be considered transference, the reaction must have two characteristics. It has to be a repetition of the past, and it must be inappropriate at the present time. Since previous intimate relationships often involve mixed feelings, including love and hate, the therapist is likely to be the recipient of these feelings as well. For example, clients who have recently lost a loved one through death or a breakup may find it difficult to trust or form a relationship with the therapist because they fear or anticipate the loss of this relationship as well. Patients also may use transference as a way to avoid disclosure. In this sense, Freud suggested that everything that a patient says in therapy should be considered to be a message to the therapist. The issue of transference is further discussed in Chapter 6.

3. *Epinosic gain (secondary gains):* These are the added benefits that result from having emotional problems or symptoms. Examples include attention, not having to go to school or work, or receiving monetary rewards ("compensation neurosis"). Sandler, Dare, and Holder (1973) point out that the revenge or gratification clients receive when others are forced to share their suffering is another example of this type of resistance.

4. *Id resistance (sometimes called repetition-compulsion resistance):* These relate to clients' unwillingness to give up behaviors that directly or indirectly satisfy the biological drives of the id. Included in this category are habits, sexual behaviors, and firmly established or gratifying behavior patterns. Freud also included here patients' desire to be treated as the therapist's "baby." Examples include wanting special favors, seeking immediate gratification, calling between sessions, and similar behaviors.

5. *Superego-resistance:* Freud believed that this type of resistance is often difficult to recognize and stems from the client's sense of guilt and need for punishment. For example, when clients start to make progress in therapy or begin to feel better, they feel guilty. As Strean (1990) points out, in a sense, patients feel more comfortable when they are miserable.

In addition to the original five types of resistance described by Freud, Sandler, Holder and Dare (1970) add the following:

1. Resistance related to therapeutic changes that may disrupt a patient's important relationships. For example, a housewife may avoid becoming more assertive because doing so might jeopardize her marriage.
2. Resistance due to the loss of the therapist when the client is "cured." This is especially strong when the client and therapist have developed a strong therapeutic relationship, or when the client lacks strong relationships in the outside world. Of course, this is likely to appear when treatment termination is being considered.
3. Resistance related to the effect of therapy on the client's self-esteem. For example, a patient may avoid some topics because of feelings of shame. This is related to superego resistance.
4. Resistance that results from faulty procedures or inappropriate treatment methods. As I will discuss, this is an adaptive type of resistance.
5. Resistance due to strong traits and characteristics that form the core structure of the client's personality. This type of resistance may emerge when changes are proposed that the client is unwilling or unable to make, and may be among the most difficult to overcome.

As Freud and many other psychoanalytic writers have pointed out, resistance has positive aspects because it indicates that progress is being made, points out the typical defenses the patient uses, and suggests to the therapist the direction that therapy should take. Freud stated that "resistances should not be one-sidedly condemned, as they include important material from the patient's past" (Freud, 1916/1963, p. 291). In order to overcome resistance, Freud suggested that two preliminary conditions must be met. To paraphrase Freud, these are as follows: (1) The patient (through therapy) must be close to uncovering the repressed material related to the resistance, and (2) he or she must have formed a good relationship (positive transference) with the therapist. Once these conditions have been met, Freud suggests that resistance can be overcome by making the unconscious material conscious and sensible through interpretation and communication (Freud, 1917/1963). However, the greater the accuracy of the interpretation, the greater the resistance will be. He says: "One must allow the patient time to become more conversant with this resistance with which he has now become acquainted, to *work through* it, to overcome it, by continuing, in defiance of it, the analytic work . . . (Freud, 1914/1958b, p. 155, emphasis in the original). Hence, in classical psychoanalysis, overcoming resistance is not part of the therapy, it *is the therapy*.

Contemporary Psychoanalysis

Over the years, psychoanalysts have refined and further described various forms of resistance. The following is a brief review of resistance as seen by more contemporary psychoanalysts. This section is limited mostly to ideas that are different from those of Freud, or ones that have been expanded.

Glover

Glover (1955) divided resistances into two groups: obvious resistance and the unobtrusive or silent mode. The obvious type of resistance is overt and straightforward. Examples include missing therapy, coming late, prolonged silences, and terminating treatment. The unobtrusive type is often difficult to recognize as resistance. It includes being a "model" patient, engaging in subtle seductive behaviors, or being overly self-demeaning. Glover also explored how various ego defense mechanisms contribute to resistance in therapy and indicates that certain resistances tend to occur with particular disorders—for example, projection with paranoia or repression with hysteria. Like Freud, he emphasizes the importance of transference resistance and points out the role of the therapist in resistance.

Reich

Reich's contribution to the concept of resistance is his extensive exploration of "character resistances" (Reich, 1949). These are described as personal traits that the patient utilizes as coping or defense mechanisms. Patients typically do not consider these traits or behavior patterns to be problems (e.g, nonassertiveness or arrogance) but, instead, utilize them as "armor" to protect themselves from the aversiveness of the outside world and to maintain the status quo. In a sense, the person's symptoms become his or her personal identity. Reich states "Economically, the character in everyday life and the character resistance in the analysis serve as a means of avoiding what is unpleasant (Unlust), of establishing and preserving a psychic (even if neurotic) balance, and finally of consuming repressed qualities of instinctual energy . . . " (Reich, 1987, p. 51). Reich gives as an example a patient who used silence to cover up his homosexual fantasies. He maintains that, to overcome resistance, the armor must be broken. To do so, the therapist must begin to analyze resistances immediately after the initiation of treatment, and the "cardinal resistance" (main or dominant form) must be confronted first. Of course, this will be a slow and painstaking process.

Greenson

Aside from Freud, Greenson (1967) has done the most to develop the concept of resistance. He suggests a comprehensive classification system for it. Specifically, he states that resistances should be classified by source (e.g., id, ego, or superego), fixation points (oral, anal, phallic), type of defense (e.g., defense mechanisms used such as repression, regression, isolation, etc.), diagnostic category (e.g., hysteria, obsessional neuroses, neurotic depression), and whether they are ego-alien or ego-syntonic. Ego-alien resistances would be recognized by the rational patient as being strange or unusual—for example, believing that the therapist does not like them, but having no support for this. These are usually easy to deal with. On the other hand, ego-syntonic resistances are habitual patterns of behavior that patients find rational or useful or that they deny or underestimate—for example, obsessive-compulsive traits or lack of assertiveness. This is similar to Reich's ideas. Greenson suggests that patients have to accept the resistance as ego-alien before it can be removed.

In addition, Greenson describes several types of "screen defenses." An example would be a patient who remembers an idea or concept (e.g., the screen) that wards off other underlying memories that are even more painful. As a possible illustration, in a case in which I served as a consultant, a patient recalled that her brother had committed suicide when she was a child, but not that it occurred after the two of them were caught engaging in sexual behavior.

Kohut

Kohut (1971) expands on the idea of narcissism as a major type of resistance. He suggests that resistance develops because psychotherapy has the potential to reawaken past fears or traumas in the patient. He states that psychotherapy has the tendency to reduce clients' self-esteem and infringe on their notion (or fantasy) of independence, thus making them feel helpless and vulnerable. Kohut suggests that a common response to this narcissistic defense is some type of (nonphysical) attack on the therapist. He explains this as follows: "The patient demonstrates through his behavior how *he* experiences the analysis, how my interpretations are received by *how* vulnerable and helpless *he* feels. One could say that he turns his passivity into activity, that he attacks *me* when *he* feels attacked" (Kohut, 1987, p. 170; emphasis in the original). Thus, Kohut generally sees resistance more as a response to the therapy process as a whole than as resisting specific unconscious material.

Similar to the focus of this book, Kohut emphasized the intersubjective nature of the patient–therapist relationship and downplayed the importance of the analyst as an detached expert observer. He also stressed the importance of an empathic climate in therapy and suggested that some forms of resistance are due to the therapist's failure to empathize with the patient's self-object needs.

Spotnitz

Spotnitz (1969, 1989) adds his own five types of resistance to those of Freud:

1. Treatment-destructive resistances, which include tardiness, missed sessions, and dropping out of therapy (similar to Glover's "obvious" type)
2. Inertia resistance, which usually occurs after the first six months of therapy and involves preserving the status quo
3. Resistance to progress, which is similar to the last type and involves a reluctance to move on and explore new issues, and a resistance to change in general
4. Resistance to cooperation, generally a resistance to forming a strong positive relationship with the therapist or to cooperating in any way
5. Resistance to termination, in which, in addition to a reluctance to terminate, the patient fights or refuses to become a fully independent functioning person

Although Spotnitz worked extensively with schizophrenics, his procedures have been extended to other populations. One of his major concepts is the idea that patients should be shown that they have the right to be resistive. This has been called "joining the resistance"—for example, telling silent patients that they have a right not to talk. He suggests that much of this resistive behavior is patients' method of dealing with internal anger and hostility, which he calls narcissistic transference resistance. In a sense, patients attack themselves in order to avoid attacking the therapist. Many of the techniques described by Spotnitz are designed to release this anger and aggression. He also suggests that if resistance in therapy cannot be overcome, it is the fault of the therapist, not the patient.

Fenichel

Otto Fenichel agrees with the Freudian concept that resistance is always present in therapy. He states: "To tell everything is much more difficult than one imagines. Even the individual who conscientiously tries to adhere to this basic rule fail's to tell many things because he considers them too unimportant, too stupid, too indiscreet, and so on. There are many who never learn to apply the basic rule because their fear of losing control is too great . . ." (1945, p. 24). He describes several types of resistance that are common in his experience. For example, patients may talk too much or too little; patients may forget to talk about certain things; patients may refuse to discuss the past or may talk of nothing but the past; patients may seem very cooperative and seemingly accept all that the therapist says, yet never change. Some patients pretend to accept what the therapist says only to be polite, and others seem honestly to accept what the therapist says, but the influence lasts only as long as the therapy hour (Fenichel describes this as the patient saying to himself, "this is all valid only as long as I lie on the couch"; p. 28). He also describes an intellectual resistance whereby patients try to refute the theoretical validity of the treatment theory, as opposed to working on real issues. Finally, Fenichel, like may other psychoanalysts, believes that the most important type of resistance, and the most difficult to overcome, is the one related to transference. He states, "the most significant category of resistance, the handling of which is the core of analysis: the transference resistance" (p. 29).

Menninger

Menninger's (1973) views of resistance are largely consistent with those of Freud. He indicates that it can be expressed by concealing facts or previous behaviors, by forgetting, by "acting out" memories rather than recalling them, or by the increase of symptoms (showing that therapy is making the patient's condition worse). He also talks at length about "erotization resistance." He describes this as occurring when patients realize that aside from symptom relief, the treatment itself is pleasurable (e.g., erotic). Citing Freud, Menninger suggests that this type of resistance is common and often results when the patient misinterprets the invitation to think and say anything as a form of seduction by the analyst. One form of this is found when the patient engages in behaviors or verbalization simply to please the therapist. In a sense, the patient is repaying the therapist for listening, being kind, showing interest, and helping him or her get better. Menninger suggests that overt or covert wishes for physical sexual gratification from the therapist are common, and goes on to describe the major categories of this resistance, which are based on erotic zones (e.g. oral, anal, phallic, and genital).

   Although I do not totally concur with this sexual explanation, I do agree that clients often say or do things in order to please the therapist. As I mentioned in Chapter 3, some cases of false memory syndrome may develop in this manner. The point is that at times the client is able to "please" the therapist and, at the same time, possibly avoid more pertinent therapeutic issues.

Langs

Langs breaks resistance down into the two broad categories: behavioral (overt) and communicative. The behavioral type includes obvious forms of resistance such as missing sessions or coming late. The communicative type involves the patient's failure to provide meaningful material for the therapy session. However, Langs (1981) extends Freud's definition of resistance to include everything that the patient *or* the therapist does that interferes with the communicative network between them. His view of resistance is notably different from that of Freud.

Langs indicates that it is important for the therapist to lay out and maintain the ground rules for therapy, such as fees, length of the session, adherence to the rule of free association, and so on. Once these are set, resistance can be defined as nonadherence to these rules. He suggests that the patient's resistance is often a response to the therapist's failure to "maintain a secure frame" (e.g., the therapist's violation of the rules or inconsistent management), which he labels counterresistance. He believes that many types of client resistances are nonpathological and appropriate defensive responses to therapist errors or improper procedures.

Langs also points out that a critical component of resistance is the decision by the therapist that the patient is being resistive. This adds a subjective component to the concept of resistance, as well as the idea that it is not totally intrapsychic. He states: "It seems best to think of all resistances as interactive" (p. 508). Langs indicates that the backbone of all client resistance is the unconscious communication between patient and therapist. He suggests that there is always an element of countertransference in the therapist's intervention and, in this sense, the therapist is always contributing to the resistance. In short, Langs views resistance as an interactional process and maintains that resistance cannot be analyzed without considering the role the therapist plays in forming or maintaining it.

As can be seen through these descriptions, most of Freud's original concepts have remained intact, although the notion of resistance has begun to move away from a totally intrapsychic model. Some of the ideas presented, especially those of Kohut and Langs, are more compatible with the ones I advocate in this book. For those who want to know more these approaches to resistance, in addition to the original works cited above, more detailed summaries are given by Sandler, Dare, and Holder

(1973); Langs (1981); Marshall (1982); Milman and Goldman (1987); Strean (1990); and Stark (1994a, 1994b).

Nonpsychoanalytic Theories

Contrary to what a number of people have written, the concept of resistance has not been ignored by nonpsychoanalytic therapists. Over the years, a great deal has been written about the topic, but the significance of resistance for psychotherapy, as well as its definition, has changed. None of the more modern therapeutic approaches have emphasized the importance of resistance as much as Freud or his followers did, and most theorists have taken a much broader view of it. For example, intrapsychic or unconscious factors are typically deemphasized, and environmental or interpersonal factors are often included as a component of its definition. The following section reviews some of these viewpoints.

Phenomenological Philosophy

Humanistic/phenomenological/existential approaches have viewed resistance in a fashion somewhat similar to Freud's in that they see it as serving a defensive function. Mahoney (1991) calls this viewpoint self-protective resistance. May (1967a, p. 95), for example, states that "sickness is precisely the method that the individual uses to preserve his being." May adds that resistance may be the client's way of avoiding his or her own uniqueness and potential, and avoiding responsibility and freedom. He states: "Thus 'social conformity' is a general form of resistance in life; and even the patient's acceptance of the doctrines and interpretations of the therapist may itself be an expression of resistance" (1967b, p. 79). He sums up his position by saying that "the purpose of psychotherapy is to set people free" (May, 1981, p. 19).

Angyal (1965) holds a similar concept of resistance and says that "Resistance is not just inertia; it is the active self-defense of the neurotic pattern" (p. 275). He suggests that resistance does not necessarily decline in the course of therapy but, rather, "As long as the therapist's interpretations touch merely the periphery of the neurosis, things may move along smoothly, but when the core patterns are approached, the neurotic pattern will not take the threat lying down" (p. 275).

Rogers (1961) has a similar view but suggests that resistance serves to protect the client's self-concept and is often expressed as an unwillingness to self-disclose. However, he does not see resistance as an inevitable part of therapy. He states: "More specifically, it grows out of unwise attempts on the part of the counselor to short-cut the therapeutic process by bringing into the discussion emotionalized attitudes which the client is not yet ready to face" (1942, p. 151). Although this is a simplification, Rogers suggests that resistance can be eliminated through a strong patient–therapist relationship and the use of therapeutic conditions such as unconditional positive regard, genuineness, and empathy, which help promote self-actualization.

The existential psychoanalyst Bugental (1965, 1978, 1987) proposes that resistance represents patients' fear of meeting their own real or authentic selves. He describes it as such: "The therapeutic task when the resistances have been in some appreciable degree confronted and worked through becomes that of supporting the client in a journey into and through hell" (1978, p. 75). Another way of saying this is that the intent of resistance is not to withhold information from the therapist but, rather, from oneself.

Bugental (1987) describes several dimensions of resistance:

1. *Interview resistance:* This is the first sign of resistance and occurs at the initial contact with the client.

2. *Life-pattern resistance:* These are forms of resistance presented in the therapy sessions that are typical behavioral patterns in the outside world. They are often similar to the interview resistance in type.

3. *Life-limiting processes:* Bugental suggests that these resistances are central to the person's problems and may be related to seeking therapy in the first place. He describes these as "life patterns which also operate to keep her from immersion in herself, which interfere with self discovery, which pervade her life outside therapy" (1987, p. 177). He equates this type as being similar to "transference neurosis."

4. *The self-and-world construct system:* This is the all-encompassing system that clients develop in order to function in the world. According to Bugental, it defines what and who we are in relation to the world around us. It includes not only all of the resistance patterns described here, but also the positive and constructive behaviors that are used to survive emotionally. Bugental agrees with Freud that the resistances presented in therapy are crucial because they show the true character of the client.

Bugental suggests that resistance in therapy serves a number of functions. It limits self-disclosure; keeps the sessions objective or impersonal; postpones feelings and thoughts until the client has "previewed" them; keeps control of the sessions in terms of direction and intensity; and avoids directly experiencing certain types of emotions. He takes the position that resistances cannot be removed unless the client is truly motivated to change, and that simple verbal feedback to clients about a resistance pattern is not likely to be effective. He also suggests that "awareness of single resistive patterns is less effective than recognition of constellations of patterns in relation to the deeper need structures they serve" (p. 183). Bugental (1987) offers some detailed and specific techniques for dealing with the types of resistance described.

The Gestalt therapist Fritz Perls originally saw resistance in a manner somewhat similar to Freud's, but eventually changed his outlook. Perls (1947/1969) believes that Freud and his followers place too much emphasis on anal resistances (withholding and refusing to let go) and ignore the other types. For Perls, the most important type of resistance is the oral type, which is related to the inhibition of aggression (Perls, 1947/1969). He states: "Freud treated his patients like children sitting on the chamber-pot, persuading, urging them to bring out whatever was in their minds without yielding to their embarrassment" (pp. 112–113). Yet, Perls believes that the methods of psychoanalysis actually contribute to resistance. For example, instead of promoting free association, Perls suggests that patients should express anything they *experience* (including feelings of shame, embarrassment, and physical sensations), but they should not be unduly forced. In this way, Perls believes that patients can truly experience their resistances, as opposed to deadening them through compulsory free association. Similarly, he does not think that it is sufficient to make unconscious material conscious; rather, it has to be reevaluated and reexperienced before the patient can accept it.

Perls holds the more contemporary view that resistance is not an impediment to the therapy process. He believes that if patients have a tendency to avoid something, it must be for a good reason. He suggests that resistances be viewed from the perspective of the client (Perls, Hefferline, & Goodman, 1951). For example, resistance might help clients suppress unwanted aspects of their personality (Perls, 1947). Perls also suggests that since therapy is aggressive in attacking clients' illness, which in some ways is their ally, resistance should be seen as a naturally occurring counteraggression (Perls, Hefferline, & Goodman, 1951).

Similar to Bugental, Perls generally views resistance as a way of avoiding awareness of various elements of oneself or one's environment. Instead of overcoming resistance, it should be analyzed and brought into clients' awareness. In this way, clients can get back in touch with previously relinquished or alienated thoughts and feelings. He suggests that psychotherapy helps clients discover why they need the resistance. However, this will not be an easy task because some of these feelings may be intolerable, and the client has worked so hard to avoid them. Yet, Perls maintains that experience is the only way that closure and healing can occur. As Breshold (1989) implies, patients often want an easy "magic cure," but successful therapy usually involves hard work and pain. Overall, Perls sees resistances as valuable energies that have been turned inward toward the self, and the purpose of therapy is to redirect them back toward the environment again. In this sense, the job of the therapist is to support the resistances rather than overcome them (Breshold, 1989).

Behaviorism

For the most part, behaviorists have not viewed resistance in the traditional manner, nor have they made it a focus of their therapy. Resistance has periodically been labeled countercontrol (Davison, 1973), resistance to direction (Hersen, 1971), reactance, nonobedience, or nonconformity (Kanfer & Schefft, 1988). Hersen (1971) suggests that behaviorists have not written more about resistance because of the manner in which therapists publish their case histories (e.g., reports are too brief to discuss resistance or other issues). Similarly, most journals do not publish reports of treatment failures.

Although behaviorists have not written a great deal about resistance, it has not been totally ignored either. An early study by Weinberg and Zaslove (1963) described three types of resistance they encountered while using systematic desensitization. They called these direct resistance, indirect resistance, and resistance related to the research setting. The first type included restlessness, boredom, or uncooperativeness. Indirect resistance involved not practicing relaxation exercises at home, not following rules or coming late to appointments, and the third type included lack of motivation or trying to please the therapist.

In another early study, D'Alessio (1968) suggested that resistance may be due to (1) patients having problems complying with authority figures or males; (2) patients wanting to have a different relationship with the therapist than what is offered (e.g., wanting sympathy, attention, love); (3) patients not really wanting to change behavior or reduce symptoms, and (4) patients wanting to impress the therapist with their intellect and abilities. It is interesting to note that both Weinberg and Zaslove (1963) and D'Alessio (1968) suggest using more traditional psychotherapy approaches such as interpretation and support, when dealing with resistance.

More recently, Munjack and Oziel (1978) divide resistance into five distinct types. In Type I, patients lack an understanding of the purpose of the intervention or how to carry it out. This would include clients who are unsophisticated or are concrete thinkers. In this case, the therapist should be careful to explain his or her expectations on a level that clients can understand.

Type II resistance results from skill deficits. An example would be a person who does not comply with a homework assignment because of poor reading ability, or a person who lacks certain interpersonal skills.

Type III resistance is characterized by a lack of motivation. Basically, the person does not want to change, does not believe change is necessary, or does not believe he or she has the ability to change. I explored this issue in depth in Chapter 2.

Type IV resistance results when the therapy makes the client feel anxious or guilty. This would include clients' reluctance to disclose embarrassing material.

Type V results from secondary gains or positive reinforcement resulting from the symptoms. These would include insurance or disability payments, getting out of work, attention, and the like. Although these categories may not be exhaustive, they are representative of the types of behaviors most therapists label as resistance.

Other behavior therapists consider resistance to be either noncompliance with treatment methods (e.g., Shelton & Levy, 1981), or the inability of the therapist to design an effective treatment program. Speaking of the latter, Lazarus and Fay (1982) suggest that "The concept of 'resistance' is probably the most elaborate rationalization that therapists employ to explain their treatment failures" (p. 115). They suggest that seven factors are responsible for most treatment failures:

1. Inappropriate therapist–patient matching or lack of rapport
2. Therapist's failure to conduct an accurate assessment
3. Therapist's failure to deal with client's social network
4. Therapist's use of incorrect techniques
5. Therapist's lack of training or experience or incorrect use of appropriate techniques
6. Extreme biological or psychological deficits in the patient
7. The desired outcome is not valued by patient (p. 120)

They also note that one of the most significant signs of resistance is not completing homework assignments. In general, they conclude that if the patient is not getting better, it is largely (though not entirely) the therapist's fault.

Lewis and Evans (1986) suggest that in order to label a client's behavior appropriately as resistive, a number of conditions must be met. First, the therapist must be working in a competent manner. This generally means that the correct diagnosis has been made and that appropriate treatment procedures have been selected (those that have been shown to be effective in the past under similar conditions) and correctly implemented. Second, there should be some objective way to measure progress, since previous research has found that subjective measures may not always be reliable (Lewis & Evans, 1986; Nisbett & Ross, 1980). A third condition is a determination that the client is not progressing at a pace deemed appropriate by the therapist. This last step may introduce some problems because the process is usually very subjective and our expectations may not be realistic. For example, a novice therapist who expects to make rapid changes in anyone with severe mental illness (e.g. schizophrenia or borderline personality disorder) is in for a great disappointment. Even with less disturbed individuals, the rate at which patients "should" be progressing may be difficult to determine. This again tends to underscore the importance of viewing resistance as an interrelational rather than an intrapsychic process.

Kanfer and Schefft (1988) generally view resistance as the discrepancy between clients' behavior and the therapist's expectations. They give several typical reasons that clients are sometimes not cooperative. The most important one is the fear of change (e.g., unwillingness to give up a known, though distressing life-style for an unknown future). Other factors include clients' lack of confidence in being able to carry out the therapeutic program or simply their lack of the necessary skills to do so; clients' tendencies to remain passive and avoid making decisions; their tendencies to avoid responsibility and to blame others for their failures; clients' poor experiences in previous therapy; secondary gains; fear of losing social networks that require them to be helpless or incompetent; failure to perceive alternatives for their lives; and their belief in fate. The authors suggest that therapists need to analyze the source of resistance before attempting to deal with it. In a similar vein, Goldstein and Higginbotham (1991) suggest that many people may be what they call "low relatability" clients. For these clients, they recommend relationship-enhancing techniques.

In an effort to further understand and better define resistance, some behavioral researchers have suggested that it be studied empirically (Hersen, 1971; Jahn & Lichstein, 1980). Under this rubric, studies have shown that behaviors related to resistance may be reduced by contracting (Baekeland & Lundwall, 1975; Kirschenbaum & Flannery, 1983), through the use of relaxation training (Goldfried, Decenteceo, & Weinberg, 1974), or through other reinforcement and behavioral techniques (Southam & Dunbar, 1986; Masek, 1982; Meichenbaum & Turk, 1987). Similarly, Chamberlain, Patterson, Reid, Kavanagh, and Forgatch (1984) have developed a system that measures resistant behaviors more objectively. Using this method with parent training interventions, they found that resistance tends to be lowest at the beginning and end of therapy, and highest in the middle stages, when the greatest amount of change is being proposed. In addition, they found that clients who had initial high levels of resistance were more likely to drop out of therapy.

Overall, it appears that behaviorists have followed Hersen's (1971) suggestion to pay more attention to the topic of resistance, and to develop strategies for addressing it in therapy.

Cognitive Model

Speaking from a cognitive-behavioral point of view and espousing his own form of therapy, Ellis (1985) has written a book dedicated entirely to the topic of resistance. Although it deals primarily with the use of rational-emotive therapy (RET) in overcoming resistance, Ellis makes a number of points that transcend any particular theory. For example, he believes that one of the strongest and basic types of resistance is low frustration tolerance, or what he terms "discomfort anxiety." This involves a basic opposition to change and a desire to maintain the status quo even when this is uncomfortable or even painful for the client (p. 11). Later, Ellis (1987) expands on this idea and suggests that humans have a general tendency to succumb to the "pleasures of the moment" rather than consider long-term effects of their behaviors. This is a theme that can be found among many other psychotherapeutic approaches as well. He also points out, as have others, that treatment does not necessarily lead to generalization and maintenance, and that this has to be specifically built into the treatment program, especially for resistive clients. Ellis maintains that clients' degree of resistance and reasons for being resistive are constantly changing and that therapists take great risks if they presume to know why a client is being resistive. He suggests that no single psychotherapeutic theory explains why a client is being resistive, so therapists should be open to other ideas or approaches. Finally, Ellis points out that therapists can often play a major role in contributing to clients' resistance and therefore need to explore how they influence or may even be the main cause of resistance (see also Newman, 1994).

Other cognitive therapists have developed their own notion of resistance. One theory stems from the idea that people organize their perceptions of the world into cognitive structures, which serve as the foundation for each person's comprehension of reality. Once formed, some of these constructs are difficult to change. For example, one of the most powerful constructs is the way an individual perceives the self. Because therapy often involves the introduction of ideas that are inconsistent with the person's self-perception, it may result in a cognitive rejection of such ideas, which is then labeled "resistance" (Kirmayer, 1990). This type of reaction is more likely to occur in brief forms of therapy where an individual may not have enough time to adjust to proposed changes.

Mahoney (1982, 1991) makes a similar point and suggests that resistance to change may actually be due to hereditary factors. He states,

"There is a sensed survival value in protecting and perpetuating old reality constructions —especially those which are more central to our experience" (1982, p. 106). The latter are the important values or beliefs a person may have or perceptions about the self regardless of whether or not these are valid. Liotti (1987) adds to this idea while discussing the role of resistance: "Its implications in the overall mental life are (1) that it affords stability to the cognitive-behavioral-emotional system (of which it is a core aspect) and (2) that it is bound to the patient's need to predict life experiences and give meaning to them" (p. 101). According to this viewpoint, without this type of stabilizing force, human behavior would be chaotic and unpredictable.

Another example of a cognitive type of resistance is called psychological reactance (Brehm, 1966). This is a person's attempt to restore lost or threatened freedom. In therapeutic situations, reactance may lead to noncompliance, which is the client's way to maintain or restore control (Dowd & Seibel, 1990). In this sense, resistance is generated by the method one uses to request change rather than the behavior that is requested to change (see Strong & Matross, 1973). To reduce reactance, Brehm (1976) suggests that therapists not come on too strong, not be too eager to persuade, and not oversell ideas. Although reactance is not a trait, people seem to differ in their "reactance potential" (Tennen, Rohrbaugh, Press, & White, 1981). As some writers have noted, if reactance were normally distributed within the population, at one extreme we would find people abnormally helpless or hopeless, and, at the other, persons who constantly oppose everyone. Both of these groups would make poor psychotherapy candidates.

Dowd and Seibel (1990) suggest that if were possible to accurately measure reactance in psychotherapy, it would aid the therapist in designing and offering compatible treatment methods. For example, paradoxical procedures might be useful for persons who are highly reactant (Tennen, Rohrbaugh, Press, & White, 1981), while those with low to average scores may respond to more traditional therapy (Dowd & Trutt, 1988). Although methods for assessing this variable have been developed (e.g., Dowd, Milne, & Wise, 1991; McDermott & Apter, 1988), it appears that most therapists have not yet made use of this capability.

Systems Theory

System theorists and strategic therapists have developed their own concepts of resistance. Although these vary depending on the model being followed, resistance is typically not viewed through the traditional linear cause-and-effect model. These therapists tend to see it instead as an interactional problem involving the various components of the system being treated. Seaburn (1989) explains it in this way: "If there is not a working relationship among all factors in therapy (therapist, client, significant others, context) movement will not occur" (p. 53). Rather than originating within the individual, resistance is said to come from diverse sources, including client–therapist interactions, family influences, and other system components (Seaburn, 1989). For example, what is labeled resistance might be an effort by the family to protect its members (Stanton & Todd, 1981). Thus, a child who is the identified client in therapy may act out whenever he senses that his parents are about to split up.

Erickson (1964) has an interesting notion of resistance in the sense that he sees it as being an integral part of the reason that the client seeks or is asked to go to treatment in the first place. For example, he describes patients who are hostile, antagonistic, and defensive, and who go out of their way to be uncooperative. However, these characteristics are part of their personality. In this case, the resistance is viewed and treated largely as another symptom.

Erickson believes that symptoms are primarily the ways that clients communicate with the therapist about their problems. While accepting these symptoms, he defines them in ways that allow for them to be changed. For example, in one of his reported cases, he relabeled a young's man impotency as being due to his new wife's overwhelming beauty. In this case, the symptom is viewed not as a psychological entity but, rather, as a way patients deal with others or themselves—for example, as a means to some end, such as to promote caring, closeness and stability (Weeks & L'Abate, 1982). In this case, the symptom is viewed in positive rather than negative terms. According to Erickson, by paradoxically accepting or even encouraging resistance, the therapist can better understand clients, establish rapport, and instill an attitude of trust. Thus, a client who is functionally paralyzed with helplessness and hopelessness is told that she is simply preparing for significant changes that lie ahead.

Haley's (1963) system of psychotherapy is based on several premises. The first is that change is not possible without a strong relationship between client and therapist. The second is that all psychotherapentic methods pose various paradoxes for the client. For example, Haley suggests that in all relationships, both parties will react in ways that will maintain the status quo. He states:

> Granting that people in ongoing relationships function as "governors" in relation to one another, and granting that it is the function of a governor to diminish change, then the first law of relationships follows: *When one person indicates a change in relation to another, the other will act upon the first to diminish and modify that change.* (1963, p. 189, emphasis in the original).

Implicit in this law is that a therapist should avoid asking clients to change, but by doing so he or she sets up a paradox: "in a framework designed to bring about change, he does not ask for change" (p. 189). Haley goes on to suggest several other paradoxes common in most if not all types of therapy:

1. Psychotherapy is said to be a voluntary relationship, yet the therapist insists that clients not miss any appointments and not terminate treatment "prematurely." Doing so invokes the label of resistance.
2. Clients are asked to form an extremely intimate relationship with the therapist and instructed to reveal "everything" to him or her, yet the therapist usually refuses to have anything to do with clients outside the session or office.
3. Clients often come to therapy because they have problems that they cannot solve, and therefore they seek the help of an expert. Frequently the first response of the "expert" is to put the client in charge.
4. "In nondirective therapy the patient is asked to be spontaneous and responsive to a man who is unresponsive and unspontaneous" (p. 187).

Because of these paradoxes and others, Haley suggests that paradoxical strategies are necessary to overcome the resistance to change. Some of these methods are explored in Chapter 4.

McHolland (1985) has come up with a number of strategies for dealing with resistance. Although these are designed to be used with adolescents, some of them may be useful for other age groups as well.

1. Determine the system the resistance serves—the client, the family, peers, or even the client–therapist system.
2. Identify the positive-protective function of the resistance and try to determine how it is positive.
3. Work with the resistance rather than against it. For example, label it in a positive way or use paradoxical techniques.
4. Try to determine the effect of change on the person's system. Will it permit change? Can it be used as an ally?

To summarize, system, strategic, and family therapists view resistance as a natural component of change and therefore try to work with it as opposed to "overcoming" it. To do so, Haley (1963) suggests that therapists must: (1) convince clients that change is possible; (2) get clients to a point where they allow the therapist to help them change, and (3) persuade clients to carry out the steps necessary for change. Some of the techniques that can be used for these purposes include hypnosis (Erickson, 1964), reframing or paradoxical interventions (DeBord, 1989;

Watzalawick, Weakland, & Fisch, 1974), and other nontraditional procedures (see Haley, 1963, 1973; Bergman, 1985).

Summary and Conclusion

As the preceding sections have shown, resistance can be viewed from a
number of different perspectives. Some professionals have tried to find
commonalities across theories in terms of overt resistive behaviors. For
example, Otani (1989) proposes that client resistance can be represented
by four broad categories of behaviors. Category A, called response quantity resistance, involves reducing the *amount* of information given to the
therapist. Some examples are silence or minimum talking. Category B,
response content resistance, restricts the *type* of information given to
the therapist. Examples are symptom preoccupation, small talk, intel-
lectualization and rhetorical questions. Category C, response style resistance, is defined as *how* the client communicates with the therapist.
Examples include thought censoring or editing, forgetting, last minute
disclosures, and seductiveness. Category D, logistic management resistance, is defined as the client breaking basic rules of counseling. Examples are poor attendance or noncompliance. Although these categories are not exhaustive, the overt behaviors that most therapists call
resistance may be similar (Otani, 1989b; Verhulst & van de Vijver, 1990).

These explanations of resistance demonstrate that many therapists
still view resistance as emanating primarily from the client. Chapter 1
introduced an alternative model that forms the basic premise of this book.
The argument was made that resistance should not be viewed as an
intrapsychic process but, rather, as one that involves the interaction of
client, therapist, and the outside social system.

Resistance is not limited to psychotherapy clients, as anyone who
has tried to teach or supervise others can attest. In fact, some of the most
"resistive" individuals may themselves be therapists who doggedly hang
on to theories or techniques that long ago stopped being useful. Most, if
not all, human endeavors that require change, effort, discomfort, and
some loss of independence result in resistance. Furthermore, change is
resisted not only by individuals, but also by organizations, corporations,
nations, or other large groups of people. Suffice to say that resistance
should be looked on as the norm rather than the exception. Resistance
can be found in medical treatment (Matthews & Hingston, 1977; DiMatteo
& DiNicola, 1982; Gerber & Nehemkis, 1986), group and family therapy
(Yalom, 1966, 1970; Anderson & Stewart, 1983), sex therapy (Weissberg
& Levay, 1981), marital therapy (Luther & Loev, 1981), and virtually all
other therapeutic relationships.

Appendix B

Reluctant Clients

Overview

Appendix B will discuss some of the factors that promote or prevent individuals from seeking professional help for their problems. A general review of treatment attrition is provided, as well as a discussion on missed psychotherapy appointments. It is important to note that terminating therapy may at times be an appropriate response. For example, sometimes the client–therapist "fit" is just not right, or clients have reached the level of change that they want at a particular point. These issues will be further discussed later.

The Reluctant Client

Assuming that psychotherapy is useful and the individual will benefit from the experience, an important issue is how to get clients who truly need treatment into a service system. Resistance to psychotherapy often appears as soon as people start to think about getting help for their problems. Lemkau, Bryant, and Brickman (1982) present the problem this way: "Prospective clients approach psychotherapy with ambivalence. Only when the pain, embarrassment or incapacitation of their symptoms is great enough to overshadow their apprehensions do they turn to a professional helper" (p. 187). Previous research is consistent with this viewpoint in that clients tend to seek therapy only for problems they consider serious, and very often many months go by between problem recognition and treatment entry (Saunders, 1993).

Even after recognizing that a problem exists, most people with psychological disorders do not seek professional help (Regier, Narrow, Rae,

Manderscheid, Locke, & Goodwin, 1993). Ellis (1985) suggests that some people simply refuse to admit to themselves that they are disturbed enough to need psychological treatment. Kushner and Sher (1991) estimate that 15 percent of Americans are in need of mental health services, yet only 3 percent actually make use of them. Using more recent data, Regier et al. (1993) estimate that about 29 percent of Americans have a diagnosable mental or substance abuse disorder, but only 6 percent make use of specialty mental health services. The difference between the number of clients who need treatment and those who actually get it has been labeled the "service gap" (Stefl & Prosperi, 1985). Some of the barriers to mental health treatment identified by Stefl and Prosperi (1985) include awareness of services, ability of getting to services, the stigma associated with treatment and affordability.

Fisher, Winer, and Abramowitz (1983, pp. 165–167) describe some potential pretherapy stages of behaviors that might help us understand why people do or do not decide to seek help for their psychological problems.

Stage 1 is called perception and identification of a problem. Before looking for help, an individual must first be aware that a psychological problem exists and that it may have some aversive consequences if not addressed. Stage 2 is called contemplating ways of helping oneself. Here individuals might wait for the problem to correct itself, try to change without the help of professionals, or decide that they can live with the problem. At stage 3,people make the decision to seek or accept help. Individuals who reach this stage have weighed the potential benefits of seeking therapy against the costs and decided that it is worth the risk. Many people, however, never reach this stage because they foresee many disadvantages associated with seeking professional help. Stage 4 is called the precipitating event. The authors maintain that individuals often need some significant event to mobilize them actually to seek help, and that without this they might be in a state of indecision for months or years. This might include their symptoms getting worse, hearing about a particular therapist, receiving positive feedback about getting help from their family, or other similar occurrence.

Stage 5 is called overt help-seeking behavior. Here,individuals will start looking for therapists and setting up appointments. Even at this level, the process can stall if the person does not have the skills necessary to find a therapist or if other factors (expense, transportation, etc.) get in the way of actually getting help.

In a similar help-seeking study, Saunders, (1993) identifies four stages similar to these. He suggests that clients' inability to recognize that a problem exists is one of the strongest barriers to seeking treatment. In addition, the time between problem recognition and actual treatment

> **Recommendations: Reducing Attrition**
> 1. Clearly explain the rationale, duration, possible results, and side effects of the treatment that you will provide, and the client's role in this process.
>
> ---
>
> **Recommendations: Reducing Attrition**
> 2. If clients have previously dropped out of treatment, thoroughly explore the reasons for this at the beginning of therapy.
>
> ---
>
> **Recommendations: Reducing Attrition**
> 3. Minimize therapist absences or session cancellations.

(which can be years) often exacerbates the symptoms, which may then make therapy much more difficult. During this gap, clients tend to use a number of coping mechanisms to deal with their problems; these include drugs and alcohol, self-help books, support groups, family or peers, and denial. People's social networks seem to be very important in that their attitude toward mental health treatment is often the deciding factor in whether professional help is sought or not. Overall, the road to psychological treatment is often a long and difficult one because individuals might get "stuck" at any one of the stages described here, or might start and terminate the process a number of times before finally getting help.

Garfield (1986) has offered a number of similar reasons that people initially reject therapy: inadequate motivation, fear of finding out they have a severe impairment, the stigma associated with seeing a therapist, and difficulty acknowledging they have a problem or need help. However, he adds that an adequate explanation for this phenomenon is currently lacking. Kushner and Sher (1991) suggest that the fear of treatment prevents many people from seeking and using mental health services. They describe a number of potential fears that the public may have about therapy, including fear of embarrassment, which would include talking about problems that are very sensitive or secret; fear of change; fear of being hospitalized or forced to use medications; fear that their symptoms will get worse; fear that therapy will bring back traumatic memories or events; and fear of being asked to engage in anxiety-producing behaviors (e.g., exposure-based treatment). They add that certain of these fears may be rational, whereas others may not. Also, some may be treatment-specific rather than person-specific. For example, individuals may not hesitate to get treatment for anxiety but may balk at pursuing treatment for a sexual disorder. The authors suggest that novel methods such as telephone counseling, outreach programs, or creative marketing techniques may be useful in reaching these types of persons, although some of these methods are controversial.

Munjack and Oriel (1978) suggest that many people resist treatment because they have little or no hope of being able to change. Without hope, they will likewise lack the motivation to seek therapy or engage in behaviors that are necessary for change. These authors point out that this lack of perceived success is usually due to a number of factors, including previous poor outcome in therapy, negative beliefs or attitudes toward psychological treatment, a pervasive feeling of hopelessness resulting from lifelong experiences, and conditions perceived as being beyond their control. The authors offer the following suggestions when facing these clients:

1. Bring their pessimism out in the open and deal with it immediately.
2. Give clients an idea of a realistic length of therapy and what they can expect at each stage.
3. Have clients predict what benefits or consequences they can expect from changing their behavior.

These issues have previously been explored.

Speaking from a psychoanalytic point of view, Strean (1990) suggests that the thought of initiating psychotherapy arouses fear of being treated like a child or being placed in a submissive position. The need for therapy may be seen as a threat to one's independence and a blow to one's self-esteem. It may also be viewed as an admission of failure in some aspect of life (such as marriage or child rearing). Often clients will make the first contact with a mental health professional even though they remain skeptical about it. He suggests that many people delay searching for a therapist for months or perhaps years, and that the initial phone contact with a client is extremely important. For example, some people may use this as an attempt to gather information that will prevent them from beginning therapy, such as finding out the fee is too high or that the therapist does not have the "right" degree or orientation. Others may make unusual or unrealistic requests of the therapist and expect these to be turned down as a way of excluding themselves from therapy. Strean suggests limiting any information over the phone to a bare minimum and convincing clients to agree to an initial face-to-face meeting instead. He also suggests that extremely reluctant clients may need time before beginning therapy, and that several preliminary phone contacts may be needed.

In a similar vein, Talmon (1990) writes that preliminary phone contacts should be considered part of the therapy process and, if possible, should be done by the therapist rather than support staff. He suggests

---

Recommendations: Reducing Attrition
4. Maintain contact with clients' families and social network and enlist their help if necessary.

Recommendations: Reducing Attrition
5. If appropriate, use brief therapy and emphasize procedures with rapid symptom relief.

Recommendations: Reducing Attrition
6. Refer clients for medications or other ancillary services when indicated.

---

that many factors may influence whether clients will decide to come to the first session or not—for example, how long the phone rings before being answered, and whether or for how long they are placed on hold. Interestingly, he suggests that clients who are asked *how* they can be helped are more likely to attend the first session.

In looking at variables that predict help seeking behaviors, Fisher, Winer, and Abramowitz (1983) conclude that middle-class persons, women, whites, Jews, and youths are most likely to seek help from professionals. However, the factors that make people with these characteristics more inclined to go into therapy are not clearly understood. Other studies have identified client variables such as motivation, age, income level, socioeconomic class, and self-referral as being positively correlated with making or keeping the first therapy appointment.

Preintake "No-Shows"

Even after clients make the decision to seek therapy, they often never make it to the first session. One study reported that approximately one-half of college students referred for counseling over an eight-year period failed to keep their first appointment (Phillips & Fagan, 1982). Another found the no-show rate at two community mental health centers to be 21 percent and 24 percent, respectively (Larsen, Nguyen, Green, & Attkisson, 1983). It appears that men may be more likely to refuse treatment than women (Hafner, 1983). Overall, between 20 and 50 percent of clients scheduled for psychotherapy never attend their sessions (Larsen et al., 1983; Garfield, 1986; Palmer & Hampton, 1987). Further, the problem is not limited to individual therapy. For example, Klein & Carroll (1986) found that 41 percent of clients referred for outpatient group therapy did not show up for the first session.

In trying to find out why clients skip their initial meetings, Noonan (1973) questioned a group of 64 clients who missed their first appointment. The following types of explanations (in order of frequency) were reported: Clients did not know why they missed; clients forgot about the appointment; condition improved; clients were anxious about receiving treatment. He also indicates that persons who identify a specific problem when they make their appointment (e.g., a phobia, obsessive thought, etc.) are more likely to attend than those with vague or evasive reasons. However, unlike some other studies, he found no relationship between missed appointments and age, gender, education, marital status, or number of days between contact and appointment (see also Orme & Boswell, 1991).

On the positive side, it is possible that more than one-third of clients who do not begin therapy improve without it (Baekeland & Lundwall, 1975; Frances & Clarkin, 1981). Of course, this is influenced by the type and severity of the psychological disorder; those with more severe impairments may show little or no improvement without therapy. Clients' premorbid or pretreatment qualities are also important. Clients who have high self-esteem, an adequate social support system, and a better education appear to be better prepared to cope with their problems without treatment. Similarly, clients who are nonpsychotic, not severely depressed, or have a crisis oriented problem are more likely to improve without treatment than are other individuals.

Frances and Clarkin (1981) indicate that many clients would be better off without therapy but suggest that most mental health professionals are reluctant to advise this. They report that clients who should not be offered treatment include those who are likely to have a negative therapeutic reaction (e.g., persons with certain personality disorders), those who enter treatment to support a lawsuit or disability claim, chronically dependent "treatment addicted" clients, and those who have made little progress in repeated previous therapy attempts. Although some of the points the authors make are valid, it may be difficult to initially screen out such clients, and for a variety of other reasons, many therapists would probably be uncomfortable with this approach. However, the interested reader should see Mays and Franks (1985) for a detailed discussion of this issue.

Treatment Attrition

Research suggests that 30 to 60 percent of outpatient psychotherapy clients drop out prematurely. One study found that over 40% of community mental health clients failed to return after the initial intake interview (Sue, McKinney, & Allen, 1976). Sue and Sue (1990) report that approxi-

---

Recommendations: Reducing Attrition

7. Make use of pretherapy orientation and client satisfaction assessments.

Recommendations: Reducing Attrition

8. Deal with clients' feelings of helplessness and hopelessness early in treatment.

---

mately half of minority group psychotherapy clients do not show up for their second appointment. Albers and Scrivner (1977) suggest that of clients seeking community mental health services, only about 5 percent enter and complete a recommended program. Mennicke, Lent & Burgoyne (1988) report that approximately 25 percent of clients in college counseling centers drop out after the intake session. Baekeland and Lundwall (1975) reviewed literally hundreds of articles related to treatment termination and found that in public psychiatric centers, 20 percent to 57 percent of clients fail to return after the first visit, and that 31 percent to 56 percent of patients attend only about four sessions. In addition to individual therapy, dropping out is also a problem with group therapy (Bostwick, 1987; McCallum, Piper, & Joyce, 1992), marital therapy (Allgood & Crane, 1991), family therapy (Lowman, DeLange, Roberts, & Brad, 1984), and in the treatment of children and adolescents (Weisz, Weiss, & Langmeyer, 1987; Suzuki, 1989).

Phillips (1985) has reviewed a large number of studies with different client groups in a variety of settings and concludes that a negatively accelerating declining attrition curve is commonly found. He prefers the use of the term *attrition* to *dropout* because clients do not necessarily leave treatment because they are unsatisfied or because they have not been helped. Specifically, Phillips reports that most people leave therapy during the first two sessions, and then continue to flow out before mutual termination occurs. Overall, he found that the mean number of psychotherapy sessions attended is 5, and approximately 80 percent of clients terminate therapy by the fifth or sixth session.

Phillips notes that the intake interview seems to be especially important since about 50 percent of clients do not return after this session. For many, this seems to be the decision point of whether to continue with therapy or not. With this in mind, one approach to reduce dropouts might be to expand the initial interview and combine assessment procedures with treatment. In this way, clients might gain enough symptom relief to motivate them to attend further sessions (see also Chapter 1). Phillips also suggests that more emphasis can be given to short-term or brief therapy, with treatment plans designed to last a maximum of five to ten sessions. This approach, which has recently become popular, seems appropriate for many clients because a number of studies indicate that few outpatients either need or want long-term psychotherapy (Bennett & Wisneski, 1979; Koss, 1979; Pekarik, 1985a; Pekarik & Wierzbick, 1986; see Budman & Gurman, 1988, and de Shazer, 1988, for a detailed description of brief psychotherapy).

Sledge, Moras, Hartley, and Levine (1990) found that the dropout rate for clients in time-limited therapy was about half that for open-ended treatment (32 percent versus 61 percent). However, as Mackenzie (1991) points out, brief therapy requires careful screening of clients who are likely to benefit from this type of approach. Although some therapists may frown on the use of time-limited treatment, with the possibility that managed care will become the norm in the provision of mental health services, planned brief psychotherapy may soon be mandated rather than an option (see Austad & Berman, 1991; Austad, 1992) .

An even more extreme approach is offering a planned one-session treatment program (e.g., Bloom, 1981). For example, Talmon (1990) found that the modal number of therapy sessions for all psychotherapists in a large medical center in California was one, and suggests formalizing this arrangement. In his book *Single-Session Therapy,* Talmon describes clients who may be suitable for this type of intervention. These include persons who have a highly specific problem; clients who can use friends or family members as natural supports; clients who need to be referred to other nonpsychotherapy services (e.g., medications, psychological testing, legal services, etc.); clients who face a truly insoluble problem, and clients who would be better off without treatment (p. 31). He also describes clients who would be unsuitable for one-session therapy, including clients with severe psychological disorders (schizophrenia, bipolar, etc.), clients who may need inpatient care, clients who are suicidal, clients who request long-term therapy, and clients with various personality disorders. His book outlines specific procedures to follow for one-session therapy.

Dropouts in the Private Sector

Koss (1979) looked at the length of psychotherapy for clients in private practice and found that the median number of sessions was eight. Fourteen percent of these clients dropped out after the first session, half by the tenth session, and two-thirds by the fifteenth. Only 20 percent of clients had twenty-five or more therapy sessions. This figure is interesting in light of the study by Howard, Kopta, Krause, and Orlinsky (1986), which shows little therapeutic improvement after the twenty-fifth ses-

> **Recommendations: Reducing Attrition**
> 9. Make contact with clients between the first and second session, which is when they are most likely to drop out.
>
> ---
>
> **Recommendations: Reducing Attrition**
> 10. Consider the behaviors of your support staff, such as being polite and answering the phone in a timely manner.

sion. In general, Koss concludes that the dropout rate for public and private clients is basically the same.

DuBrin and Zastowny (1988) looked at 426 private practice patients in New York State who did not request a time-limited contract (fewer than nine sessions) and found results similar to those of Koss. Specifically, 13 percent did not show up for the second session, and an additional 104 patients (25 percent) completed 8 or fewer sessions and were classified as dropouts.

Dropout for Clients with Severe Impairments

Premature termination seems to be even more likely for clients with severe psychiatric impairments. For example, approximately 75 percent of schizophrenic patients drop out of outpatient services (Meichenbaum & Turk, 1987; Corrigan, Liberman, and Engel, 1990). Axelrod and Wetzler report that between 30 percent and 64 percent of recently discharged psychiatric patients fail to attend their first aftercare appointment, and only about 30 percent complete this program. A similar trend is found in drug and alcohol programs, where 20 percent to 60 percent of outpatients miss the first session (Phillips, 1985) and up to 75 percent of the patients drop out before the fourth session (Baekeland & Lundwall, 1975). The same pattern is seen with posttraumatic stress disorders, where one study found the dropout rate to be 81 percent (Burstein, 1986).

Even in inpatient facilities, this problem cannot be completely avoided because clients can drop out of treatment through elopement or can sign themselves out against medical advice. In fact, about 35 percent of inpatients do so (Corrigan, Liberman & Engel, 1990; Chandrasena, 1987). Baekeland and Lundwall (1975) report that inpatients most likely to elope are young, single, African American, court-referred, antisocial, and those with a previous history of elopement or previous inpatient admissions.

Chandrasena (1987) adds unemployment, admission on a Friday, and treatment with neuroleptic drugs to this list.

Factors Affecting Treatment Attrition

Lemkau, Bryant, and Brickman (1982, p. 192) maintain that one of the most important factors related to dropout rates is clients' lack of commitment to therapy. They suggest that this commitment goes through various stages and changes over time. The first phase is one of exploration, where the aversive consequences of symptoms and hope for relief set the stage for seeking help and attending the initial sessions. In the second stage, the costs of therapy (emotional, financial, or effort) become apparent. The client often becomes ambivalent and must decide whether these costs make it worth continuing with therapy. As was discussed, this is when most clients drop out of therapy. In this case, the decision to remain depends on whether clients perceive the rewards of therapy to be reachable and worth the effort. The third stage is the resolution of this ambivalence, with a renewed sense of commitment and enthusiasm. The fourth stage is often marked by boredom and uninterest, where again the positive and negative aspects of therapy are assessed, followed by the fifth and last stage, where a sense of completion and fulfillment prevail.

Supported by social-psychological literature, the authors make a number of suggestions for increasing clients' commitment to therapy. The first step is based on the idea that the more effort that is voluntarily employed in pursuing a freely chosen course of action, the stronger the attraction to that course becomes. Thus, the goal is to produce in the client a perception of a high degree of choice of engaging in target behaviors with minimal extrinsic justification. A second suggestion is based on the foot-in-the-door technique, where making a commitment to a small request makes it more likely that commitment to a larger request will follow. For example, the authors describe a procedure whereby clients make a commitment to attend only three therapy session initially, as opposed to a commitment to an unspecified lengthy course. Having complied with this request, clients are more likely to remain in therapy afterward. Another suggestion is to promote client responsibility for solving their own problems, with the therapist acting as a consultant. Of course, these approaches may need to be shaped up, and this procedure is not appropriate for all clients. Finally, the authors point out that clients' expectations of therapy have both potentially positive and negative consequences. Clients must have high expectations in order to work hard and continue in therapy, but unrealistically high expectations or not be-

---

Recommendations: Reducing Missed Appointments
1. Schedule the intake appointment within seven days of contact, and personally contact clients several days before your first meeting.

Recommendations: Reducing Missed Appointments
2. Try to set up appointments that are most convenient for clients and, if possible, schedule appointments at the same day and hour every week.

---

ing ready for setbacks may lead to dissatisfaction or dropout. The authors suggest distinguishing the ultimate (long-term) goals of therapy from the more immediate course.

In a related manner, clients' readiness for therapy can be assessed through the transtheoretical model of change described in Chapter 2. One study (Smith, Subich, & Kalodner, 1995) found that premature terminators and nonterminators can be distinguished by the stage of change in which they enter therapy. More specifically, clients who enter therapy in the precontemplation stage are more likely to drop out than are those who are in more advanced stages of change. This appears to be a very viable line of research.

In their comprehensive study of premature termination, Baekeland and Lundwall (1975) examine three major issues: (1) the average or typical dropout, (2) why clients typically drop out of treatment, and (3) what happens to dropouts when they leave therapy. These authors generally found that dropping out of therapy is related to three major factors: (1) intrapsychic characteristics such as personality traits; (2) therapist factors such as the therapist's attitudes toward clients; and (3) environmental factors such as family attitudes toward therapy. A summary of their findings follows.

To describe a typical dropout, the authors suggest that three categories of clients can be classified as dropouts: (1) patients who fail to return; (2) patients who refuse to return; and (3) patients who are dropped from treatment because of lack of response, poor cooperation, or similar problems. They found that a number of variables are related to dropping out of therapy. One is age, with younger patients being more likely to drop out. A second factor is gender, with females more likely to drop out of therapy than men. However, this difference may be due to the fact that men are less likely to seek or initiate therapy in the first place, and thus, those who do end up in therapy may be more motivated or committed to attend. A third factor is socioeconomic status, with education, occupation, and income being important. Generally speaking, members of low-income, poorly educated, and unemployed groups are at risk of dropping out. Race has also been studied extensively, and it appears that African Americans and other minorities are more likely to drop out of therapy than are white clients. However, client–therapist matching appears to be an important factor here, as well as other factors which were discussed in Chapter 8. Additional client characteristics related to dropping out are persons who are hospital-referred as opposed to being privately or self-referred. Studies show that self-referred clients are only half as likely to drop out of treatment as "other"-referred patients (Pekarik, 1985). Persons who have dropped out of therapy in the past; persons who are homeless, single, living alone, or not affiliated with any formal groups or organizations; and persons with a below-average IQ are also more likely to drop out.

The clinical features associated with dropouts are both low and high levels of depression, paranoid and sociopathic disorders, substance and alcohol abuse, highly aggressive or passive-aggressive personality characteristics, and greater pathology in general. Low levels of motivation and "psychological mindedness" (see Hall, 1992, for a review of this concept), as well as high levels of defensiveness, are also correlated with dropping out (Baekeland & Lundwall, 1975).

These authors also found that therapist characteristics are important. For example, therapists with greater experience tend to have lower dropout rates. Depending on the setting, however, clients with the most severe problems are sometimes referred to the least experienced therapists, so this finding may be biased. Therapists who appear unconcerned or bored, or who seem to dislike their clients, also lead to more dropouts. In addition, therapists who have negative feelings about the use of medication; who cancel appointments; or who are too permissive, introverted, or detached are likely to lose clients. Finally, male therapists and those who have negative expectations of client improvement are also more likely to have their clients drop out.

Procedural factors that may lead to dropouts are interruptions in the therapy process, therapist substitutions and patient–therapist mismatches. For the last factor, therapists who are similar to their clients in various ways or who share the same treatment assumptions are less likely to have their clients drop out. Of course, it is important to remember that it is usually an elaborate combination of therapist, client, and social/environmental variables that lead to attrition.

In looking at what happens to clients after they drop out of therapy, Baekeland and Lundwall report that the news is not totally negative. Between 20 percent and 40 percent of clients who drop out end up in ser-

Recommendations: Reducing Missed Appointments
3. Give clients cards with dates and times of appointment, and make use of telephone and mail reminders.

Recommendations: Reducing Missed Appointments
4. In cases of chronic missed appointments, contract with clients or obtain verbal or written commitments to attend sessions.

vices elsewhere. Second, clients drop out for all kinds of reasons. Some clients drop out after the initial crisis is over or after they have reached their own treatment goals. These, of course, may be different from those of the therapist. For example, Pekarik (1985) suggests that one reason for high dropout rates is that clients expect and desire treatment to last a significantly shorter time than their therapists do. Also, in at least some cases, clients who drop out are not treatment failures because many of them may have benefited significantly from the therapy. For example, Bloom (1981) has reported that approximately 70 percent of clients who had only one intake session reported satisfaction with their encounter. However, other studies suggest that clients who drop out after one or two sessions do not benefit much from therapy (Tutin, 1987; Pekarik, 1985b).

Additional studies of premature terminations have had mixed results. Cross and Warren (1984) looked at environmental factors that might influence premature termination. They found no differences between continuers and dropouts on factors such as adjustment, external support, stress, or family attitudes toward therapy, but they did find that continuers were more satisfied with the treatment they received. DuBrin and Zastowny (1988) looked at a number of different variables and found that client characteristics such as lower levels of education and occupation were correlated with dropping out of therapy, but age and sex were not. The authors suggest that dropouts are generally difficult to predict.

Looking at clients being treated for depression, Persons, Burns, and Perloff (1988) found that clients with a personality disorder, high Beck Depression Inventory scores (above 20) at the beginning of therapy, lower education, and an absence of endogenous symptoms were statistically more likely to drop out. Other factors such as age, sex, employment status, drug or alcohol diagnosis, medication use, or serious medical problems were not related to dropping out. They also found that clients who did not do homework assignments were more likely to terminate treatment.

McCallum, Piper, and Joyce (1992) found that low levels of "psychological mindedness" predicted dropping of short-term group therapy, but failed to identify any other variables. Beckham (1992) found that initial positive levels of rapport between client and therapist were related to continuing therapy, and that high numbers of missed sessions predicted dropping out, but again most of the variables studied were not found to be useful for prediction. Frayn (1992) identifies a high degree of early motivation, good impulse control, and high frustration tolerance as predictors of persons who remain in psychoanalytic psychotherapy, but not factors such as gender or diagnosis.

Garfield (1986) warns that research findings in this area are inconsistent because of various methodological problems. For example, there is no formal consensus on the definition of a dropout or treatment "continuer." Garfield's definition of a dropout includes someone who has been accepted for therapy, attends at least one session, but fails to return to future planned treatment sessions. However this view is not routinely held, and a universally accepted number of therapy sessions differentiating a dropout from a continuer has yet to be established. For example, Talmon (1990) may not consider a client who attended only one therapy session as a dropout, whereas, at the other extreme, Frayn (1992) views anyone who ceases treatment before nine months as a premature terminator. Further, Pekarik (1985b) argues that definitions of dropouts based on treatment duration (e.g., number of sessions attended) can be misleading and should not be used. These types of issues weaken the ability to make consistent generalizations from previous research findings.

Recently, Wierzbicki and Pekarik (1993) conducted a meta-analysis of 125 dropout studies conducted between 1974 and 1990, which included children and adults, public, private and university settings, individual and group/family therapy, and a wide distribution of diagnoses. They found that the average dropout rate across all of the studies was approximately 47 percent, which is similar to previous studies. The authors point out that therapist judgments may be the best method of defining dropouts, and that failure to attend scheduled sessions may produce conservative levels. They also found that dropping out was significantly related to minority status (African Americans and other minorities), low education, and low socioeconomic status. Dropout rates also increase for young, female, and married clients, but this is not statistically significant. Although these authors found some of the same variables related to dropouts as earlier studies, they conclude that simple client or therapist demographic variables may not be sufficient in identifying dropouts. They suggest that more complex psychological variables such as treatment expectations, clients' intentions, and differences between clients' and therapists' value systems, may provide more useful results.

Recommendations: Reducing Missed Appointments
5. If memory is a problem, enlist the help of the family to remind clients of appointments. Follow up on the reasons that clients missed the appointment prior to the next session.

Recommendations: Reducing Missed Appointments
6. Use personalized rather than standard reminders (e.g., form letters). In order to protect clients' confidentiality, use a "neutral" return address on the envelope (e.g., a post office box instead of "Smith's Psychological Services").

Despite these limitations, the widespread problems associated with premature termination have prompted clinicians to attempt to deal with it. One suggested approach is to screen clients before accepting them for psychotherapy. For example, one could eliminate clients with some of the variables described (e.g., low IQ, education, or socioeconomic level) that correlate with dropping out. Of course, such a procedure might be limited by practical as well as ethical concerns. As noted, studies have been inconsistent in identifying variables that predict attrition, and in general dropouts may be difficult to screen out.

A related manner for reducing premature terminations deals with developing instruments that can predict continuation in therapy. Although some studies report some success in this area (e.g., Balch & Ross, 1975; Heilbrun, 1961), the consistency of research findings has again been a problem. For example, personality tests such as the MMPI or the Rorschach have been studied extensively in this regard (Baekeland & Lundwall, 1975), but thus far consistent results have been lacking (Garfield, 1986; Walters, Solomon, & Walden, 1982). Some studies have found the psychopathic deviate scale (pd) of the MMPI to correlate with dropping out (Pekarik, Jones, & Blodgett, 1986), but others failed to replicate this finding (DuBrin & Zastowny, 1988). Overall, this process has been less than successful. An interesting finding related to the use of pretherapy personality tests is that clients who comply with completing these assessments appear to be more likely to continue in therapy than those who do not comply (Wolff, 1967; Garfield, 1986).

Another approach to reduce attrition might be to provide pretherapy training for clients (Garfield, 1986; Orlinsky & Howard, 1986). For example, some programs have been developed to help prepare members of low socioeconomic groups for therapy (e.g., Heitler, 1973; 1976; Strupp & Bloxom, 1973). Despite some promising initial results with this approach (Orne & Wender, 1968), other studies suggest that such programs have little or no effect on dropout rates (Levitt & Fisher, 1981), and subsequent investigations have been mixed (see Tinsley, Bowman & Ray, 1988, for a review). One investigation found that pretherapy orientation significantly reduces early dropouts with clients of lower socioeconomic status, but showed less clear effects with treatment outcome (Larsen, Nguyen, Green, & Attkisson, 1983). Another study found that the use of a pretherapy videotape designed to reduce anxiety and prepare clients for psychotherapy had some immediate and short-term effects on anxiety and treatment knowledge, but no long-term consequences for outcome (Deane, Spicer, Leathem, 1992). These latter authors point out, however, that since this procedure is simple and requires little effort or cost, its use is warranted. Unfortunately, despite the potential usefulness of pretherapy interventions, a recent survey of a large group of private psychotherapists conducted by the author in Pennsylvania indicates that only 2 percent use these procedures in their practice.

Missed Therapy Appointments

Another problem seen frequently in psychotherapy is missed appointments. Such behaviors may strain the client–therapist relationship, reduce staff motivation, increase costs, reduce treatment effectiveness, and generally interfere with the treatment process. I have already talked about clients who miss their intake appointments. The rates for missing subsequent meetings are similar (e.g., 17 percent to 52 percent; Benjamin-Bauman, Reiss, & Bailey, 1984; Macharia, Leon, Rowe, Stephenson, & Haynes, 1992). In a recent study, Sparr, Moffitt, and Ward (1993) found that approximately 20 percent of clients in their sample missed therapy appointments at one time or another, which made up about 9 percent of scheduled visits. However, over 80 percent kept the next scheduled appointment. The major reasons given for these are similar to Noonan's (1973) findings as reported. The primary excuse is that the client "forgot about it." Other frequent reasons given for missed appointments include weather conditions, sickness, lack of transportation, lack of a babysitter, schedule conflicts, unforeseen circumstances, and inconvenient time of appointment (DiMatteo & DiNicola, 1982).

Various procedures have been used to reduce missed appointments. Larsen et al. (1983) were able to reduce first-session no-shows by almost half by scheduling sessions within four days of initial contact and by having the therapist call to confirm the appointment when it was made by another staff member. In a review of the literature, Macharia et al. (1992) found that three general categories of interventions have been used for this purpose, including cuing (letter or telephone prompts), reducing perceived barriers (automatic appointments, helping clients with problem solving), and increasing motivation (contracting). These authors found that letter or telephone prompts were used most often and were effective when done one week or less before the next appointment. They also found that contracting increased appointment keeping by 14 percent. Other studies suggest that telephone reminders may be more effective than mail reminders, but these of course require more time. Meichenbaum and Turk (1987) advise that missed appointments can be reduced by arranging to have a member of the family help out—for example, by transporting or reminding the client about the appointment. Similarly, transportation can be arranged through various social agencies. These authors also suggest that the method used to remind clients should be personalized rather than standard. Form letters should be avoided. In addition, they suggest that the type of contact (telephone, mail, etc.) should be rotated, and that the highest frequency of contact should be at the beginning of therapy.

Summary

This chapter reviewed some of the factors that lead to or prevent individuals from seeking professional help for their problems. Some of the identified barriers to mental health treatment include cost, awareness and availability of services, stigma, a high degree of self-reliance, and anxiety or fear of treatment. Factors that increase the probability of treatment include having a clear awareness that a problem exists and a precipitating event. It appears that whites, women, and members of the middle class are more likely to seek therapy than those from other groups.

Getting those who need help into treatment might be facilitated if therapists took a more active role in recruiting clients. However, most therapists seem to be reluctant or unable to do this. Despite the influence of the community mental health movement, clinical services have generally retained the *waiting mode* of service delivery (that is, you wait until the client contacts you) as opposed to the *seeking* mode or outreach model.

The area of treatment attrition was also reviewed. Dropping out of therapy can have serious consequences for both clients and staff, including potentially poor outcome for clients who drop out, wasted time and reduced income for therapists, and possibly reduced job satisfaction or burnout (Pekarik, 1985). Despite hundreds of research studies, it is clear that we still cannot consistently predict which clients are more likely to drop out of therapy, nor do we totally understand what can be done to help clients complete their program once they begin. However, the many suggestions given in this appendix can be used as a starting point for this latter task.

Appendix C

Client Credibility and Deception

Overview

To a large extent, the effectiveness of psychotherapy depends on clients being honest and open with the therapist. Of course, *honesty* is a relative term—I doubt that any human relationship is totally honest. For the most part, however, psychotherapists expect clients to be truthful with them. As part of this discussion, I will also talk about malingering. Malingering is not often viewed as a type of resistance, and in its pure form I agree that it probably is not. However, if we expand its scope to include all levels of deception, I believe it should be included. One of the easiest ways that clients can be resistive is simply by not telling the therapist the truth. Although clients may have many reasons for doing so, the fact remains that an essential part of psychotherapy is honesty.

Along the same lines, as Rogers (1988) points out, "diagnoses of mental disorders rely heavily on the honesty, accuracy, and completeness of clients' self report; distortions, both intentional and unintentional, complicate greatly the assessment process" (p. 1). Because assessment is the cornerstone of the treatment process, false information can have significant effects on treatment outcome and effectiveness. Over and above this, clients' credibility permeates the entire therapeutic relationship. It is difficult to form a close relationship (both inside and out of therapy) with someone you cannot trust. This is why I believe this topic is important.

As part of this discussion, I will also talk about *dissimulation*. This is another term that is used to describe individuals who intentionally distort or misrepresent psychological symptoms. It includes faking "good" as well as faking "bad" (Rogers, 1988). Although they are not totally equivalent, to simplify matters, I will use the terms *deception, malingering,* and *dissimulation* somewhat interchangeably in this appendix.

Malingering

Malingering is defined by the DSM-IV (American Psychiatric Association, 1994) as the "intentional production of false or grossly exaggerated physical or psychological symptoms, motivated by external incentives . . ." (p. 683). It is similar to but not the same as factitious disorder with psychological symptoms. In the latter case, the symptoms are apparently under the individual's voluntary control, and the immediate goal is that of assuming the role of a client. However, the ultimate motives for this behavior are not obvious or well understood. In contrast, with malingering the motives are usually easy to figure out, and the deception often extends beyond the person's role as a client. Also, there seems to be a bias in the sense that most professionals do not feel that malingering needs to be treated at all, whereas this view is not quite as strong with factitious disorders. In some cases, however, it may be difficult to differentiate between the two.

Other disorders that may be mistaken for malingering are Ganser and Munchausen syndromes. In Ganser syndromes, clients present with a sudden onset of psychosis. Symptoms typically include hallucinations and a clouding of consciousness, and episodes are frequently accompanied by amnesia. However, there is often a rather quick resolution with complete return to normal mental functioning. Ganser syndrome has not been shown to be under voluntary control, and most researchers believe it is a stress-related brief psychosis. On the other hand, Munchausen syndrome is a rare, chronic, and extreme variety of factitious disorder, where clients often induce physical symptoms with drugs, bloodletting, or other means. It is a strange hybrid of malingering and conversion disorder.

Client Credibility

One of the factors that makes a client's credibility difficult to assess is that it can fall along a wide continuum. Therefore, it should generally be viewed as a continuous rather than a dichotomous variable. In practice, however, it may help to break deception down into the following types or degrees:

1. *Pure malingering:* All symptoms are made up.
2. *Partial malingering:* Existing symptoms are exaggerated, or previous symptoms are falsely said to remain. For example, you may have a client with schizophrenia who really is psychotic but may make up symptoms at times (e.g., prior to being discharged, he may complain of hearing voices again).
3. *False imputation:* Actual symptoms exist, but the cause given for these is not true. For example, symptoms that are due to stresses at home are blamed on conditions at work.
4. *Unreliability:* The client's responses are not honest, but no clarification can be made regarding intention. In addition, clients may be honest but report distorted information because of poor memory, inaccurate perceptions, or similar reasons. I would also include "unconscious" distortions and deceptions in this category.
5. *Unsystematic deception:* This is probably the most common type found in therapy. The client is generally honest but may lie in response to certain questions, or may hold certain types of information from the therapist. This type is probably the most difficult to uncover.
6. *Defensiveness:* This is the opposite of malingering and involves deception by minimizing psychological symptoms.

Although many professionals do not think about deception when there is a clear DSM Axis I diagnosis, I am not sure this is always a good rule to follow because it can occur in virtually anyone. Cunnien (1988, p. 32) suggests that deception should be considered when (1) the client is involved in any type of legal action; (2) there appears to be lack of cooperation with assessment; (3) there are obvious incentives for deception (Social Security or veterans' benefits, obtaining drugs, etc.); (4) you suspect voluntary control over symptoms in that symptoms get worse under observation, or (5) symptoms fail to respond to otherwise effective treatment strategies.

Rogers (1988, Chapter 14) gives a detailed description of how various types of deception can be assessed. The following is a brief summary:

1. Clients attempting to malinger tend to skip subtle symptoms and endorse only blatant ones.
2. An unlikely number of symptoms or unexpected symptom severity is often indicated.
3. Clients endorse rare or unusual symptoms.
4. Individuals may report an unusually sudden onset or sudden resolution.
5. Malingerers tend to overplay their inability to complete tasks. Even severely impaired clients can complete simple cognitive tests.

6. There tends to be an inconsistency between reported and observed symptoms—for example, reporting paranoia in the absence of any observable signs or symptoms.
7. There is often a theatrical or overdramatic quality to their presentation.
8. There tends to be an inconsistency of symptoms across time. For example, these individuals often forget which symptoms they endorsed or their severity. A careful check after a few days may give them away.
9. Malingerers tend to be nonselective in their endorsement of symptoms, and thus odd combinations often result (e.g., hallucinations in the absence of delusions).
10. Improbable or absurd symptoms are reported (e.g., a client claims he cannot remember his wife's name).
11. There tends to be an unrealistic degree of precision. For example, a client reports spending two hours and fifteen minutes each day staring at a wall.
12. There may be an endorsement of total or extreme honesty (e.g., most normal people will acknowledge minor deceptions).
13. In the interview, the client often asks you to repeat questions, and responses are slow, vague, and indirect. In addition, responses tend to be carefully thought out.

Deception of Specific Disorders

One way to test for deception is by comparing persons you suspect of faking with clients who truly have various psychiatric symptoms. The next section describes more specific signs of deception and malingering for several categories of disorders and compares these with authentic signs and symptoms. This review is based on research articles by Atkinson, Henderson, Sparr, and Deale (1982); Asaad and Shapiro (1986); Beaber, Marston, Michelli, and Mills (1985); Binder (1986); Binder and Pankratz (1987); Oltmanns and Maher (1988); Perconte and Goreczny (1990); Resnick (1988a, 1988b); Rogers (1988); and Rogers (1990).

Psychosis

This is a frequent target of malingering and deception. People usually attempt to fake psychosis in one of these five conditions:

1. Criminals may try to show they are incompetent to stand trial or to be executed or may try to indicate they were insane at the time of the crime. This is also used by those who want to be transferred to a psychiatric setting from jail.
2. Civilians may fake psychosis to avoid the draft (which is not currently valid), or military personnel may do so to avoid combat duty or to be discharged.
3. People may fake psychosis to obtain financial gain (e.g., Social Security, veterans', or other insurance benefits).
4. Some may fake psychosis to obtain food and shelter (e.g., to be admitted to a psychiatric hospital or similar program for free services).
5. Finally, some may fake psychosis to obtain prescription drugs.

A common way of faking psychosis is by claiming to have various hallucinations. Hallucinations are seen most often in schizophrenic disorders although they are seen in others as well (e.g., major depression, bipolar or organic disorders, substance abuse). In genuine cases of schizophrenia, clients typically have auditory hallucinations. About 20 percent of schizophrenics also report visual hallucinations, but these tend to be more characteristic of organic disorders or substance abuse. Hallucinations are almost always coupled with delusions and rarely occur independently. These tend to be intermittent rather than continuous; in persons with schizophrenia, the voices are said to come from outside the client's head. Usually, the message that is given is clear (as opposed to vague noises or sounds), and does not appear to be fabricated. For example, it is unlikely that a person will have a command hallucination to "stick someone up" to "go rape somebody."

Although command hallucinations are very common in schizophrenia, most clients are able to ignore them and not act on them. Many schizophrenics have developed strategies to deal with their voices, and they often report that the hallucinations decrease when they engage in activities such as smoking, watching TV, or working. In multiple personalities, the voices are usually reported to come from inside the head as opposed to outside; in schizophrenia, visual hallucinations remain constant regardless of whether the eyes are open or closed. When symptoms are questionable, it may help to have the person clarify some of these points.

Persons faking psychosis tend to present symptoms that are exaggerated and bizarre. They often have no previous history of treatment or hospitalization, which tends to be unlikely unless the person is relatively young. When asked to repeat an idea, they often will do it exactly, as opposed to cases of true schizophrenia where clients often get lost or tangential. Malingerers will often answer "I don't know" when asked about various symptoms, or respond very slowly in order to have time to think about an answer. Malingerers also have problems with the more subtle signs of schizophrenia, such as impaired relatedness, blunted affect, or concreteness. Often their symptoms do not seem to fit any known diagnostic entity (malingering should always be considered and evaluated in cases of atypical psychosis). Other signs to be investigated are acute onset of delusions or renunciation of delusional ideas. As most professionals know, delusional ideas tend to be fixed and very difficult to eliminate even with medications or other forms of treatment. In true schizophrenia, the behavior of the client is often consistent with the delusional ideas, whereas this may not be the case for malingerers. For example, a person who is truly paranoid, may appear frightened, may not want to eat, or may refuse to sit with his back to the door. In addition, malingerers have a hard time keeping up their act as they get tired, and sometimes it helps to get information from reliable clients who may be able to catch them off guard.

Posttraumatic Stress Disorder (PTSD)

This is a diagnosis that has caused a great deal of controversy since being introduced to the DSM-III in 1980. National service organizations have widely distributed lists of PTSD symptoms, and this perhaps has made it easier for veterans to fake this disorder.

This section deals primarily with faked PTSD associated with veterans, although others may fake this disorder as well. The motivation for malingering PTSD is usually one of five reasons: (1) to obtain Veterans Administration (VA) compensation, (2)t to be admitted to a VA hospital, (3) for self-ingratiating purposes, (4) to reduce punishment for criminal behavior, or (5) to obtain Social Security disability benefits.

In cases where malingering is suspected, official military records should be obtained. There are a number of case studies of persons malingering PSTD who have never been in combat or, in some cases, never been in the service. When possible, the veteran's spouse or family should be contacted in order to confirm symptoms and get an idea of premorbid functioning. Although an antisocial personality disorder does not rule out PTSD, these individuals should be carefully evaluated. Unfortunately, many persons with true PTSD have many symptoms associated with antisocial personality disorders, such as poor work history, drug abuse, and reckless behavior, so again it is important to get premorbid functioning levels and discover when these types of behaviors began.

A common complaint of veterans malingering PSTD is an expressed fear that they will lose control and hurt others. This threat is sometimes enough to get them admitted to a psychiatric hospital or to achieve other goals. Malingerers tend to overplay their Vietnam experience, whereas the opposite tends to be true for real cases. Malingerers also tend to blame most or all of their problems on Vietnam, as opposed to true cases where the person tends to blame him- or herself or to have an intense level of guilt. In the first interview session, in true cases, clients may be resistant to blaming their problems on Vietnam, but this is often not the case for malingers.

Veterans with true PTSD have intrusive recollections and dreams that often report themes of helplessness, rage, or guilt, whereas in malingerers the reported themes are anger toward authority figures, grandiosity, and power. True PTSD clients generally downplay symptoms, whereas malingerers overplay them. Malingerers often reports that they think of nothing other than Vietnam and enjoy telling combat stories. In true PTSD, veterans may try to avoid environmental conditions associated with the trauma, such as crowds, hot rainy days, camping, or other environmental conditions that may be similar to those of Vietnam; malingerer is not likely to report this. Finally, malingerers often show intense anger toward authority figures, whereas in true cases the anger is often turned inward. Of course, all of these are generalizations, and each case should be evaluated independently.

Organic Disorders

Individuals generally fake or exaggerate organic disorders in order to receive various types of compensation. This is likely to be done after an automobile or work-related accident where head injuries are involved. This is a controversial area because even mild head injuries in the absence of unconsciousness can at times cause real and persistent symptoms, so care must be taken not to accuse someone falsely of deception. Some common symptoms after a true head injury include dizziness, headaches, insomnia, fatigue, and memory and concentration problems (the last two being the most common). Loss of everyday knowledge or skills is rare. Perseveration is a relatively common feature of more severe organic impairment and is very difficult to fake. Persons who are faking head injuries tend to give near but incorrect answers to almost all questions, as opposed to truly impaired individuals who sometimes give correct answers or give very obviously incorrect responses. Unless it is very severe or in the later stages, even persons with true organic disorders remember things like the names of their spouses, their ages and addresses, personal identity, relatives' names, and other personal facts about themselves and their families. Malingerers are more likely to "forget" these. Similarly, long-term memory tends to remain intact for a relatively long period in true organicity. A relatively easy and effective procedure for detecting false memory disorders is called symptom validity Testing (Binder & Pankratz, 1987). This involves a forced-choice design of two alternative responses, with below-chance performance indicating deception. For example, you present the individual with either a red or a black pencil, remove it, and after distraction have him or her recall the color. After one hundred trials, by chance the person should be correct about 50 percent of the time. Those who are exaggerating symptoms are likely to perform below chance levels. The procedure is also useful for detecting other types of deception.

Affective Disorders

Persons with true depression often report that their symptoms are worse in the early morning hours, and fakers tend not to know this. True depression often shows general physical signs of slowing, such as constipation or low energy, in addition to the emotional symptoms.

Mania is difficult to fake. Premature ending of a manic phase due to fatigue is clear sign of malingering. Grandiose or paranoid delusions are more common in bipolar disorders than in other types of affective conditions. Common themes are being a renowned or great person, having special powers or wealth, or being chosen to accomplish a great task. Manic episodes tend *not* to be preceded by major life stressors. Lithium and some antidepressive drugs may take several weeks to be effective. Responding "too quickly" to medications may be a sign of faking.

Implications

It is difficult to judge the magnitude of the problem that deception plays in psychotherapy. Some researchers have estimated that about 25 percent of clients engage in significant levels of deception, but of course this would depend on the treatment setting, typical clientele, and how deception is defined and measured. Also, some professionals argue that what clients say in therapy is not crucial because it is the process and not the content of psychotherapy that is important. However, I believe that deception can and does play an important role in psychotherapy and should be given some consideration. For example, deception may be one of the least likely factors we think about when clients are not progressing in treatment. In this case, in addition to the evaluation of deception for the specific disorders outlined here, therapists may want to be more alert to various levels of dishonesty in the typical treatment process. Normally, we should expect clients to be more open and honest as the relationship progresses, but this does not always occur. This topic is beyond the scope of this section, but various signs of dishonesty such as speech patterns, emotional expressions, tone of voice, embarrassment, slips of the tongue, or elevated rate of breathing may be apparent. The interested reader is referred to Ekman (1985); Ekman, Friesen, and O'Sullivan (1988); and Ford, King, and Hollender (1988).

Compensation Dissonance

There is a different type of problem possibly involving some level of deception, that I have not yet seen in the literature but which both my colleagues and I have experienced in practice. I believe it may become a growing problem for psychotherapy as more people are placed on workmen's compensation or disability benefits. The situation can occur in different scenarios and may involve either physical or psychological symptoms. It often occurs when a person is placed off work on a disability or is involved in litigation relating to an accident or injury. It appears to be a hybrid of "compensation neurosis," secondary gains, and cognitive dissonance.

For example, let's say you have two people riding on a public transportation bus. One of them is a sociopath, and the other is a perfectly normal, law-abiding, and generally truthful person. The bus gets into a minor accident, and both people are tossed around a bit. They are both taken to the hospital, where no serious injuries are found, but the results nonconclusive. Both passengers experience some ill-defined but generally mild back pain as a result of the accident. There is nothing seriously wrong with either person, but the sociopath decides that he is going to use this opportunity to sue the bus company for a lot of money, and he somehow convinces the normal person to go along.

Two years later, the bus company settles with both of them out of court for a large sum of money. After getting the money, and assuming that nothing can be done to him, if you ask the sociopath if there is really something wrong with his back, he is likely to say "no" and experience no other symptoms. If you ask the other person if there is something wrong, however, he is likely to honestly say yes, and in fact his symptoms will persist for a number of years afterward.

Because I have never seen this problem officially investigated, I am not sure of its prevalence, but I am convinced that it does occur. At times it may start off with real symptoms, but the longer the person is off work, or on disability (or treated differently because of the symptoms), the more difficult it becomes for him or her to get well. I do not see this as malingering because the symptoms are not consciously faked and subjectively may be real. In a sense, after receiving some compensation (special treatment, time off work, etc.), the individual is placed in a situation where perhaps unconsciously he or she has to justify the circumstances (current and past) and cannot allow him- or herself to improve. In effect, some government entitlement programs may prevent some clients from making significant improvements. Because I do not have any objective data on this problem, I will not comment on it further here, but will leave it open to future investigation.

References

Abramowitz, S.I., Berger, A., & Weary, G. (1982). Similarity between clinician and client: Its influence on the helping relationship. In T.A. Wills (Ed.), *Basic processes in helping relationships* (pp. 357–379). New York: Academic Press.

Achterberg-Lawlis, J. (1982). The psychological dimensions of arthritis. *Journal of Consulting and Clinical Psychology, 50,* 984–992.

Adler, A. (1929). *The practice and theory of individual psychology.* London: Routledge and Kegan Paul.

Albers, R.J., & Scrivner, L.L. (1977). The structure of attrition during appraisal. *Community Mental Health Journal, 13,* 325–332.

Allen, J.G. (1974). When does exchanging personal information constitute self-disclosure? *Psychological Reports, 35,* 195–198.

Allgood, S.M., & Crane, D.R. (1991). Predicting marital therapy dropouts. *Journal of Marital and Family Therapy, 17,* 73–79.

Altman, I. (1973). Reciprocity of information exchange. *Journal for the Theory of Social Behavior, 3,* 249–261.

Altman, I., & Taylor, D.A. (1973). *Social penetration: The development of interpersonal relationships.* New York: Holt, Rinehart & Winston.

American Psychiatric Association. (1994). *Diagnostic and statistical manual of mental disorders* (4th ed.). Washington, DC: Author.

Anderson, J.L. (1979). Patients' recall of information and its relation to the nature of the consultation. In D.J. Oborne, M.M. Gruneberg, & J.R. Eiser (Eds.), *Research in psychology and medicine* (Vol. 2, pp. 238–246). London: Academic Press.

Anderson, C.M., & Stewart, S. (1983). *Mastering resistance: A practical guide to family therapy.* New York: Guilford Press.

Andreasen, N.C., & Carpenter, W.T. (1993). Diagnosis and classification of schizophrenia. *Schizophrenia Bulletin, 19,* 199–214.

Angyal, A. (1965). *Neurosis and treatment: A holistic theory.* New York: Viking Press.

Ankuta, G.Y., & Abeles, N. (1993). Client satisfaction, clinical significance and meaningful change in psychotherapy. *Professional Psychology: Research and Practice. 24,* 70–74.

Archer, R.L. (1979). Role of personality and the social situation. In G.J. Chelune, (Ed.) *Self-disclosure* (pp. 28–58). San Francisco: Jossey-Bass.

Archer, R.L. (1987). Commentary: Self-disclosure, a very useful behavior. In V.J. Derlega & J.H. Berg (Eds.), *Self-disclosure: Theory, research and therapy* (pp. 329–342). New York: Plenum Press.

Archer, R.L,. & Burleson, J.A. (1980). The effects of timing and responsibility of self-disclosure on attraction. *Journal of Personality, 38,* 120–130.

Arieti, S. (1974). *Interpretation of schizophrenia* (2nd ed.). New York: Basic Books.

Arkin, R.M., & Baumgardner, A.H. (1985). Self-handicapping. In J.H. Harvey & G. Weary (Eds.), *Attribution: Basic issues and applications* (pp. 169–202). New York: Academic Press.

Asaad, G., & Shapiro, B. (1986). Hallucinations: Theoretical and clinical overview. *American Journal of Psychiatry, 143,* 1088–1097.

Ascher, L.M. (1989). *Therapeutic paradox.* New York: Guilford Press.

Atkinson, R.M., Henderson, R.G., Sparr, L.F., & Deale, S. (1982). Assessment of Viet Nam veterans for posttraumatic stress disorder in veterans administration disability claims. *American Journal of Psychiatry, 139,* 1118–1121.

Atwood, G.E., & Stolorow, R.D. (1993). *Faces in a cloud.* Northvale, NJ: Jason Aronson.

Austad, C.S. (1992). Managed health care and its effects on the practice and evolution of psychotherapy: Pros and cons. *Psychotherapy in Private Practice, 11,* 11–14.

Austad, C.S., & Berman, W.H. (1991). *Psychotherapy in managed health care: The optimal use of time and resources.* Washington, DC: American Psychological Association.

Averill, J.R. (1982). *Anger and aggression: An essay on emotion.* New York: Springer-Verlag.

Axelrod, S., & Wetzler, S. (1989). Factors associated with better compliance with psychiatric aftercare. *Hospital and Community Psychiatry, 40,* 397–401.

Bachrach, L.L. (1982). Young adult chronic patients: An analytical review of the literature. *Hospital and Community Psychiatry, 33,* 189–197.

Bachrach, L.L. (1988). Defining chronic mental illness: A concept paper. *Hospital and Community Psychiatry, 39,* 383–388.

Baekeland, F.B., & Lundwall, L. (1975). Dropping out of treatment: A critical review. *Psychological Bulletin, 82,* 738–783.

Bain, D.J.G. (1976). Doctor–patient communication in general practice consultations. *Medical Education, 10,* 125–131.

Balch, P., & Ross, A.W. (1975). Predicting success in weight reduction as a function of locus of control: A unidimensional and multidimensional approach. *Journal of Consulting and Clinical Psychology, 43,* 119.

Balswick, J. (1988). *The inexpressive male.* Lexington, MA: Lexington Books.

Bankoff, E.A., & Howard, K.I. (1992). The social network of the psychotherapy patient and effective psychotherapy process. *Journal of Psychotherapy Integration, 2,* 273–294.

Bandura, A. (1977). Self-efficacy: Toward a unified theory of behavioral change. *Psychological Review, 84,* 191–215.

Bateson, G. (1979). *Mind and nature.* New York: Elsevier-Dutton.

Baumeister, R.F., & Scher, S.J. (1988). Self-defeating behavior patterns among normal individuals: Review and analysis of common self-destructive tendencies. *Psychological Bulletin, 104,* 3–22.

Baumgardner, A.H. (1991). Claiming depressive symptoms as a self-handicap: A protective self-presentation strategy. *Basic and Applied Social Psychology, 12,* 97–100.

Beaber, R.J., Martson, A., Michelli, J., & Mills, M.J. (1985). A brief test for measuring malingering in schizophrenic individuals. *American Journal of Psychiatry, 142,* 1478–1481.

Beck, A.T. (1976). *Cognitive therapy and the emotional disorders.* New York: International Universities Press.

Becker, M.H. (1976). Sociobehavioral determinants of compliance. In D.L. Sacket & R.B. Haynes (Eds.), *Compliance with therapeutic regimens* (pp. 40–50). Baltimore: Johns Hopkins University Press.

Becker, M.H. (1979). Understanding patient compliance: The contributions of attitudes and other psychosocial factors. In S.J. Cohen (Ed.), *New Directions in patient compliance.* (pp. 1–31). Lexington, MA: Lexington Books.

Becker, M.H., & Maiman, L.A. (1980). Strategies for enhancing patient compliance. *Journal of Community Health, 6,* 113–137.

Beckham, E.E. (1992). Predicting patient dropout in psychotherapy. *Psychotherapy, 29,* 177–182.

Bellack, A.S., & Mueser, K.T. (1986). A comprehensive treatment program for schizophrenia and chronic mental illness. *Community Mental Health Journal, 22,* 175–189.

Bellack, A.S., & Mueser, K.T. (1993). Psychosocial treatment for schizophrenia. *Schizophrenia Bulletin, 19,* 317–336.

Beiser, M. (1985). The grieving witch: A framework for applying principles of cultural psychiatry to clinical practice. *Canadian Journal of Psychiatry, 30,* 130–141.

Benjamin-Bauman, J., Reiss, M. L., & Bailey, J. S. (1984). Increasing appointment keeping by reducing the call-appointment interval. *Journal of Applied Behavior Analysis, 17,* 295–301.

Bennett, M.J. (1989). The catalytic function in psychotherapy. *Psychiatry, 52,* 351–364.

Bennett, M.J., & Wisneski, M.J. (1979). Continuous psychotherapy within an HMO. *American Journal of Psychiatry, 136,* 1283–1287.

Bennett, S.K. (1994). The American Indian: A psychological overview. In W.J. Lonner & R. Malpass (Eds.), *Psychology and culture* (pp. 35–39). Boston: Allyn and Bacon.

Berg, J.N. (1987). Responsiveness and self-disclosure. In V.J. Derlega and J.H. Berg (Eds.), *Self-Disclosure: Theory, Research and Therapy* (pp. 101–130). New York: Plenum Press.

Berg, J.N., & Derlega, V.J. (1987). Themes in the study of self-disclosure. In

V.J. Derlega & J.H. Berg (Eds.), *Self-Disclosure: Theory, Research and Therapy* (pp.1–8). New York: Plenum Press.

Bergman, J.S. (1985). *Fishing for barracuda*. New York: Norton.

Berman, J. (1979). Counseling skills used by Black and White male and female counselors. *Journal of Counseling Psychology, 26,* 81–84.

Berman, J.S., & Norton, N.C. (1985). Does professional training make a therapist more effective? *Psychological Bulletin, 98,* 401–407.

Berzins, J.I. (1977). Therapist–patient matching. In A.S. Gurman & A.M. Razin (Eds.), *Effective psychotherapy: A handbook of research* (pp. 222–251). New York: Pergamon Press.

Betts, G.R., & Remer, R. (1993). The impact of paradoxical interventions on perceptions of the therapist and ratings of treatment acceptability. *Professional Psychology: Research and Practice, 24,* 164–170.

Beutler, L.E., & Clarkin, J.F. (1990). *Systematic treatment selection*. New York: Brunner/Mazel.

Beutler, L.E., & Consoli, A.J. (1993). Matching therapist's stance to clients' characteristics. *Psychotherapy, 30,* 417–422.

Beutler, L.E., Crago, M. & Arizmendi, T.G. (1986). Therapist variables in psychotherapy process. In S.L. Garfield & A.E. Bergin (Eds.), *Handbook of psychotherapy and behavior change* (3rd ed., pp. 257–310). New York: Wiley.

Binder, J.L., & Strupp, H.H. (1993). Recommendations for improving psychotherapy training based on experiences with manual guided research: An introduction. *Psychotherapy, 30,* 571–572.

Binder, L.M. (1986). Persisting symptoms after mild head injury: A review of the postconcussive syndrome. *Journal of Clinical and Experimental Neuropsychology, 8,* 323–346.

Binder, L.M., & Pankratz, L. (1987). Neurological evidence of a factitious memory complaint. *Journal of Clinical and Experimental Neuropsychology, 9,* 167–171.

Blackwell, B. (1976). Treatment adherence. *British Journal of Psychiatry, 129,* 513–531.

Blackwell, B. (1982). Treatment and compliance. In J.H. Greist, J.W. Jefferson, & R.L. Spotzer (Eds.), *Treatment of mental disorders* (pp. 501–516). Oxford University Press.

Block, C.B. (1981). Black Americans and the cross-cultural counseling and psychotherapy experience. In A.J. Marsella & P.B. Pedersen (Eds.), *Cross-cultural counseling and psychotherapy* (pp. 177–194). New York: Pergamon Press.

Bloom, B.L. (1981). Focused single-session therapy: Initial development and evaluation. In S.H. Budman (Ed.), *Forms of brief therapy* (pp. 167–218). New York: Guilford.

Bostwick, G.J. (1987). "Where's Mary?" A review of the group treatment dropout literature. *Social Work with Groups, 10,* 117–132.

Boulanger, G. (1988). Working with the entitled patient. *Journal of Contemporary Psychotherapy, 18,* 124–144.

Braaten, E. B., Otto, S., & Handelsman, M. (1993). What do people want to know about psychotherapy? *Psychotherapy, 30,* 565–570.

Brand, F.N., Smith, R.T., & Brand, P.A. (1977). Effect of economic barriers to medical care on patients' noncompliance. *Public Health Reports, 91,* 72–78.

Brehm, J.W. (1966). *A theory of psychological reactance.* New York: Academic Press.

Brehm, S.S. (1976). *The application of social psychology to clinical practice.* Washington, DC: Hemisphere.

Breshgold, E. (1989). Resistance in Gestalt therapy: An historical theoretical perspective. *The Gestalt Journal, 12*(2), 73–102.

Breslin, N.A. (1992). Treatment of schizophrenia: Current practice and future promise. *Hospital and Community Psychiatry, 43,* 877–885.

Brody, D.S. (1980a). The patient's role in clinical decision making. *Annals of Internal Medicine, 93,* 718–722.

Brody, D.S. (1980b). Feedback from patients as means of teaching the non-technological aspects of medical care. *Journal of Medical Education, 55,* 34–41.

Brown, J.E., & Slee, P.T. (1986). Paradoxical strategies: The ethics of intervention. *Professional Psychology: Research and Practice, 17,* 487–491.

Brownell, K.D., & Foreyt, J.P. (1985). Obesity. In D. Barlow (Ed.), *Clinical handbook of psychological disorders* (pp. 299–343). New York: Guilford Press.

Budman, S.H., & Gurman, A.S. (1988). *Theory and practice of brief psychotherapy.* New York: Guilford Press.

Bugental, J.F.T. (1965). *The search for authenticity.* New York: Rinehart & Winston.

Bugental, J.F.T. (1978). *Psychotherapy and process.* Reading, MA: Addison Wesley.

Bugental, J.F.T. (1987). *The art of psychotherapy.* New York: Norton.

Burstein, A. (1986). Treatment noncompliance in patients with post-traumatic stress disorder. *Psychosomatics, 27,* 37–41.

Chamberlain, P., Patterson, G., Reid, J., Kavanagh, K., & Forgatch, M. (1984). Observation of client resistance. *Behavior Therapy, 15,* 144–155.

Cantor, N. & Fleeson, W. (1991). Life tasks and self-regulatory processes. In M.L. M,aeher & P.R. Pintrich (Eds.), *Advances in motivation and achievement* (Vol. 7., pp. 327–369). Greenwich, CT: JAI Press.

Cantor, N., & Kihlstrom, J.F. (1987). *Personality and social intelligence.* Englewood Cliffs, NJ: Prentice Hall.

Carpenter, B.N. (1987). The relationship between psychopathology and self-disclosure. In V.J. Derlega & J.H. Berg (Eds.), *Self-Disclosure: Theory, Research and Therapy* (pp. 203–227). New York: Plenum Press.

Carpenter, W.T., Heinrichs, D.W., & Wagman, A.M.I. (1988). Deficit and nondeficit forms of schizophrenia: The concept. *American Journal of Psychiatry, 145,* 578–583.

Cassata, D.M. (1978). Health communication theory and research: An overview of the communication specialist interface. In B.D. Ruben (Ed.), *Communication yearbook 2* (pp. 495–504). New Brunswick, NJ: Transaction Books.

Cerney, M.S., & Buskirk, J.R. (1991). Anger: The hidden part of grief. *Bulletin of the Menninger Clinic, 55,* 228–237.

Chamberlain, P, Patterson, G., Reid, J., Kavanagh, K., & Forgatch, M. (1984). Observation of client resistance. *Behavior Therapy, 15,* 144–155.

Chandransena, R. (1987). Premature discharge. *Canadian Journal of Psychiatry, 32,* 259–263.

Chelune, G.J. (1975). Self-disclosure: An elaboration of its basic dimensions. *Psychological Reports,* 1975, *36,* 79–85.

Chelune, G.J. (1977). Sex differences, repression-sensitization and self-disclosure. A behavioral look. *Psychological Reports, 40,* 667–670.

Chelune, G.J. (1979). Measuring openness in interpersonal communication. In G.J. Chelune, (Ed.) *Self-Disclosure* (pp. 1–27). San Francisco: Jossey-Bass, 1979.

Chelune, G.J. (1987). A neuropsychological perceptive of interpersonal communication. In V.J. Derlega & J.H. Berg (Eds.), *Self-Disclosure: Theory, research and therapy* (pp. 9–34). New York: Plenum Press.

Chiauzzi, E.J. (1991). *Preventing relapse in the addictions: A biopsychosocial approach.* New York: Pergamon Press.

Coates, D., & Winston, T. (1987). Dilemma of distress disclosure. In V.J. Derlega & J.H. Berg (Eds.), *Self-disclosure: Theory, research and therapy* (pp. 229–255). New York: Plenum Press.

Cochran, S.D. (1984). Preventing medical noncompliance in the outpatient treatment of bipolar affective disorders. *Journal of Consulting and Clinical Psychology, 52,* 873–878.

Cody, J., & Robinson, A. (1977). The effect of low-cost maintenance medication of the rehospitalization of schizophrenic outpatients. *American Journal of Psychiatry, 134,* 73–76.

Conoley, J.C., & Bonner, M. (1991). The effects of counselor fee and title on perceptions of counselor behavior. *Journal of Counseling and Development, 69,* 356–358.

Conoley, C.W., Padula, M.A., Payton, D.S., & Daniels, J.A. (1994). Predictors of client implementation of counselor recommendations: Match with problem, difficulty level, and building on client strengths. *Journal of Counseling Psychology, 41,* 3–7.

Corrigan, P.W. (1990). Consumer satisfaction with institutional and community care. *Community Mental Health Journal, 26,* 151–165.

Corrigan, P.W., & Jakus, M.R. (1993). The patient satisfaction interview for partial hospitalization programs. *Psychological Reports, 72,* 387–390.

Corrigan, P.W., Liberman, R.P., & Engel, J.D. (1990). From noncompliance to collaboration in treatment of schizophrenia: Strategies that facilitate collaboration between practitioner and patient. *Hospital and Community Psychiatry, 41,* 1203–1211.

Coursey, R.D. (1989). Psychotherapy with persons suffering from schizophrenia: The need for a new agenda. *Schizophrenia Bulletin, 15,* 349–353.

Cozby, P.C. (1972). Self-disclosure, reciprocity and liking. *Sociometry,* 1972, *35,* 151–160.

Cozby, P.C. (1973). Self-disclosure: A literature review. *Psychological Bulletin, 79,* 73–91.

Cross. D.G., & Warren, C.F. (1984). Environmental factors associated with continuers and terminators in adult out-patient therapy. *British Journal of Medical Psychology, 57,* 363–369.

Cullari, S. (1994). *A manual to conduct therapeutic relationships with individuals who have persistent mental disorders.* Unpublished manuscript.

Cummings, C., & Nehemkis, A.M. (1986). How society contributes to noncompliance. In K.E. Gerber & A.M. Nehemkis (Eds.), *Compliance: The dilemma of the chronically ill* (pp. 213–225). New York: Springer.

Cummings, K.M., Becker, M.H., & Maile, M.C. (1980). Bringing the models together: An empirical approach to combining variables used to explain health actions. *Journal of Behavioral Medicine, 3,* 123–145.

Cunnien, A.J. (1988). Psychiatric and medical syndromes associated with deception. In R. Rogers (Ed). *Clinical assessment of malingering and deception* (pp.13–33). New York: Guilford Press.

D'Alessio, G. (1968). The concurrent use of behavior modification and psychotherapy. *Psychotherapy: Theory, research and practice, 5,* 154–159.

D'Zurilla, T.J. (1986). *Problem solving therapy.* New York: Springer.

Davidson, P.O. (1982). Issues in patient compliance. In T. Millon, C. Green, & R. Meagher (Eds.), *Handbook of clinical health psychology* (pp. 417–434). New York: Plenum Press.

Davis, H. (1984). Impossible clients. *Journal of Social Work Practice* (May), 28–48.

Davis, J.D. (1978). When boy meets girl: Sex roles and the negotiation of intimacy in an acquaintance exercise. *Journal of Personality and Social Psychology, 36,* 684–692.

Davison, G. (1973). Counter-control in behavior modification. In L. Hamerlynck, L. Hand, & E. Mash (Eds.), *Behavioral change: Methodology, concepts, and practice* (pp. 153–167). Champaign, IL: Research Press.

DeBord, J.B. (1989). Paradoxical interventions: A review of the recent literature. *Journal of Counseling and Development, 67,* 394–398.

Deane, F.P., Spicer, J., & Leathem, J. (1992). Effects of videotaped preparatory information on expectations, anxiety, and psychotherapy. *Journal of Consulting and Clinical Psychology, 60,* 980–984.

Deffenbacker, J.L,. & Stark, R.S. (1992). Relaxation and cognitive-relaxation treatments of general anger. *Journal of Counseling Psychology, 39,* 158–167.

Derlega, V.J., & Berg, J.H. (1987). *Self-disclosure: Theory, research and therapy.* New York: Plenum Press.

Derlega, V.J., & Chaikin, A.L. (1975). *Sharing intimacy: What we reveal to others and why.* Englewood Cliffs, NJ: Prentice-Hall.

Derlega, V.J., & Grzelak, J. (1979). Appropriateness of self-disclosure. In G. J. Chelune (Ed.), *Self-disclosure* (pp. 151–176). San Francisco: Jossey-Bass.

Derlega, V.J., Metts, S, Petronio, S., & Margulis, S.T. (1993). *Self-disclosure.* Newbury Park, CA: Sage.

Derlega, V.J., Wilson, M., & Chaikin, A.L. (1976). Friendship and disclosure reciprocity. *Journal of Personality and Social Psychology, 34,* 578–582.

Derlega, V.J., Winstead, B.A., Wong, P.T.P., & Hunter, S. (1985). Gender effects in an initial encounter: A case where men exceed women in disclosure. *Journal of Social and Personality Relationships, 2,* 25–44.

de Shazer, S. (1988). *Clues: Investigating solutions in brief therapy.* New York: W.W. Norton.

DeVoge, J.T., & Beck, S. (1978). The therapist–client relationship in behavior therapy. *Progress in Behavior Modification, 6,* 203–248.

DiGiacomo, J., Cullari, S., Krohn, E., & Kelley, J. (1994). *Therapeutic relationships with hospitalized schizophrenics.* Unpublished manuscript.

DiGiuseppe, R., Tafrate, R., & Eckhardt, C. (1994). Critical issues in the treatment of anger. *Cognitive and Behavioral Practice, 1,* 111–132.

DiMatteo, M.R. (1979). A social-psychological analysis of physician-patient rapport: Toward a science of the art of medicine. *Journal of Social Issues, 35,* 12–33.

DiMatteo, M.R., & DiNicola, D.D. (1982). *Achieving patient compliance: The psychology of the mental practitioner's role.* New York: Pergamon Press.

Diamond, R.E., & Hellkamp, D.T. (1969). Race, sex, ordinal position of birth, and self disclosure in high school students. *Psychological Reports, 25,* 235–238.

Dindia, K., & Allen, M. (1992). Sex differences in self-disclosure: A meta-analysis. *Psychological Bulletin, 112,* 106–118.

Dorken, H., VandenBos, G.R., Henke, C., Cummings, N., & Pallak, M.S. (1993). Impact of law and regulation on professional practice and use of mental health services: An empirical analysis. *Professional Psychology: Research and Practice, 24,* 256–265.

Doster, J.A., & Nesbitt, J.G. (1979). Psychotherapy and self-disclosure. In G.J. Chelune (Ed.), *Self-disclosure* (pp. 177–224). San Francisco: Jossey-Bass.

Dowd, E.T., & Milne, C.R. (1986). Paradoxical interventions in counseling psychology. *Counseling Psychology , 14,* 237–282.

Dowd, E.T., Milne, C.R., & Wise, S.L. (1991). The therapeutic reactance scale: A measure of psychological reactance. *Journal of Counseling and Development, 69,* 541–545.

Dowd, E.T., & Seibel, C.A. (1990). A cognitive theory of resistance and reactance: Implications for treatment. *Journal of Mental Health Counseling, 12,* 458–469.

Dowd, E.T., & Trutt, S.D. (1988). Paradoxical interventions in behavior modification: In M. Hersen, R.M. Eisler, & R.E. Miller (Eds.), *Progress in behavior modification* (pp. 96–130). Newbury Park, CA: Sage.

Draguns, J.G. (1980). Psychological disorders of clinical severity. In H.C. Triandis & J.G. Draguns (Eds.), *Handbook of cross-cultural psychology: Vol. 6. Psychopathology* (pp. 99–174). Boston: Allyn and Bacon.

Draguns, J.G. (1990). Normal and abnormal behavior in cross-cultural perspective: Specify the nature of their relationship. In J. Berman (Ed.), *Cross-cultural perspectives: Nebraska symposium on motivation 1989* (pp. 235–277). Lincoln: University of Nebraska Press.

Draguns, J.G. (1995). Cultural influences upon psychopathology: Clinical and practical implications. *Journal of Social Distress and the Homeless, 3*(2), 88–99.

DuBrin, J.R., & Zastowny, T.R. (1988). Predicting early attrition from psychotherapy: An analysis of a large private-practice cohort. *Psychotherapy, 25,* 393–408.

Dunbar, J.M. (1979). Issues in assessment. In S.J. Cohen (Ed.), *New directions in patient compliance* (pp. 41–57). Lexington, MA: Lexington Books.

Dunbar, J.M., & Agras, W.S. (1980). Compliance with medical instructions. In J.M. Ferguson & C.B. Taylor (Eds.), *The comprehensive handbook of behavioral medicine* (Vol. 3., pp. 115–145). New York: Spectum Publications.

Durlak, J.A. (1979). Comparative effectiveness of paraprofessional and professional helpers. *Psychological Bulletin, 86,* 80–92.

Dweck, C.S., & Leggett, E.L. (1988). A social-cognitive approach to motivation and personality. *Psychological Review, 95,* 256–273.

Edwards, E.D., & Edwards, M.E. (1980). American Indians: Working with individuals and groups. *Social Casework: The Journal of Contemporary Social Work, 61,* 498–506.

Ehrlich, H.J., & Graeven, D.B. (1971). Reciprocal self-disclosure in a dyad. *Journal of Experimental Social Psychology, 7,* 389–400.

Ekman, P. (1985). *Telling lies.* New York: W.W. Norton.

Ekman, P., Friesen, W.V., & O'Sullivan, M. (1988). Smiles when lying. *Journal of Personality and Social Psychology, 54,* 414–420.

Ellis, A. (1985). *Overcoming resistance.* New York: Springer Publishing Company.

Ellis, A. (1987). The impossibility of achieving consistently good mental health. *American Psychologist, 42,* 364–375.

Ellsworth, P.C. (1994). Sense, culture, and sensibility. In S. Kitayama & H.R. Markus (Eds.). *Emotion and culture* (pp. 23–50). Washington, DC: American Psychological Association.

Eisler, R.M., & Frederiksen, L.W. (1980). *Perfecting social skills: A guide to interpersonal behavior development.* New York: Plenum Press.

Epstein, L.H., & Cluss, P.A. (1982). A behavioral medicine perspective on adherence to long-term medical regimens. *Journal of Consulting and Clinical Psychology, 50,* 960–971.

Epstein, L.H., & Masek, B.J. (1978). Behavioral control of medicine compliance. *Journal of Applied Behavior Analysis, 11,* 1–9.

Eraker, S.A., Kirscht, J.P., & Becker, M.H. (1984). Understanding and improving patient compliance. *Annals of Internal Medicine, 100,* 258–268.

Erdelyi, M.H. (1985). *Psychoanalysis: Freud's cognitive science.* New York: Freeman.

Erickson, M.H. (1964). A hypnotic technique for resistant patients: The patient, the technique, and its rationale and field experiments. *Journal of Clinical Hypnosis, 7,* 8–32.

Essex, D., Fox, J., & Groom, J. (1981). The development, factor analysis, and revision of a client satisfaction form. *Community Mental Health Journal, 17,* 226–235.

Feigenbaum, W.M. (1977). Reciprocity in self-disclosure within the psychological interview. *Psychological Reports, 40,* 15–26.

Fenichel, O. (1945). *The psychoanalytic theory of neurosis.* New York: W.W. Norton.

Flesher, S. (1990). Cognitive rehabilitation in schizophrenia: A theoretical review and model of treatment. *Neuropsychology Review, 1,* 223–245.

Firestone, P. (1982). Factors associate with children's adherence to stimulant medication. *American Journal of Orthopsychiatry, 52,* 447–457.

Fischer, E.H., Winer, D., & Abramowitz, S.I. (1983). Seeking professional help for psychological problems. In A. Nadler, J.D. Fisher, & B.M. DePaulo (Eds.), *New directions in helping* (Vol. 3, pp.163–185). New York: Academic Press.

Folensbee, R., Draguns, J.G., & Danish, S.J. (1986). Impact of two types of counselor intervention on Black American, Puerto Rican and Anglo-American analogue clients. *Journal of Counseling Psychology, 33,* 446–453.

Ford, C.V., King, B.H., & Hollender, M.H. (1988). Lies and liars: Psychiatric aspects of prevarication. *American Journal of Psychiatry, 145,* 554–562.

Ford, M.E. (1992). *Motivating humans: Goals, emotions, and personal agency beliefs.* Newbury Park, CA: Sage Publications.

Ford, M.E., & Nichols, C.W. (1987). A taxonomy of human goals and some possible applications. In M.E. Ford & D.H. Ford (Eds.), *Humans as self-constructing living systems* (pp. 289–311). Hillsdale, NJ: Lawrence Erlbaum.

Ford, M.E., & Nichols, C.W. (1991). Using goal assessments to identify motivational patterns and facilitate behavioral regulation and achievement. In M.L. Maeher & P.R. Pintrich (Eds.), *Advances in motivation and achievement* (pp. 51–84). Greenwich, CT: JAI Press.

Ford, M.E., & Nichols, C.W. (1992). *Manual: Assessment of personal goals.* Palo Alto, CA: Consulting Psychologist Press.

Foulks, E.F., Persons, J.B., & Merkel, R.L. (1986). The effect of patients' beliefs about their illness on compliance in psychotherapy. *American Journal of Psychiatry, 143,* 340–344.

Fox, R.E. (1995). The rape of psychotherapy. *Professional Psychology: Research and Practice, 26,* 147–155.

France, A. (1988). *Consuming psychotherapy.* London: Free Association Books.

Frances, A., & Clarkin, J.F. (1981). No treatment as the prescription of choice. *Archives of General Psychiatry, 38,* 542–545.

Frank, J.D. (1961). *Persuasion and healing.* Baltimore: John Hopkins University Press.

Frank, J.D. (1982). Therapeutic components shared by all psychotherapies. In J.H. Harvey & M.M. Parks (Eds.), *Psychotherapy research and behavior change* (pp. 9–37). Washington, DC: American Psychological Association.

Frayn, D.H. (1992). Assessing factors associated with premature psychotherapy termination. *American Journal of Psychotherapy, 46,* 250–261.

Fremont, S., & Anderson, W. (1986). What client behaviors make counselors angry? An exploratory study. *Journal of Counseling and Development, 65,* 67–70.

French, J.R.P., & Raven, B.H. (1959). The bases of social power. In D. Cartwright (Ed.), *Studies in social power* (pp. 150–167). Ann Arbor, MI: Institute for Social Research, University of Michigan.

Frese, F.J. (1993). Twelve aspects of coping for persons with schizophrenia. *Innovations and Research, 2,* 39–46.

Freud, S. (1955). Studies on hysteria (with Josef Breuer). In J. Strachey (Ed. & Trans.), *The standard edition of the complete psychological works of Sigmund Freud* (Vol. 2) *[Standard edition].* London: Hogarth Press. (Original work published 1895).

Freud, S. (1953). On psychotherapy. *Standard edition* (Vol. 7, pp. 255-266). (Original work published 1905).

Freud, S. (1955). Beyond the pleasure principle. *Standard edition* (Vol. 18, pp. 7–64). (Original work published 1920).

Freud, S. (1957a). Five lectures on psychoanalysis. *Standard edition* (Vol. 11, pp. 3–56). (Original work published 1910).

Freud, S. (1957b). On the history of the psycho-analytic movement. *Standard edition* (Vol. 14, pp. 7–66). (Original work published 1914).

Freud, S. (1958a). The dynamics of transference. *Standard edition* (Vol. 12, pp. 99–108). (Original work published 1912).

Freud, S. (1958b). Remembering, repeating and working through. *Standard edition* (Vol. 12, pp. 147–156). (Original work published 1914).

Freud, S. (1959). The question of lay analysis. *Standard edition* (Vol. 20, pp. 183–251). (Original work published 1926)

Freud, S. (1963a). Introductory lectures on psychoanalysis. Lecture XIX. *Standard edition* (Vol. 16, pp. 286–302). (Original work published 1916).

Freud, S. (1964). Analysis terminable and interminable. *Standard edition* (Vol. 23, 216– 253). (Original work published 1937).

Friedman, S. (1993). *The new language of change.* New York: Guilford Press.

Garfield, S.L. (1986). Research on client variables in psychotherapy. In S.L. Garfield & A.E. Bergin (Eds.), *Handbook of psychotherapy and behavior change* (3rd ed., pp. 213–256). New York: John Wiley.

Gerber, W.D., & Nehemkis, A.M. (Eds.) (1986). *Compliance: The dilemma of the chronically ill.* New York: Springer.

Gillum, R.E. & Barsky, A.J. (1974). Diagnosis and management of patient non-compliance. *Journal of American Medical Association, 228,* 1563–1567.

Glover, E. (1955). *The technique of psychoanalysis.* New York: International Universities Press.

Glynn, S., & Mueser, K.T. (1986). Social learning for chronic mental patients. *Schizophrenia Bulletin, 12,* 648–668.

Goldberg, C. (1986). *On being a psychotherapist.* New York: Gardner Press.

Goldfried, M.R. (1982). Resistance and clinical behavior therapy. In P. Wachtel (Ed.), *Resistance* (pp. 95–115). New York: Plenum.

Goldfried, M.R., Decenteceo, E.T., & Weinberg, L. (1974). Systematic rational restructuring as a self-control technique. *Behavior Therapy, 5,* 247–254.

Goldstein, A.P., & Higginbotham, H.N. (1991). Relationship enhancing methods. In F.H. Kanfer & A.P. Goldstein (Eds.), *Helping people change* (4th Ed., pp. 20–69). New York: Pergamon Press.

Good, B.J. (1993). Culture, diagnosis, and comorbidity. *Culture, Medicine, and Psychiatry, 16,* 427–446.

Gordis, L. (1979). Conceptual and methodological problems in measuring patient compliance. In R.B. Haynes, D.W. Taylor, & D.L. Sackett (Eds.), *Compliance in health care* (pp. 23–45). Baltimore: Johns Hopkins University Press.

Gottlieb, B.H. (1981). *Social networks and social support.* Beverly Hills, CA: Sage Publications.

Green, M.F. (1993). Cognitive remediation in schizophrenia: Is it time yet? *American Journal of Psychiatry, 150,* 178–187.

Greenberg, G. (1984). Reflections on being abrasive: Two unusual cases. *The Psychotherapy Patient, 1,* 55–60.

Greenson, R.R. (1965). The working alliance and the transference neurosis. *Psychoanalytic Quarterly, 34,* 155–181.

Greenson, R.R. (1967). *The technique and practice of psychoanalysis.* New York: International University Press.

Gunderson, J.G. (1978). Patient–therapist matching: A research evaluation. *American Journal of Psychiatry, 135,* 1193–1197.

Hafner, R.J. (1983). Behavior therapy for agoraphobic men. *Behavior Research and Therapy, 21,* 51–56.

Haley, J. (1963) *Strategies of psychotherapy.* New York: Grune & Stratton.

Haley, J. (1973). *Uncommon therapy: The psychiatric techniques of Milton H. Erickson, M.D.* New York: Norton.

Hall. J.A. (1992). Psychological mindedness: A conceptual model. *American Journal of Psychotherapy, 46,* 131–140.

Halverson, C.F., & Shore, R.E. (1969). Self-disclosure and interpersonal functioning. *Journal of Consulting and Clinical Psychology, 33,* 213–217.

Hamilton, J.D., Decker, N., & Rumbaut, R.D. (1986). The manipulative patient. *American Journal of Psychotherapy, 60,* 189–200.

Handelsman, M.M. (1990). Do written consent forms influence clients' first impression of therapists? *Professional Psychology: Research and Practice, 21,* 451–454.

Hanna, F.J., & Puhakka, K. (1991). When psychotherapy works: Pinpointing an element of change. *Psychotherapy, 28,* 598–607.

Hanson, R.W. (1986). Physician–patient communication and compliance. In K.E. Gerber & A.M. Nehemkis (Eds.), *Compliance: The dilemma of the chronically ill* (pp. 182–212).. New York: Springer.

Hargrove, D.S., & Spaulding, W.D. (1988). Training psychologists for work with the chronically mentally ill. *Community Mental Health Journal, 24,* 283–295.

Harris, G.A., & Watkins, D. (1987). *Counseling the involuntary and resistant client.* College Park, MD: American Correctional Association.

Haynes, R.B. (1976). A critical review of the "determinants" of patient compliance with therapeutic regimens. In D.L. Sacket & R.B. Haynes (Eds.), *Compliance with therapeutic regimens* (pp. 26–39). Baltimore: Johns Hopkins University Press.

Haynes, R.B. (1979). Introduction. In R.B. Haynes, D.W. Taylor, & D.L. Sackett (Eds.), *Compliance in health care.* Baltimore: Johns Hopkins University Press.

Haynes, R.B., Taylor, D.W., & Sackett, D.L. (1979). *Compliance in health care.* Baltimore: Johns Hopkins University Press.

Heilbrun, A.B. (1961). Male and female personality correlates of early termination in counseling. *Journal of Counseling Psychology, 8,* 31–36.

Heitler, J.B. (1973). Preparation of lower-class patients for expressive group psychotherapy. *Journal of Consulting and Clinical Psychology, 41,* 251–260.

Heitler, J.B. (1976). Preparatory techniques in initiating expressive psychotherapy with lower class, unsophisticated patients. *Psychological Bulletin, 83,* 339–352.

Hendrick, S.S. (1981). Self-disclosure and marital satisfaction. *Journal of Personality and Social Psychology, 40,* 1150–1159.

Hendrick, S.S. (1987). Counseling and self-disclosure. In V.J. Derlega & J.H. Berg (Eds.), *Self-disclosure: Theory, research and therapy* (pp. 303–327). New York: Plenum Press.

Hendrick, S.S. (1988). Counselor self-disclosure. *Journal of Counseling and Development, 66,* 419–424.

Heppner, P.P., & Claiborn, C.D. (1989). Social influence research in counseling: A review and critique. *Journal of Counseling Psychology, 36,* 365–387.

Hersen, M. (1971). Resistance to direction in behavior therapy: Some comments. *The Journal of Genetic Psychology, 118,* 121–127.

Higginbotham, H.N., West, S., & Forsyth, D. (1988). *Psychotherapy and behavior change: Social, cultural and methodological perspectives.* New York: Pergamon Press.

Higgins, R.L., & Harris, R.N. (1988). Strategic "alcohol" use: Drinking to self-handicap. *Journal of Social and Clinical Psychology, 6,* 191–202.

Hill, C.T., & Stull, D.E. (1987). Gender and self-disclosure. In V.J. Derlega & J.H. Berg (Eds.), *Self-Disclosure: Theory, research and therapy* (pp. 81–100). New York: Plenum Press.

Horowitz, M.J. (Ed.). (1991). *Person schemas and maladaptive interpersonal patterns.* Chicago: University of Chicago Press.

Horvath, A.O., & Luborsky, L. (1993). The role of the therapeutic alliance in psychotherapy. *Journal of Consulting and Clinical Psychology, 61,* 561–573.

Howard, K.I., Kopta, S.M., Krause, M.S., & Orlinsky, D.E. (1986). The dose-effect relationship in psychotherapy. *American Psychologist, 41,* 159–164.

Howe, D. (1993). *On being a client.* London: Sage.

Ivey, A.E., & Authier, J. (1978). *Microcounseling* (2nd ed.). Springfield, IL: Charles C Thomas.

Ivey, A.E., Ivey, M.B., & Simek-Morgan, L. (1993). *Counseling and psychotherapy: A multicultural perspective* (3rd ed.). Boston: Allyn and Bacon.

Jahn, D.L., & Lichstein, K. L. (1980). The resistive client: A neglected phenomenon in behavior therapy. *Behavior Modification, 4,* 303–320.

Janis, I.L. (1983). The role of social support in adherence to stressful decisions. *American Psychologist, 38,* 143–160.

Janis, I.L., & Mann, L. (1977). *Decision making: A psychological analysis of conflict, choice, and commitment.* New York: Free Press.

Jenkins, A.H. (1982). *The psychology of Afro-Americans.* New York: Pergamon Press.

Jenkins, J.H., & Karno, M. (1992). The meaning of "expressed emotion". Theoretical issues raised by cross-cultural research. *American Journal of Psychiatry, 149,* 9–21.

Jones, A.C. (1985). Psychological functioning in Black Americans: A conceptual guide for use in psychotherapy. *Psychotherapy, 22,* 363–369.

Jourard, S.M. (1971). *The transparent self* (rev. ed.). New York: Van Nostrand Reinhold.

Jourard, S.M. (1974). *Healthy personality.* New York: Macmillan.

Jourard, S.M., & Resnick, J.L. (1970). The effect of high revealing subjects on the self-disclosure of low revealing subjects. *Journal of Humanistic Psychology, 10,* 84–93.

Kalman, T.P. (1983). An overview of patient satisfaction with psychiatric treatment. *Hospital and Community Psychiatry, 34,* 48–54.

Kanfer, F.H., & Gaelick-Buys, L. (1991). Self-management methods. In F.H. Kanfer & A.P. Goldstein (Eds.), *Helping people change* (pp. 305–360). New York: Pergamon Press.

Kanfer, F.H., & Goldstein, A.P. (1991). *Helping people change.* New York: Pergamon Press.

Kanfer, F.H., & Schefft, B. K. (1988). *Guiding the process of therapeutic change.* Champaign, IL: Research Press.

Kaplan, K.J., Firestone, I. J., Klein, K.W., & Sodkoff, C. (1983). Distancing in dyads: A comparison of four models. *Social Psychology Quarterly, 46,* 108–115.

Karpf, F.B. (1953). *The psychology and psychotherapy of Otto Rank.* New York: Philosophical Library.

Kasl, S.V. (1975). Issues in patient adherence to health regimes. *Journal of Human Stress, 1,* 5–18.

Katz, J.H. (1985). The sociopolitical nature of counseling. *The Counseling Psychologist, 13,* 615–625.

Kelman, H.C. (1961). Processes of opinion change. *Public Opinion Quarterly, 25,* 57–78.

Kendall, P.C., Kipnis, D., & Otto-Salaj, L. (1992). When clients don't progress: Influences on and explanations for lack of therapeutic progress. *Cognitive Therapy and Research, 16,* 269–281.

Kiesler, D.J. (1982). Interpersonal theory of personality and psychotherapy. In J. Anchin & D.J. Kiesler (Eds.), *Handbook of interpersonal psychotherapy* (pp. 3–24). Elmsford, NY: Pergamon Press.

Kirmayer, L.J. (1990). Resistance, reactance, and reluctance to change: A cognitive attributional approach to strategic interventions. *Journal of Cognitive Psychotherapy: An International Quarterly, 4,* 83–104.

Kirschenbaum, D.S. & Flanery, R.C. (1983). Behavioral contracting: Outcomes and elements. In M. Hersen, R.M. Eisler, & P.M. Miller (Eds.), *Progress in behavior modification* (Vol. 15, pp. 217–275). New York: Academic Press.

Kirscht, J.P., & Rosenstock, I.M. (1979). Patients' problems in following recommendations of health experts. In G. Stone, F. Cohen, & N. Adler (Eds.), *Health psychology* (pp. 189–215). San Francisco: Jossey-Bass.

Kitano, H.H. (1989). A model for counseling Asian Americans. In P.B. Pedersen, J.G. Draguns, W.J. Lonner, & J.E. Trimble (Eds.), *Counseling across cultures* (3rd ed., pp. 139–152). Honolulu: University of Hawaii Press.

Kitayama, S., & Markus, H.R. (1994). *Emotion and culture.* Washington, DC: American Psychological Association.

Klein, R.H., & Carroll, R.A. (1986). Patient characteristics and attendance patterns in outpatient group psychotherapy. *International Journal of Group Psychotherapy, 36,* 115–132.

Kleinginna, P.R., & Kleinginna, A.M. (1981). A categorized list of motivation definitions, with a suggestion for a consensual definition. *Motivation and Emotion, 5,* 263–291.

Kleinman, A. (1980). *Patients and healers in the context of culture.* Berkeley: University of California Press.

Kleinman, A. (1988). *Rethinking psychiatry.* New York: Free Press.

Kohut, H. (1971). *The analysis of the self.* New York: International Universities Press.

Kohut, H. (1987). Narcissism as a resistance and as a driving force in psychoanalysis. In D.S. Milman & G.D. Goldman (Eds.), *Techniques of working with resistance* (pp. 167–178). Northvale, NJ: Jason Aronson.

Kopel, S., & Arkowitz, H. (1975). The role of attribution and self-perception in behavior change: Implications for behavior therapy. *Genetic Psychology Monographs, 92,* 175–212.

Koss, M.P. (1979). Length of psychotherapy for clients seen in private practice. *Journal of Consulting and Clinical Psychology, 47,* 210–212.

Kottler, J.A. (1992). *Compassionate therapy.* San Francisco: Jossey-Bass.

Kottler, J.A., & Blau, D.S. (1989). *The imperfect therapist: Learning from failure in therapeutic practice.* San Francisco: Jossey-Bass.

Kris, A. (1990). The analyst's stance and the method of free association. *Psychoanalytic Study of the Child, 45,* 25–41.

Kushner, M.G., & Sher, K.J. (1991). The relationship of treatment fearfulness and psychological service utilization: An overview. *Professional Psychology: Research and Practice, 22,* 196–203.

LaCave, L.J., & Black, G. (1989). Reframing to deal with patient resistance. *American Journal of Psychotherapy, 43,* 68–76.

Landrine, H. (1992). Clinical implications of cultural differences: The referential versus the indexical self. *Clinical Psychology Review, 12,* 401–415.

Langs, R. (1981). *Resistances and interactions.* New York: Jason Aronson.

Larke, J. (1985). Compulsory treatment: Some practical methods of treating the mandated client. *Psychotherapy, 22,* 262–268.

Larsen, D.L., Clifford, C.C., Hargreaves, W.A., & Nguyen, T.D. (1979). Assessment of client/patient satisfaction: Development of a general scale. *Evaluation and Program Planning, 2,* 197–207.

Larsen, D.L., Nguyen, T.D., Green, R.S., & Attkisson, C.C. (1983). Enhancing the utilization of outpatient mental health services. *Community Mental Health Journal, 19,* 305–320.

Lazarus, A.A. (1993). Tailoring the therapeutic relationship, or being an authentic chameleon. *Psychotherapy, 30,* 404–407.

Lazarus, A.A., & Fay, A. (1982). Resistance or rationalization? A cognitive-behavioral perspective. In P. Wachtel (Ed.), *Resistance* (pp. 115–133). New York: Plenum Press.

Leary, T. (1957). *Interpersonal diagnosis of personality.* New York: Ronald Press.

Lebow, J. (1982). Consumer satisfaction with mental health treatment. *Psychological Bulletin, 91,* 244–259.

Leet-Pellegrini, H., & Rubin, J.Z. (1974). The effects of six bases of power upon compliance, identification, and internalization. *Bulletin of the Psychonomic Society, 3,* 68–70.

Lefley, H.P. (1989). Counseling refugees: The North American experience. In P.B. Pedersen, J.G. Draguns, W.J. Lonner, & J.E. Trimble (Eds.), *Counsel-*

ing across cultures (3rd ed., pp. 243–266). Honolulu: University of Hawaii Press.

Lemkau, J.P., Bryant, F.B., & Brickman, P. (1982). Client commitment to the helping relationship. In T.A. Wills (Ed.), *Basic processes in helping relationships* (pp. 187–207). New York: Academic Press.

Leong, F.T. (1986). Counseling and psychotherapy with Asian-Americans: Review of the literature. *Journal of Counseling Psychology, 33,* 196–206.

Levanthal, H., Diefenbach, M., & Leventhal, E.A. (1992). Illness cognition: Using common sense to understand treatment adherence and affect cognition interactions. *Cognitive Therapy and Research, 16,* 143–163.

Levinson, P. McMurray, L., Podell, P., & Weiner, H. (1978). Causes for the premature interruption of psychotherapy by private practice patients. *American Journal of Psychiatry, 135,* 826–830.

Levitt, E.E., & Fisher, W.P. (1981). The effects of an expectancy state on the fate of applications and psychotherapy in an outpatient setting. *Journal of Clinical Psychiatry, 42,* 234–237.

Levy, R.L. (1983). Social support and compliance: A selective review and critique of treatment integrity and outcome measurement. *Social Science and Medicine, 17,* 1329–1338.

Levy, R.L. (1986). Social support and compliance: Salient methodological problems in compliance research. *Journal of Compliance in Health Care, 1,* 184–198.

Lewis, W.A., & Evans, J.W. (1986). Resistance: A reconceptualization. *Psychotherapy, 23*(3), 426–433.

Lewis-Fernandez, R., & Kleinman, A. (1994). Culture, personality and psychopathology. *Journal of Abnormal Psychology, 103,* 67–71.

Ley, P. (1979). The psychology of compliance. In D.J. Oborne, M.M. Gruneberg, & J.R. Eiser (Eds.), *Research in psychology and medicine* (Vol. 2, pp. 187–229). London: Academic Press.

Ley, P. (1982). Giving information to patients. In R.J. Eiser (Ed.), *Social psychology and behavioral science* (pp. 339–373). New York: Wiley.

Lietaer, G. (1984). Unconditional positive regard: A controversial basic attitude in client-centered therapy. In R.F. Levant & J.M. Shlien (Eds.), *Client-centered therapy and the person centered approach: New directions in theory, research, and practice* (pp. 41–58). New York: Praeger.

Linehan, M.M. (1993a). *Cognitive-behavioral treatment of borderline personality disorder.* New York: Guilford Press.

Linehan, M.M. (1993b). *Skills training manual for treating borderline personality disorder.* New York: Guilford Press.

Liotti, G. (1987). The resistance to change of cognitive structures: A counter proposal to psychoanalytic metapsychology. *Journal of Cognitive Psychotherapy: An International Quarterly, 1,* 87–104.

Lipman, A.A., & Simon, F.A. (1985). Psychiatric diagnosis in a state hospital: Manhattan State Revisited. *Hospital and Community Psychiatry, 36,* 368–373.

Littlefield, R.P. (1979). Self-disclosure among some Negro, white, and Mexican-American adolescents. *Journal of Counseling Psychology, 21,* 133–136.

Locke, E.A., & Latham, G.P. (1990). *A theory of goal setting and task performance.* Englewood Cliffs, NJ: Prentice Hall.

Locke, E.A., Shaw, K.N., Saari, L.M., & Latham, G.P. (1981). Goal setting and task performance: 1969-1980. *Psychological Bulletin, 90,* 125–152.

Loftus, E.F., & Ketcham, K. (1994). *The myth of repressed memory.* New York: St. Martin's Press.

Lonner, W.J., & Malpass, R. (1994). *Psychology and culture.* Boston: Allyn and Bacon.

Lowman, R.L., DeLange, W.H., Roberts, T.K., & Brady, C.P. (1984). Users and "teasers": Failure to follow through with initial mental health service inquiries in a child and family treatment center. *Journal of Community Psychology, 12,* 253–262.

Luborsky, L., Singer, B., & Luborsky, L. (1975). Comparative studies of psychotherapies: Is it true that "Everyone has won and all must have prizes"? *Archives of General Psychiatry, 69,* 684–694.

Luther, G., & Loev, I. (1981). Resistance in marital therapy. *Journal of Marital and Family Therapy,* (Oct.), 475–480.

Macharia, W.M., Leon, G., Rowe, B.H., Stephenson, B.J., & Haynes, R.B. (1992). An overview of interventions to improve compliance with appointment keeping for medical services. *Journal of the American Medical Association, 267,* 1813–1817.

Mackenzie, K.R. (1991). Principles of brief intensive psychotherapy. *Psychiatric Annals, 21,* 398–404.

Mahoney, M.J. (1982). Psychotherapy and human change processes. In J.H. Harvey & M.M. Parks (Eds.), *Psychotherapy research and behavior change* (pp. 73–122). Washington, DC: American Psychological Association.

Mahoney, M.J. (1991). *Human change processes: The scientific foundations of psychotherapy.* New York: Basic Books.

Mahoney, M.J., & Norcross, J.C. (1993). Relationship styles and therapeutic choices: A commentary. *Psychotherapy, 30,* 423–426.

Mahoney, M.J., & Thoresen, C.E. (1974). *Self-control: Power to the person.* Monterey, CA: Brooks/Cole.

Maluccio, A.N. (1979). *Learning from clients.* New York: Free Press.

Manthei, R.J., & Matthews, D.A. (1982). Helping the reluctant client engage in counselling. *British Journal of Guidance and Counselling, 10,* 45–51.

Markus, H.R., & Kitayama, S. (1994). The cultural construction of self and emotion: Implications for social behavior. In S. Kitayama & H.R. Markus (Eds.), *Emotion and culture* (pp. 89–130). Washington, DC: American Psychological Association.

Markus, H.R., & Nurius, P. (1986). Possible selves. *American Psychologist, 41,* 954–969.

Marlatt, G.A. (1982). Relapse prevention: A self-control program for the treatment of addictive behaviors. In R.B. Stuart (Ed.), *Adherence, compliance, and generalization in behavioral medicine* (pp. 329–378). New York: Brunner/Mazel.

Marlott, G. A., & Gordon, J.R. (1985). *Relapse prevention: Maintenance strategies in the treatment of addictive behaviors.* New York: Guilford Press.

Marshall, G.N. (1991). A multidimensional analysis of internal health locus of control beliefs: Separating the wheat from the chaff? *Journal of Personality and Social Psychology, 61,* 483–491.

Marshall, R.J. (1982). *Resistant interactions. Child, family and psychotherapist.* New York: Human Services Press.

Marston, A.R. (1984). What makes therapist run? A model for analysis of motivational styles. *Psychotherapy: Theory, Research and Practice, 21,* 456–459.

Marston, M. (1977). Nursing management of compliance with medication regimens. In I. Barofsky (Ed.), *Medication compliance: A behavioral management approach* (pp. 139–164). Thorofare, NJ: C.B. Slack.

Masek, B.J. (1982). Compliance and medicine. In D.M. Doleys, R.L. Meredith, & A.R. Ciminero (Eds.), *Behavioral medicine: Assessment and treatment strategies* (pp. 527–545). New York: Plenum Press.

Matthews, D., & Hingston, R. (1977). Improving patient compliance: A guide for physicians. *Medical Clinics of North America, 61,* 429–433.

May, P.R.A. (1968). *Treatment of schizophrenia: A comparative study of five treatment methods.* New York: Science House.

May, R. (1967a). *Psychology and the human dilemma.* Princeton: Von Nostrand.

May, R. (1967b). Contributions of existential psychotherapy. In R. May, E. Angel, & H. Ellenberger (Eds.), *Existence: A new direction in psychiatry and psychology* (pp. 37–91). New York: Clarion Books. (Original work published 1958).

May, R. (1981). *Freedom and destiny.* New York: Norton.

Mays, D.T., & Franks, C.M. (1985). Negative outcome: Historical context and definitional issues. In D.T. Mays & C.M. Franks (Eds.), *Negative outcome in psychotherapy and what to do about it* (pp.1–19). New York: Springer.

McCallum, M., Piper, W.E., & Joyce, A.S. (1992). Dropping out from short-term group therapy. *Psychotherapy, 29,* 206–215.

McClelland, D.C. (1987). *Human motivation.* Cambridge: Cambridge University Press.

McDermott, M., & Apter, M.J. (1988). The negativism dominance scale. In M.J. Apter, J.H. Kerr, & M Cowles (Eds.), Progress in reversal theory (pp. 373–376). Amsterdam: North-Holland.

McGoldrick, M., Pearce, J.K., & Giordano, J. (Eds.). (1982). *Ethnicity and family therapy.* New York: Guilford Press.

McHolland, J.D. (1985). Strategies for dealing with resistant adolescents. *Adolescence, 20,* 349–368.

McLeod, J. (1990). The client's experience of counselling and psychotherapy: A review of the research literature. In D. Mearns & W. Dryden (Eds.), *Experiences of counselling in action* (pp. 66–79). London: Sage.

Meichenbaum, D. (1977). *Cognitive-behavior modification.* New York: Plenum Press.

Meichenbaum, D., & Turk, D.C. (1987). *Facilitating treatment adherence.* New York: Plenum Press.

Mennicke, S.A., Lent., R.W., & Burgoyne, K.L. (1988). Premature termination from university counseling centers: A review. *Journal of Counseling and Development, 66,* 458–465.

Menninger, K.A. (1973). *Theory of psychoanalytic technique* (2nd ed.). New York: Basic Books.

Miller, W.R. (1985). Motivation for treatment. *Psychological Bulletin, 98,* 84–107.

Miller, W.R. (1989). Increasing motivation for change. In R.K. Hester & W.R. Miller (Eds.), *Handbook of alcoholism: Treatment approaches* (pp. 67–271). New York: Pergamon Press.

Miller, L.C., Berg, J.H., & Archer, R.L. (1983). Openers: Individuals who elicit intimate self-disclosure. *Journal of Personality and Social Psychology, 44,* 1234–1244.

Miller, W.R., & Rollnick, S. (1991). *Motivational interviewing: Preparing people to change addictive behavior.* New York: Guilford Press.

Miller, M.J., & Wells, D. (1990). On being "attractive" with resistant clients. *Journal of Humanistic Education and Development, 29,* 86–90.

Milman, D.S., & Goldman, G. D. (1987). *Techniques of working with resistance.* Northvale, NJ: Jason Aronson.

Mook, D.G. (1987). *Motivation: The organization of action.* New York: Norton.

Moon, J.R., & Eisler, R.M. (1983). Anger control: An experimental comparison of three behavioral treatments. *Behavior Therapy, 14,* 493–505.

Mueser, K.T., & Berenbaum, H. (1990). Psychodynamic treatment of schizophrenia: Is there a future? *Psychological Medicine, 20,* 253–262.

Munjack, D.J., & Oziel, L.J. (1978). Resistance in the behavioral treatment of sexual dysfunctions. *Journal of Sex and Marital Therapy, 4,* 122–138.

Murgatroyd, S., & Apter, M.J. (1986). A structural-phenomenological approach to eclectic psychotherapy. In J.C. Norcross (Ed.), *Handbook of eclectic psychotherapy* (pp. 260–281). New York: Bruner/Mazel.

Nash, J.L., & Cavenar, J.O. (1976). Free psychotherapy: An inquiry into resistance. *American Journal of Psychiatry, 133,* 1066–1069.

Natterson, J. (1991). *Beyond countertransference.* Northvale, NJ: Jason Aronson.

Newman, C.F. (1994). Understanding client resistance: Methods for enhancing motivation to change. *Cognitive and Behavioral Practice, 1,* 47–69.

Nisbett, R. & Ross, L. (1980). *Human inference: Strategies and shortcomings of social judgment.* Englewood Cliffs, NJ: Prentice-Hall.

Noonan, J.R. (1973). A follow-up of pretherapy dropouts. *Journal of Community Psychology, 1,* 43–44.

Norcross, J.C. (1993). Tailoring relationship stances to client needs: An introduction. *Psychotherapy, 30,* 402–403.

Novaco, R.W. (1975). *Anger control.* Lexington, MA: Lexington Books.

Oldfield, S. (1983). *The counseling relationship: A study of the client's experience.* London: Routledge & Kegan Paul.

Oltmanns, T.F., & Maher, B.A. (1988). *Delusional beliefs.* New York: Wiley.

Orlinsky, D.E., & Howard, K.I. (1986). Process and outcome in psychotherapy. In S.L. Garfield & A.E. Bergin (Eds.), *Handbook of psychotherapy and behavior change* (3rd. ed., pp. 311-384). New York: Wiley.

Orlinsky, D.E., Grawe, K., & Parks, B. (1994). Process and outcome in psychotherapy—*noch einmal.* In A. Bergin & S. Garfield (Eds.), Handbook of psychotherapy and behavior change (4th ed., pp. 270–376). New York: Wiley.

Orme, D.R., & Boswell, D. (1991). The pre-intake dropout at a community mental health center. *Community Mental Health Journal, 27,* 375–379.

Orne, M.T., & Wender, P.H. (1968). Anticipatory socialization for psychotherapy: Method and rationale. *American Journal of Psychiatry, 124,* 1202–1212.

Otani, A. (1989a). Resistance management techniques of Milton H. Erickson, M.D.: An application to nonhypnotic mental health counseling. *Journal of Mental Health Counseling, 11,* 325–334.

Otani, A. (1989b). Client resistance in counseling: Its theoretical rationale and taxonomic classification. *Journal of Counseling and Development, 67,* 458–561.

Owen, I.R. (1992). Applying social constructionism to psychotherapy. *Counseling Psychology Quarterly, 5,* 385–402.

Palmer, D., & Hampton, P.T. (1987). Reducing broken appointments in a community mental health center. *Community mental Health Journal, 23,* 76–78.

Palombo, J. (1987). Spontaneous self-disclosures in psychotherapy. *Clinical Social Work Journal, 15,* 107–120.

Paniagua, F.A. (1995). *Assessing and treating culturally diverse clients.* Thousand Oaks, CA: Sage.

Parrish, J.M. (1986). Parent compliance with medical and behavioral recommendations. In N.A. Krasnegor, J.D. Araseth & M.F. Cataldo (Eds.), *Child Health Behavior: A behavioral pediatrics perspective* (pp. 453–501). New York: Wiley.

Pedersen, D.M., & Breglio, V. J. (1968). The correlation of two self-disclosure inventories with actual self-disclosure: A validity study. *Journal of Psychology, 68,* 291–298.

Pedersen, P.B., Draguns, J.G., Lonner, W.J., & Trimble, J.E. (1989). *Counseling across cultures* (3rd ed.). Honolulu: University of Hawaii Press.

Pekarik, G. (1985a). Coping with dropouts. *Professional Psychology: Research and Practice, 16,* 114–123.

Pekarik, G. (1985b). The effects of employing different termination classifications criteria in dropout research. *Psychotherapy, 22,* 86–91.

Pekarik, G. (1992). Relationship of clients' reasons for dropping out of treatment to outcome and satisfaction. *Journal of Clinical Psychology, 48,* 91–98.

Pekarik, G., Jones, D.L., & Blodgett, C. (1986). Personality and demographic characteristics of dropouts and completers in a nonhospital residential alcohol treatment program. *International Journal of the Addictions, 21,* 131–137.

Pekarik, G., & Wierzbicki, M. (1986). The relationship between client's expected and actual treatment duration. *Psychotherapy, 23,* 532–534.

Pelham, W., & Murphy, H.A. (1986). Attention deficit and conduct disorders. In M. Hersen (Ed.). *Pharmacological and behavioral treatments: An integrative approach* (pp. 108–148). New York: Wiley.

Perconte, S.T., & Goreczny, A.J. (1990). Failure to detect fabricated posttraumatic stress disorder with the use of the MMPI in a clinical population. *American Journal of Psychiatry, 147,* 1057–1060.

Perls, F.S. (1969). *Ego, hunger and aggression.* New York: Vintage Books. (Original work published 1947)

Perls, F., Hefferline, R.F., & Goodman, P. (1951). *Gestalt therapy: Excitement and growth in the human personality.* New York: Julian Press.

Perris, C. (1989). *Cognitive therapy with schizophrenic patients.* New York: Guilford Press.

Persons, J.B., Burns, D.D., & Perloff, J.M. (1988). Predictors pf dropout and outcome in cognitive therapy for depression in a private practice setting. *Cognitive Therapy and Research, 12,* 557–575.

Pervin, L.A. (1983). The status and flow of behavior: Toward a theory of goals. In M. Page (Ed.), *Personality: Current theory and research* (pp. 1–53). Lincoln: University of Nebraska Press.

Pervin, L.A. (1991). Self-regulation and the problem of volition. In M.L. Maeher & P.R. Pintrich (Eds.), *Advances in motivation and achievement* (pp. 1–20). Greenwich, CT: JAI Press.

Phillips, E. L. (1985). *Psychotherapy revised: New frontiers in research and practice.* Hillsdale, NJ: Lawrence Erlbaum Associates.

Phillips, E.L., & Fagan, P.J. (1982). *Attrition: Focus on the intake and first therapy interviews.* Paper presented at the 90th Annual Convention of the American Psychological Association, Washington, D.C.

Pinder, C.C. (1984). *Work motivation: Theory, issues, and applications.* Glenview, IL: Scott, Foresman.

Pipes, R.B., & Davenport, D.S. (1990). *Introduction to psychotherapy.* Englewood Cliffs, NJ: Prentice-Hall.

Podell, R.N., & Gary, L.R. (1976). Compliance: A problem in medical management. *American Family Physician, 13,* 74–80.

Polansky, N.A. (1965). The concept of verbal accessibility. *Smith College Studies in Social Work, 36,* 1–44.

Ponterotto, J.G., & Pedersen, P.B. (1993). *Preventing prejudice.* Newbury Park, NY: Sage.

Pool, V.E., & Elder, S.T. (1986). A selected review of the literature and an empirical analysis of drug treatment compliance by schizophrenic patients. *International Review of Applied Psychology, 35,* 547–576.

Prince, R. (1980). Variations in psychotherapeutic procedures. In H.C. Triandis & J.G. Draguns (Eds.), *Handbook of cross-cultural psychology: Vol. 6. Psychopathology* (pp. 291–349). Boston: Allyn and Bacon.

Prochaska, J., & DiClemente, C. (1984). *The transtheoretical approach: Crossing the traditional boundaries of therapy.* Homewood, IL: Dow Jones/Irwin.

Prochaska, J., & DiClemente, C. (1986). The transtheoretical approach. In J.C. Norcross (Ed.), *Handbook of eclectic psychotherapy* (pp. 163–200). New York: Brunner/Mazel.

Prochaska, J., DiClemente, C., & Norcross, J.C. (1992). In search of how people change: Applications to addictive behaviors. *American Psychologist, 47,* 1102–1114.

Razin, A.M. (1977). The A-B variable: Still promising after twenty years? In A.S. Gurman & A.M. Razin (Eds.), *Effective psychotherapy: A handbook of research* (pp. 291–324). New York: Pergamon Press.

Read, S.J., & Miller, L.C. (1989). Inter-personalism: Toward a goal-based theory of persons in relationship. In L. Pervin (Ed.), *Goal concepts in personality and social psychology* (pp. 413–472). Hillsdale, NJ: Lawrence Erlbaum.

Regier, D.A., Narrow, W.E., Rae, D.S., Manderscheid, R.W., Locke, B.Z., & Goodwin, F.K. (1993). The de facto US mental and addictive disorders service system. *Archives of General Psychiatry, 41,* 971–978.

Reich, W. (1949). *Character analysis* (3rd ed.). New York: Orgone Institute Press.

Reich, W. (1987). Character resistances. In D.S. Milman & G.D. Goldman (Eds.), *Techniques of working with resistance* (pp. 41–116). Northvale, NJ: Jason Aronson.

Reimers, T.M., Wacher, D.P., & Koeppl, G. (1987). Acceptability of behavioral interventions: A review of the literature. *School Psychology Review, 16,* 212–227.

Resnick, P.J. (1988a). Malingered psychosis. In R. Rogers (Ed). *Clinical assessment of malingering and deception* (pp. 84–103). New York: Guilford Press.

Resnick, P.J. (1988b). Malingering of posttraumatic stress disorders. In R. Rogers (Ed). *Clinical assessment of malingering and deception.* New York: Guilford Press.

Ridley, C.R. (1984). Clinical treatment of the nondisclosing Black client. *American Psychologist, 39,* 1234–1244.

Ridley, C.R. (1989). Racism in counseling as an aversive behavioral process. In P.B. Pedersen, J.G. Draguns, W.J. Lonner, & J.E. Trimble (Eds.), *Counseling across cultures* (3rd ed., pp. 55–78). Honolulu: University of Hawaii Press.

Ridley, C.R., Mendoza, D.W., Kanitz, B.E., Angermeier, L., & Zenk, R. (1994). Cultural sensitivity in multicultural counseling: A perceptual schema model. *Journal of Counseling Psychology, 41,* 125–136.

Ritchie, M.H. (1986). Counseling the involuntary client. *Journal of Counseling and Development, 64,* 516–518.

Robbins, J.M., Beck, P.R., Mueller, D.P., & Mizener, D.A. (1988). Therapists' perceptions of difficult patients. *Journal of Nervous and Mental Disorders, 176,* 490–497.

Robertson, M.H. (1988). Assessing and intervening in client motivation for psychotherapy. *Journal of Integrative and Eclectic Psychotherapy, 7,* 319–329.

Rodin, J., & Janis, I.L. (1979). The social power of health care practitioners as agents of social change. *Journal of Social Issues, 35,* 60–81.

Rodin, J., & Salovey, P. (1989). Health psychology. In M.R. Rosenzweig & L.W. Porter (Eds.), *Annual review of psychology* (Vol. 40, pp. 533–580). Palo Alto, CA: Annual Reviews.

Rogers, C.R. (1942). *Counseling and psychotherapy.* Boston: Houghton Mifflin.

Rogers, C.R. (1951). *Client-centered therapy.* Boston: Houghton Mifflin.

Rogers, C. R. (1961). *On becoming a person.* Boston: Houghton Mifflin.

Rogers, R. (1988). (Ed). *Clinical assessment of malingering and deception.* New York: Guilford Press.

Rogers, R. (1990). Models of feigned mental illness. *Professional Psychology: Research and Practice, 21,* 182–188.

Rokach, A. (1987). Anger and aggression control training: Replacing attack with interaction. *Psychotherapy, 24,* 353–362.

Rokeach, M. (1973). *The nature of human values.* New York: Free Press.

Romig, C.A., & Gruenke, C. (1991). The use of metaphor to overcome inmate resistance to mental health counseling. *Journal of Counseling & Development, 69,* 414–418.

Rooney, R.H. (1992). *Strategies for work with involuntary clients.* New York: Columbia University Press.

Rosenbaum, R.L., Horowitz, M.J., & Wilner, N. (1986), Clinical assessments of patient difficulty. *Psychotherapy, 23,* 417–425.

Rosenfeld, L.B., Civikly, J.M., & Herron, J.R. (1979). Anatomical and psychological sex differences. In G.J. Chelune (Ed.), *Self-disclosure* (pp. 80–109). San Francisco: Jossey-Bass.

Rosenstock, I.M. (1974). Historical origins of the health belief model. *Health Education Monographs, 2,* 328.

Ruocchio, P.J. (1989). How psychotherapy can help the schizophrenic patient. *Hospital and Community Psychiatry, 40,* 188–190.

Sack, R.T. (1988). Counseling responses when clients say "I don't know." *Journal of Mental Health Counseling, 10,* 179–187.

Sackett, D.L, & Haynes, R.B. (1976). *Compliance with therapeutic regimens.* Baltimore: Johns Hopkins University Press.

Sackett, D.L., & Snow, J.C. (1979). The magnitude of compliance and noncompliance. In R.B. Haynes, D.W. Taylor, & D.L. Sackett (Eds.), *Compliance in health care* (pp. 11–22). Baltimore: Johns Hopkins University Press.

Sandler, J., Dare, C., & Holder, A. (1973). *The patient and the analyst.* New York: International Universities Press.

Sandler, J., Holder, A., & Dare, C. (1970). Brief psychoanalytic concepts: V. Resistance. *British Journal Of Psychiatry, 117,* 215–221.

Saunders, S.M. (1993). Applicant's experience of the process of seeking therapy. *Psychotherapy, 30,* 554–564.

Schachter, S., & Singer, J. (1962). Cognitive, social and psychological determinants of emotional state. *Psychological Review, 69,* 379–399.

Schorr, D., & Rodin, J. (1982). Perceived control in practitioner-patient relationships. In T.A. Wills (Ed.), *Basic processes in helping relationships* (pp. 155–186). New York: Academic Press.

Seaburn, D. B. (1989). Treating "resistant" behavior: Contributions of systems theory. *Psychotherapy Patient, 4,* 51–60.

Searles, H. (1977). *Countertransference and related subjects.* New York: International Universities Press.

Seligman, L. (1990). *Selecting effective treatments.* San Francisco: Jossey-Bass.

Seltzer, L.F. (1986). *Paradoxical strategies in psychotherapy: A comprehensive overview and guidebook.* New York: Wiley.

Selvini-Palazzoli, M., Cecchin, G., Prata, G. & Boscolo, L. (1978). *Paradox and counterparadox.* New York: Jason Aronson.

Sermat, V., & Smyth, M. (1973). Content analysis of verbal communication in the development of a relationship: Conditions influencing self-disclosure. *Journal of Personality and Social Psychology, 26,* 332–346.

Sexton, T.L., & Whiston, S.C. (1994). The status of the counseling relationship: An empirical review, theoretical implications and research directions. *The Counseling Psychologist, 22,* 6–78.

Shaffer, D.R., Pegalis, L.J., & Cornell, D.P. (1992). Gender and self-disclosure revisited: Personal and contexual variations in self-disclosure to same sex acquaintances. *Journal of Social Psychology, 132,* 307–315.

Shapiro, J.G., & Swensen, C.H. (1977). Self-disclosure as a function of self-concept and sex. *Journal of Personality Assessment, 41,* 144–149.

Shelton, J.L., & Levy, R.L. (1981). *Behavioral assignments and treatment compliance: A handbook of clinical strategies.* Champaign, IL: Research Press.

Shlien, J.M. (1984). A countertheory of transference. In R.F. Levant & J.M. Shlien (Eds.), *Client-centered therapy and the person-centered approach* (pp. 153–181). New York: Praeger.

Shoham-Salomon, V., & Rosenthal, R. (1987). Paradoxical interventions: A meta analysis. *Journal of Counseling and Clinical Psychology, 55,* 22–28.

Sledge, W.H., Moras, K., Hartley, D., & Levine, M. (1990). Effect of time-limited psychotherapy on patient dropout rates. *American Journal of Psychiatry, 147,* 1341–1347.

Sloane, R.B., Staples, F.R., Cristol, A.H., Yorkson, N.J., & Whipple, K. (1975). *Psychotherapy versus behavior therapy.* Cambridge, MA: Harvard University Press.

Smith, K.J., Subich, L.M., & Kalodner, C. (1995). The transtheoretical model's stages and processes of change and their relation to premature termination. *Journal of Counseling Psychology, 42,* 34–39.

Southam, M.A., & Dunbar, J.M. (1986). Facilitating patient compliance with medical interventions. In K. Holroyd & T. Creer (Eds.), *Self-management of chronic disease* (pp. 163–188). New York: Academic Press.

Sparr, L.F., Moffitt, M.C., & Ward, M.F. (1993). Missed psychiatric appointments: Who returns and who stays. *American Journal of Psychiatry, 150,* 801–806.

Spence, D.P. (1994). The failure to ask the hard questions. In P.F. Talley, H.H. Strupp, & S.F. Butler (Eds.), *Psychotherapy research and practice: Bridging the gap* (pp. 19–38). New York: Basic Books.

Spotnitz, H. (1969). *Modern psychoanalysis of the schizophrenic patient.* New York: Grune & Stratton.

Spotnitz, H. (1989). Therapeutic countertransference: Interventions with the schizophrenic patient. *Modern Psychoanalysis, 14,* 3–20.

Srull, T.K., & Wyer, R.S. (1986). The role of chronic and temporary goals in social information processing In R.M. Sorrentino & E.T. Higgins (Eds.), *Handbook of motivation and cognition* (pp. 503–549). New York: Guilford Press.

Stanton, M.D., & Todd, T.C. (1981). Engaging "resistant" families in treatment. *Family Process, 20,* 261–293.

Stark, M. (1994a). *Working with resistance.* Northvale, NJ: Jason Aronson.

Stark, M. (1994b). *A primer on working with resistance.* Northvale, NJ: Jason Aronson.

Stefl, M.E., & Prosperi, D.C. (1985). Barriers to mental health service utilization. *Community Mental Health Journal, 21,* 167–178.

Stiles, W.B. (1987). I have to talk to somebody. In V.J. Derlega & J.H. Berg (Eds.), *Self-disclosure: Theory, research and therapy.* New York: Plenum Press.

Stiles, W.B., Putnam, S.M., Wolf, M.H., & James, S.A. (1979). Vernal response mode profiles of patients and physicians in medical screening interviews. *Journal of Medical Education, 54,* 81–89.

Stiles, W.B., Shuster, P.L., & Harrigan, J.A. (1992). Disclosure and anxiety: A test of the fever model. *Journal of Personality and Social Psychology, 63,* 980–988.

Stokes, J.P. (1987). Relation of loneliness and self-disclosure. In V.J. Derlega & J.H. Berg, (Eds.), *Self-disclosure: theory, research and therapy* (pp. 175–201). New York: Plenum Press.

Stoltenberg, C.D., Leach, M.M., & Bratt, A. (1989). The elaboration likelihood model and psychotherapeutic persuasion. *Journal of Cognitive Psychotherapy: An International Quarterly, 3,* 181–199.

Stone, G.C. (1979). Patient compliance and the role of the expert. *Journal of Social Issues, 35,* 34–59.

Storch, R.S., & Lane, R.C. (1989). Resistance in mandated psychotherapy: Its function and management. *Journal of Contemporary Psychotherapy, 19,* 25–38.

Strean, H.S. (1990). *Resolving Resistances in Psychotherapy.* New York: Brunner/ Mazel.

Stricker, G. (1990). Self-disclosure and psychotherapy. In G. Stricker & M. Fisher (Eds.), *Self-disclosure in the therapeutic relationship* (pp. 277–289). New York: Plenum Press.

Strong, S.R., & Matross, R.P. (1973). Change processes in counseling and psychotherapy. *Journal of Counseling Psychology, 20,* 25–37.

Strupp, H.H., & Bloxom, A.L. (1973). Preparing lower-class patients for group psychotherapy: Development and evaluation of a role induction film. *Journal of Consulting and Clinical Psychology, 41,* 373–384.

Strupp, H.H., Fox, R.E., & Lessler, K. (1969). *Patients view their psychotherapy.* Baltimore: Johns Hopkins University Press.

Sue, D.W. (1977). Counseling the culturally different: A conceptual analysis. *Personality and Guidance Journal, 55,* 422–425.

Sue, D.W. (1981). Evaluating process variables in cross-cultural counseling and psychotherapy. In A.J. Marsell & P.B. Pedersen (Eds.), *Cross-cultural counseling and psychotherapy* (pp. 102–125). Elmsford, NY: Pergamon Press.

Sue, S., McKinney, H.L., & Allen, D.B. (1976). Predictors of the duration of therapy for clients in the community mental health system. *Community Mental Health Journal, 12,* 365–375.

Sue, D.W., & Sue, D. (1990). *Counseling the culturally different: Theory and practice* (2nd ed.). New York: Wiley.

Suinn, R.M. (1990). *Anxiety management training.* New York: Plenum Press.

Sullivan, H.S. (1940). *Conceptions of modern psychiatry.* New York: Norton.

Sullivan, H.S. (1965). *Collected works.* New York: Basic Books.

Sutton, S.R. (1982). Fear-arousing communication: A critical examination of theory and research. In R.J. Eiser (Ed.), *Social psychology and behavioral science* (pp. 303–337). New York: Wiley.

Svartberg, M., & Stiles, T.C. (1992). Predicting patient change from therapist competence and patient–therapist complementarity in short-term anxiety-provoking psychotherapy: A pilot study. *Journal of Consulting and Clinical Psychology, 60,* 304–307.

Suzuki, R. (1989). Adolescents' dropout from individual psychotherapy—Is it true? *Journal of Adolescence, 12,* 197–205.

Swoboda, J.S., Dowd, E.T., & Wise, S.L. (1990). Reframing and restraining directives in the treatment of clinical depression. *Journal of Counseling Psychology, 37,* 254–260.

Szasz, T.S. (1970). *Ideology and insanity: Essays on the psychiatric dehumanization of man.* Garden City, NY: Anchor Books.

Szasz, T.S., & Hollender, M.H. (1956). A contribution to the philosophy of medicine: The basic models of the doctor–patient relationship. *Archives of Internal Medicine, 97,* 585–592.

Talmon, M. (1990). *Single-session therapy.* San Francisco: Jossey-Bass.

Tanner, B.A. (1982). A multi-dimensional client satisfaction instrument. *Evaluation and Program Planning, 5,* 161–167.

Tansey, M.J., & Burke, W.F. (1989). *Understanding countertransference.* Hillsdale, NJ: Analytic Press.

Taylor, G.J. (1984). Psychotherapy with the boring patient. *Canadian Journal of Psychiatry, 29,* 217–222.

Taylor, S.E., Lichtman, R.R., & Wood, J.V. (1984). Compliance with chemotherapy among breast cancer patients. *Health Psychology, 3,* 553–562.

Tennen, H., Rohrbaugh, M., Press, S., & White, L. (1981). Reactance theory and therapeutic paradox: A compliance–defiance model. *Psychotherapy: Theory, Research and Practice, 18,* 14–23.

Tice, D.M. (1991). Esteem protection or enhancement? Self-handicapping motives and attributions differ by trait self-esteem. *Journal of Personality and Social Psychology, 60,* 711–725.

Tinsley, H.E.A., Bowman, S.L., & Ray, S.B. (1988). Manipulation of expectancies about counseling and psychotherapy: Review and analysis of expectancy manipulation strategies and results. *Journal of Counseling Psychology, 35,* 99–108.

Thompson, B.J., & Hill, C.E. (1993). Clients perceptions of therapist competence. *Psychotherapy Research, 3,* 124–130.

Tracey, T.J. (1993). An interpersonal stage model of the therapeutic process. *Journal of Counseling Psychology, 40,* 396–409.

Triandis, H.C. (1994a). Major cultural syndromes and emotion. In S. Kitayama & H.R. Markus (Eds.). *Emotion and culture* (pp. 285–306). Washington, DC: American Psychological Association.

Triandis, H.C. (1994b). Culture and social behavior. In W.J. Lonner & R. Malpass (Eds.), *Psychology and culture* (pp. 169–173). Boston: Allyn and Bacon.

Trimble, J.E., & Fleming, C.M. (1989). Providing counseling services for Native American Indians: Clients, counselor and community characteristics. In P.B. Pederson, J.G. Draguns, W.J. Lonner, & J.E. Trimble (Eds.), *Counseling across cultures* (3rd ed., pp. 177–204). Honolulu: University of Hawaii Press.

Tseng, W., & McDermott, J.F. (1981). *Culture, mind and therapy.* New York: Brunner/Mazel.

Tulipan, A.B. (1983). Fees in psychotherapy: A perspective. *Journal of the American Academy of Psychoanalysis, 11,* 445–463.

Turk, D.C., Salovey, P., & Litt, M.D. (1986). Adherence: A cognitive-behavioral perspective. In K.E. Gerber & A.M. Nehemkis (Eds.), *Compliance: The dilemma of the chronically ill* (pp. 44–72). New York: Springer.

Tutin, J. (1987). A multivariate analysis of dropout status by length of stay in a rural community mental health center. *Community Mental Health Journal, 23,* 40–52.

Valins, S. (1970). The perception and labeling of bodily changes as determinants of emotional behavior. In P. Black (Ed.), *Physiological correlates of emotion* (pp. 229–243). New York: Academic Press.

Verhulst, J.C.R.M., & Van de Vijver, F.J.R. (1990). Resistance during psychotherapy and behavior therapy. *Behavior Modification, 14*(2), 172–187.

Vondracek, F.W., & Marshall, M.J. (1971). Self-disclosure and interpersonal trust. An exploratory study. *Psychological Reports, 28,* 235–240.

Voth, H.M., & Orth, M.H. (1973). *Psychotherapy and the role of the environment.* New York: Behavioral Publications.

Wallston, B.S., & Wallston, K.A. (1984). Social psychological models of health behavior. In A. Baum, S.E. Taylor, & J.E. Singer (Eds.), *Handbook of psychology and health: Social psychological aspects of health* (Vol. 4, pp. 23–53). Hillsdale, NJ: Lawrence Erlbaum.

Walters, G.C., Solomon, G.S., & Walden, V.R. (1982). Use of the MMPI in predicting persistence in groups of males and female outpatients. *Journal of Clinical Psychology, 38,* 80–83.

Waltz, J., Addis, M.E., Koerner, K., & Jacobson, N.S. (1993). Testing the integrity of a psychotherapy protocol: Assessment of adherence and competence. *Journal of Consulting and Clinical Psychology, 61,* 620–630.

Watts, C.A., Scheffler, R., & Jewell, N.P. (1986). Demand for outpatient mental health services in a heavily insured population: The case of the Blue Cross and Blue Shield Association's Federal Employees Health Benefits Program. *Health Services Research, 21,* 267–289.

Watzlawich, P., Weakland, J., & Fisch, R. (1974). *Change: Principles of problem formation and problem resolution.* New York: Norton.

Webb, E.J., Cambell, D.T., Schwartz, R.D., & Sechrest, L. (1966). *Unobtrusive measures: Nonreactive research in the social sciences.* Chicago: Rand McNally.

Weeks, G.R., & L'Abate, L. (1982). *Paradoxical psychotherapy: Theory and practice with individuals, couples and families.* New York: Bruner/Mazel.

Weinberg, N.H., & Zaslove, M. (1963). "Resistance" to systematic desensitization of phobias. *Journal of Clinical Psychology, 19,* 179–181.

Weiner, B. (1986). Attribution, emotion, and action. In R.M. Sorrentino & E.T. Higgins (Eds.), *Handbook of motivation and cognition* (pp. 281–312). New York: Guilford Press.

Weiner, B. (1992). *Human motivation: Metaphors, theories and research.* Newbury Park, CA: Sage Publications.

Weissberg, J.H., & Levay, A.N. (1981). The role of resistance in sex therapy. *Journal of Sex and Marital Therapy, 712,* 125–130.

Weisz, J.R., Weiss, B., & Langmeyer, D.B. (1987). Giving up on child psychotherapy: Who drops out? *Journal of Consulting and Clinical Psychology, 55,* 916–918.

Whitcher-Alagna, S. (1983). Receiving medical help: A psychological perspective on patient reactions. In A. Nadler, J.D. Fisher, & B.M. DePaulo (Eds.), *New directions in helping* (Vol. 3, pp. 131–162). New York: Academic Press.

Wierzbicki, M., & Pekarik, G. (1993). A meta-analysis of psychotherapy dropout. *Professional Psychology: Research and Practice, 24,* 190–195.

Wise, R.A., & Rompre, P.P. (1989). Brain dopamine and reward. In M.R. Rosenzweig & L.W. Porter (Eds.), *Annual review of psychology* (Vol. 40, pp. 191–225). Palo Alto, CA: Annual Review.

Whitehorn, J.C., & Betz, B.J. (1954). The study of psychotherapeutic relationships between physicians and schizophrenic patients. *American Journal of Psychiatry, 111,* 321–331.

Wilensky, R. (1983). *Planning and understanding: A computational approach to human reasoning.* Reading, MA: Addison-Wesley.

Wills, T.A. (1982). *Basic processes in helping relationships.* New York: Academic Press.

Winell, M. (1987). Personal goals: The key to self-direction in adulthood. In M.E. Ford & D.H. Ford (Eds.), *Humans as self-constructing living systems* (pp. 261–287). Hillsdale, NJ: Lawrence Erlbaum.

Wohl, J. (1989). Cross-cultural psychotherapy. In P.B. Pedersen, J.G. Draguns, W.J. Lonner, & J.E. Trimble (Eds.), *Counseling across cultures* (3rd ed., 79–114). Honolulu: University of Hawaii Press.

Wolff, W.M. (1967). Psychotherapeutic persistence. *Journal of Consulting Psychology, 31,* 429.

Worthy, M., Gary, A.L., & Kahn, G.M. (1969). Self-disclosure as an exchange process. *Journal of Personality and Social Psychology, 13,* 59–63.

Wright, J.H., & Davis, D. (1994). The therapeutic relationship in cognitive-behavioral therapy: Patient perceptions and therapist responses. *Cognitive and Behavioral Practice, 1,* 25–45.

Yoken, C., & Berman, J.S. (1987). Third-party payment and the outcome of psychotherapy. *Journal of Consulting and Clinical Psychology, 55,* 571–576.

Yalom, I.D. (1966). A study of group therapy dropouts. *Archives of General Psychiatry, 14,* 393–414.

Yalom, I.D. (1970). *The theory and practice of group psychotherapy.* New York: Basic Books.

Yau, T.Y., Sue, D., & Hayden, D. (1992). Counseling style preference of international students. *Journal of Counseling Psychology, 39,* 100–104.

Name Index

Subject Index

Interrelational approach, 9–11
Intersubjectivity, theory of, 4, 132
Involuntary clients, 118–121

Learning, 15, 33
Legitimate power, 98
Life goals, 30–32
Locus of control, 76–77
Loneliness, 53

Maintenance (of change), 17, 18, 23, 100, 214
Maintenance-growth goal, 32
Malingering, 236–243.
Managed care. *See* HMO
Mania, 243
Marital problems, 53
Maturation, 15, 76
Measurements:
  biological, 72
  direct observation, 72
  outcome, 62, 134
  self-disclosure, 45–46
  self-reports, 71–72
  subjective ratings, 72
Mechanist movement, 2
Medications, 41, 71, 91, 221
  antidepressants, 243
  compliance and, 73
  psychotherapy and, 149–151, 154
  psychotropic drugs, 148, 149, 153
  and schizophrenia, 160, 163
  treatment setting and, 84
Memory, 2, 4–5, 170, 240. *See also* False-memory syndrome; Repressed memory
Mental disorders (illness), 3, 58
  assessment of, 153–156
  and client–therapist relationship, 156
  culture and, 172–176
  and minority groups, 188
  psychotherapy and, 149–159, 213
  resistance and, 148–149, 152
  symptoms of, 148–149
  treatment of, 152–153
Mental health services, 91, 170, 220, 221
Mental retardation, 123, 151
Mexican Americans 48
  and self-disclosure, 48
Microskills approach. 193–195
Minorities (ethnic and racial), 169–170, 173, 182, 184–193. *See also* Culture; Multicultural groups; specific racial and ethnic groups
  attrition rate of, 183, 225, 232–233
  and microskills approach, 193–195
  and resistance, 171
Mirroring, 131

MMPI, 233
Modeling, 165
Motivation, 12–42, 108, 140
  and change, 18–19, 41–42, 70
  definition of, 24–26, 41–42
  and drop-out rate, 136
  as a dynamic, 13
  goal-based model of, 28–35
  human behavior and, 26–28
  and resistance, 12–16, 208, 212
Multicultural groups. *See also* Minorities
  attrition and, 225
  treatment of, 185–186
Munchausen syndrome, 237

Narcissism, 118, 174, 204–205
Native Americans, 184–187
  as clients, 170, 179, 180, 182, 194
  treatment recommendations for, 186–187
Neurological disorders, 118, 154
Neurotransmitters, 39. *See also* Brain; Dopamine
  drugs (medications) and, 41
Neutrality, 131
Nonverbal communication, 56, 186

Objectivity, 132-134
Organic disorders, 85, 118, 123, 148–149, 151, 154, 240. *See also* Biological disorders
  client deception and, 242–243
Outcome:
  expectations of, 103
  and goals, 28, 212
  measurements of, 62, 134
  treatment adherence and, 72

Paradoxical interventions, 103–107, 108, 216–217
Paranoia, 85, 230, 243
Paranoid schizophrenia, 174
Parents, 91
Passivity, 23
Peer pressures, 102
Peer support, 122
Performance goals, 33
Perseveration, 79–80
Personality, 138
  self-disclosure and, 46–48
Personality disorders, 85, 174, 230, 233. *See also* Borderline personalities
Personality tests, 233
Person-centered therapy, 11
Phenomenological philosophy, 208–211
Phobias, 85
Physical change (in humans), 15–16
Physiology, 2